Cary,
Joseph Warren: physician, politician, patriot.

| DATE DUE | | | |
|---|---|---|---|
| AUG 2 3 1999 | | | |
| | | | |
| | | | |
| | | | |
| | | | |
| | | | |
| | | | |
| | | | |
| | | | |
| | | | |
| | | | |
| | | | |

BREWER STATE JR. COLLEGE
LIBRARY
TUSCALOOSA CAMPUS
DISCARD

# JOSEPH WARREN

*Physician, Politician, Patriot*

# JOSEPH WARREN

*Physician, Politician, Patriot*

by John Cary

*University of Illinois Press, Urbana, 1961*

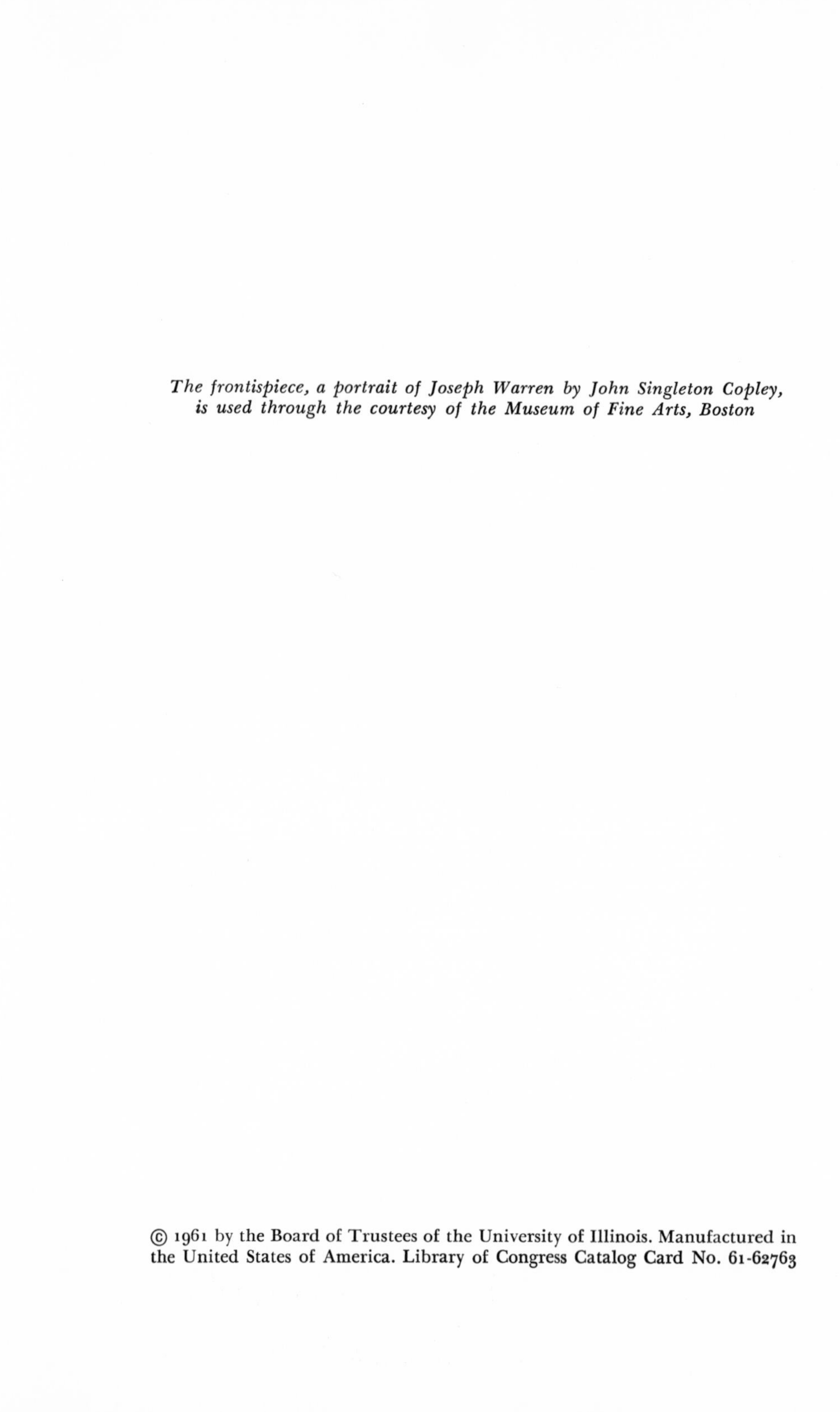

*The frontispiece, a portrait of Joseph Warren by John Singleton Copley, is used through the courtesy of the Museum of Fine Arts, Boston*

 Manufactured in the United States of America. Library of Congress Catalog Card No. 61-62763

*To my parents*

JOHN BERNARD CARY

MARY BESCHTA CARY

# Preface

Historians of the revolutionary period cherish the hope that their studies of propaganda, nationalism, trade, and other subjects may have permanently corrected the myopic view that "taxation without representation" provides a single and satisfactory account of the causes of the War for Independence. Thus far, however, they have had to cope as best they could with the knowledge that a gross nearsightedness distorts our vision of the men who led the revolutionary movement. Otis, Hancock, Adams, Henry, Jefferson, and a few other major figures dominate the picture, with Christopher Gadsden, James Bowdoin, William Henry Drayton, and a host of other men existing as outlines, altogether too vague outlines, in a shadowy background. In some cases, of course, the obscurity is deserved and the prominence richly merited; too often, however, history has dealt unfairly with some and been inordinately generous to others. For one such man, Joseph Warren, the obscurity came late.

In the mid-nineteenth century, when the only full biography of Warren was published, his name was as well known as that of Samuel Adams. Fourteen counties in the United States were named after Warren, and hospitals, streets, and bridges in Massachusetts still pay tribute to his former fame. The Warren family, which included among its members the founder of Harvard Medical School and the first American surgeon to operate upon an anesthetized patient, was still the most eminent family of doctors in the United States, and Joseph Warren had been the first to enter this profession. Also, Warren's orations had been reprinted several times, and nineteenth-century Americans loved good oratory. Largely, however, his fame arose from his death in the Battle of Breed's Hill, where he fought as a common soldier, though he had just been appointed a major general. This dramatic death, at an early age, was responsible for the creation of a legend which obscured the importance of the man.

In 1865 the publication of Richard Frothingham's *Life and Times of Joseph Warren* did much to correct this. Since that time, Warren's reputation has suffered a sharp decline, largely because Warren did not live to play a part in those movements which have most interested twentieth-century colonial historians—the discussions that led to the Declaration of Independence and the establishment of the new government after the war. As a result, most people who have heard of Warren in our own day know of him only as the man who sent Paul Revere on his midnight ride to Lexington. Few but colonial historians are aware of his political activities: as one of the most vigorous propagandists in Massachusetts' revolutionary party; as a key figure in both the *Liberty* incident and the tea crisis; as the man who wrote the Suffolk Resolves, which pledged America to a defensive war; and as the chief executive who shaped the Bay Colony's policy and tried to organize the raw militia besieging Boston into an army capable of meeting the well-trained British troops.

My own opinion, that Joseph Warren ranks with Samuel Adams as one of the two most important leaders in the Massachusetts revolutionary movement, might as well be stated at the outset. He was the most charming leader of them all, and his personality made him a more effective political leader than most. On the other hand, this study of Warren is not an exercise in knocking over statues of Hancock and Otis, so that Warren may ascend a pedestal. If the hint appears in these pages that it is time to reevaluate the role of some of the leaders of the revolution in Massachusetts, it has not been my primary concern to attempt this in a study of only one of them.

Much more is said in these pages of nationalism and politics, taxes and, without apology, patriotism, than of tiewigs and kneebuckles or hot rum and love affairs. Warren's political orations receive more space than do his children. In large part, this is due to the sources that time has allowed to survive. Because of the small amount of personal material available, Frothingham filled many of his pages with general history, and, as he realized, Warren was often lost from sight. Though additional material has been uncovered since 1865, it has been largely on his professional and political life, and any biographer of Warren is confronted with the same difficulty of getting at his personal life that Frothingham faced. A personal, belletristic biography of Warren cannot be written, and this book is intended only as a new look at his public career.

The librarians and archivists of the following institutions, among many, were helpful in granting permission and extending aid for the use of their collections: Massachusetts Historical Society, Boston Public Library, New York Public Library, William L. Clements Library, the Harvard University Libraries and Archives, University of Illinois Library, Masonic Library in Boston, Massachusetts Archives, and the Probate, Court Record, and Deeds Offices of Suffolk County. Dr. Richard Warren kindly extended permission for the use of the portion of the Warren papers in the family's possession. Mr. Malcolm Freiberg and Mr. Bernhard Knollenberg read the manuscript and made a number of valuable suggestions. My wife, Kathryn D. Cary, assisted with typing and proofreading. Professor Louise B. Dunbar of the University of Illinois directed this study when it was a doctoral thesis. Her enthusiasm for another's work is one of the hallmarks of a fine teacher, and she was unsparing in giving of her vast knowledge of Colonial America. She devoted many hours to the reading of this biography, and it has profited much from her suggestions.

# Contents

# New England Boyhood

## CHAPTER I

Peter Warren, the family's first American ancestor, was born, no one knows where, in the year of grace 1631, just one year after the ship *Arbella* set her canvas to the English wind and sailed to found the new colony of Massachusetts Bay in New England. Some of his descendants claimed that he was a son of Richard Warren of the *Mayflower,* but proof of that is sadly lacking.[1] More likely, he was born in Old England and migrated to the New World as a youth or, perhaps, was a sailor who jumped ship here. The land to the west of the Atlantic sounded its siren call in the ears of England's young men for many a strange reason. Of most who came, it might at least be said that they had adventurous hearts and fair constitutions to survive the ocean passage.

What we do know is that Peter Warren was a sailor, perhaps by

[1] Genealogical chart, prepared by John C. Warren, Warren MSS, I (Massachusetts Historical Society Library). A genealogist employed by the Warren family provided a reasonable explanation of its origins. A Henry Tucker married an Elizabeth Warren in 1623. Peter married a Tucker, and his kinship to Elizabeth, as brother or nephew perhaps, is likely. This Elizabeth Warren was of Ashburton Parish in Devonshire, and Peter might also have been. Peter Warren named one of his daughters Elizabeth. Edward L. Smith to John C. Warren, Boston, Aug. 15, 1899, *ibid.*

choice, perhaps by necessity. In 1654 he was working for Matthew Cannedge, a fisherman, on the lonely island of Monhegan, about eleven miles east-southeast of Pemaquid Point, Maine. French and Spanish fishermen had lowered their nets in these waters at the opening of the seventeenth century, and the Gorges and Mason families held an English charter to the region. By 1654 the General Court of Massachusetts had announced that colony's claim to the area, and occasionally exercised some authority there. Thus, when young Warren was called as a witness in the investigation of the murder of his employer, it was the Bay Colony governor before whom he appeared.

Peter Warren told his story succinctly and vividly. He had called at Cannedge's home on an October evening in 1654. One Gregory Cassell, who "was in drink," was quarreling with Cannedge "and did strike him on the nose and make him bleed." After a bit, Warren took his gun and went off shooting for an hour, returning to the house to find a crowd about Cannedge, who was bleeding badly. Cassell had "strucke him on the head with an hammer as he was about to mend his shooes," and seven weeks later the victim died.[2]

The details of the case, of course, are of little interest here. But this murder in a small fishing settlement, remote from Boston, did effect an important change in Peter Warren's life and was to have some significance for his descendants. Peter Warren was the founder in America of the Roxbury branch of the Warren family. From him was descended a long line of distinguished doctors, perhaps the most eminent family of medical men in American history. His great-grandson was Dr. Joseph Warren, whom nineteenth-century Americans knew as one of their noblest heroes and whose life story is written here. How does one account for this? What was the road from the poor fisherman at a Massachusetts outpost to the Harvard-educated doctor who became known as an outstanding revolutionary leader? The first step was the unfortunate murder of Matthew Cannedge. Having lost his employment, Peter was transformed from a bachelor sailor at isolated Monhegan into a married property holder at Boston, the center of New England life. He purchased a house and lot in Auchmuty Lane (now Essex

[2] John F. Cronin, ed., *Records of the Court of Assistants of the Colony of the Massachusetts Bay, 1630-1692* (Boston, 1928), III, 62.

Street), and on August 1, 1660, married Sarah Tucker, daughter of Robert Tucker of Dorchester. Their first child, a son, was born a year later; Joseph, the second-born and first of four direct descendants so christened, was born on February 19, 1663.[3] This Joseph Warren, who is designated by his title "housewright," was the grandfather of Dr. Joseph Warren, the subject of this biography.

As his family grew, Peter kept a weather eye open for a further source of income. In 1669 he found employment as bellman for Boston, a job for the winter months when the town's maritime pursuits were least active. During the winter the regular watchman did not patrol, but the bellman was to "goe up and downe throughout the towne by the space of five howers in the night, beginning at eleaven, and soe to contynue till four." Peter Warren held the post from 1669 until 1678, after which it ceased to exist. His political interest is seen in his signing of a petition in October, 1664, praying for continuance of the colony's charter rights, upon the occasion of the arrival of two commissioners sent to Massachusetts by Charles II.[4] Thus early, close as they were to their English background, the Warrens were beginning to acquire an American orientation, which would lead Dr. Joseph Warren to a vigorous fight for the right of Massachusetts to govern itself, free from English interference.

The Warren family furnished their house with the bare necessities of a family of their station in seventeenth-century Boston—featherbeds, tables, chairs and "cushings," and other furniture. Small luxuries—eight shillings worth of table linen, a looking glass, and two shillings worth of books—were purchased from time

[3] Deed executed March 28, 1659, and entered Dec. 17, 1664, Suffolk Deeds, IV, 235 (Suffolk County Courthouse, Boston); "Boston Marriages," New England Historical and Genealogical Society, *Register,* XIX, No. 1 (Jan., 1865), 31; "Boston Records," *ibid.,* XVI, No. 1 (Jan., 1862), 45; James Savage, *A Genealogical Dictionary of the First Settlers of New England* (Boston, 1862), IV, 426-427, for data on Peter's other wives and his children. The Warrens, with the titles used to distinguish them, were: Peter (1631-1704), whose son was Joseph Warren, housewright (1663-1729), whose son was Joseph, Selectman of Roxbury (1696-1755), whose sons were Dr. Joseph Warren, the subject of this biography (1741-75), Samuel (1743-1805), Ebenezer (1748-1824), and John (1753-1815).

[4] Robert F. Seybolt, *The Town Officials of Colonial Boston, 1634-1775* (Cambridge, Mass., 1939), pp. 19, 38-54; Julius H. Tuttle, "The Boston Petitions of 1664," Mass. Hist. Soc., *Proceedings,* LII (1918-19), 312-316.

to time. Also, Peter Warren seems to have added rooms to the house and acres to the land he had bought for fourteen pounds. He signed a petition asking repeal of a law requiring that all building be done in brick, and by the time of his death on November 15, 1704, his house and lands were valued at £140.[5]

Peter Warren had put the family on the road to a modest prosperity, and the provisions of a typical New England will aided in keeping the estate intact by passing the property on to the eldest son. Warren's third wife, Esther, refused to serve as executor of the estate, and the task fell to her stepson Joseph, eldest of the five surviving children. The will granted half of the movable property to Esther, the remainder to the son. The widow was allowed to use the house and land until her death or remarriage, at which time they were to pass to Joseph. He was then to give forty shillings to each of the children—Ebenezer, Peter, Robert, and Hannah.[6]

In his early twenties, Joseph Warren decided to follow the plow instead of the sea. In 1686 he paid ninety-five pounds to John Levens for a house, barn, six acres of farm land, and two acres of salt marsh in the village of Roxbury.[7] His wife, Deborah Williams, was a Roxbury girl, the daughter of Samuel and Theoda and the sister of the Reverend John Williams, who recorded his perils at the hands of Indian captors after the Deerfield Massacre. For Joseph and Deborah Warren, as for most New Englanders of that day, farming was just a subsistence enterprise. Joseph's trade was carpentry and he is listed in surviving records as a housewright. Three and one-half acres of the modest farm were sold in 1702 for the "valuable price of seven pound." In 1714, Joseph Warren sold his father's house in Boston for eighty pounds, much less than its value, but with the provision that Peter's widow could live there for the rest of her life without paying rent to the new owner. But there were purchases of land also. One might have to work at a trade to live, but the goal was land ownership. Six acres adjoining the farm on the west were purchased for sixty pounds in

[5] Suffolk County Probate Records, XV (June 20, 1704), 360-361 (Suffolk County Courthouse, Boston); New Eng. Hist. and Geneal. Soc., *Register,* XVI, No. 1 (Jan., 1862), 84-87.

[6] Suffolk County Probate Records, XV (June 20, 1704), 360-361.

[7] Deed executed Feb. 15, 1686/7, entered Oct. 13, 1738, Suffolk Deeds, LVII, 30-31.

1703 and, by 1725, ten and three-quarters additional acres had been acquired for £210.[8]

Besides removing the family to Roxbury and beginning its long association with farming, Joseph Warren developed the type of religious affiliation which many New Englanders found so influential in their lives. Peter Warren's three wives were all members of the Old South Church, but Peter seems not to have joined. In Roxbury the meeting house of the First Church stood hard by the farm as a reminder of one's spiritual duties. Small as the town was, the congregation soon began to outgrow the building. In 1690, to enlarge the accommodations, Warren and seven other members were granted "the backward seate in the lower front galery in the meeting house and liberty to make it according to their own minds, upon their own cost and charge (not doing any damage to any other seate)." Deborah was admitted to full communion with the First Church on November 13, 1698, and Joseph Warren on August 17, 1718.[9]

Deborah and five children survived Joseph Warren, housewright, when he died on July 13, 1729, aged sixty-six. Samuel, the first-born, had died less than a month after birth. The eldest son then, and joint administrator with Deborah of her husband's estate, was Joseph, born on February 2, 1696 N.S.[10] All of the movables were bequeathed to the widow, and the buildings and land of the estate passed to the son. He was to pay eight pounds per year to his mother, keep "one cow for her both summer and winter," procure for her two barrels of cider and a cord of firewood each year, and allow one room in the house for her use. To each of the other four children, Joseph was to pay sixty-five pounds.[11] This second Joseph is distinguished from his father, the house-

[8] All deeds are in Suffolk Deeds. The dates of entry, volume, and page are: Warren to Payson, Feb. 14, 1722, XXXVI, 211; Williams to Warren, Oct. 13, 1738, LVII, 32; Cheney to *id.*, Oct. 13, 1738, LVII, 32-33; Warren to Hill, April 15, 1714, XXVIII, 65-66; Parker to Warren, Oct. 13, 1738, LVII, 33-34; Williams to *id.*, April 11, 1732, XLVI, 210.

[9] Walter E. Thwing, *History of the First Church in Roxbury, Massachusetts, 1630-1904* (Boston, 1908), p. 73; Boston. *A Report of the Boston Record Commissioners, Containing the Roxbury Land and Church Records* (Boston, 1881), pp. 102, 104, cited hereafter as Boston. *Roxbury Land and Church Records.*

[10] Roxbury. *Vital Records of Roxbury to the End of the Year 1849* (Salem, Mass., 1925), I, 352; II, 657.

[11] Suffolk County Probate Records, XXVII (Jan. 2, 1728/9), 258-259.

wright, by his title "selectman," and it is he who was the father of Dr. Joseph Warren.

The rising position and fortune of the Warren family become apparent by comparing the life of Joseph Warren II with that of his grandfather Peter, the rugged sailor of Monhegan Island. Through the purchase of further acres of land and his election to town and church offices, Joseph Warren II became a man of substance and stature in the town of Roxbury. A year after his father's death, he bought eight acres of land from Soloman Kneeland for £151 16*s*. Further deeds record purchases by Joseph Warren "husbandman" and, indicating his rising position, by Joseph Warren "gentleman" five years later. By 1755 he owned a farm of more than ninety acres, with a "mansion house" and barn valued at £1,345.[12]

The personality of Joseph Warren, selectman, can only be glimpsed in the scattered records which remain of his life. He was an active church member, being admitted to full communion in his father's church on March 29, 1724. In 1738 he was elected precinct treasurer of the First Church, a permanent post which he held until his death. When there were discussions of erecting a new meeting house in 1736, Warren was named one of a committee of thirteen, which included the Honorable Paul Dudley and Colonel Heath, to chart plans. It is unlikely that Joseph Warren attended school beyond the lower grades, but he was interested in scripture and works on religion. His library included several Bibles, Willard's *Body of Divinity,* Dodridge's *Rise and Progress of Religion in the Soul of Man,* and other divinity books.[13]

Joseph Warren II also assumed an important role in town affairs, and it was doubtless from his father that Dr. Joseph Warren gained much of his interest in public affairs and his sense of civic

[12] Deeds in Suffolk Deeds as follows: Kneeland to Warren, Sept. 22, 1737, LIV, 241; Bowles to *id.*, Oct. 13, 1738, LVII, 34; Stevens to *id.*, March 10, 1742, LXV, 178; Gridley to *id.*, March 26, 1747, LXXIII, 127-128; Warren to Holbrook, July 6, 1764, CI, 272; Cheney to Warren, Feb. 18, 1756, XXCVIII, 65-66. Suffolk County Probate Records, LI (May 24, 1756), 316.

[13] Boston. *Roxbury Land and Church Records*, p. 105; Thwing, *First Church in Roxbury*, pp. 80, 146; Suffolk County Probate Records, LI (May 24, 1756), 633. A grandson, who heard much about the family from his father, Dr. John Warren, said that his grandfather "studied the scriptures with great zeal, and impressed upon his children a deep love and veneration for the *Bible*." Edward Warren, *The Life of John Warren, M. D.* (Boston, 1874), pp. 1-2.

duty. Roxbury, of course, presented a smaller political arena than did Boston, and one might be fined twenty pounds Old Tenor there for refusing to serve in a town office. Still, the number of important families in Roxbury was impressive, and Warren's election to office indicates the respect in which he was held. In 1749 the town meeting chose him surveyor of highways and member of a select committee; the following year he was one of three instructed "to search the town books, to know what right the town has in the training place." On March 4, 1750/1, the town meeting elected Joseph Warren as one of the five selectmen. As such he directed the petty affairs which constituted the business of a New England town. The selectmen, for example, approved a petition to the Massachusetts Council for reimbursement of Roxbury citizens for their care of an indigent Indian woman.[14] Limited though the power of a selectman was—and it was no more so than that of his counterpart in Boston and other towns—the position was one of the most important that Roxbury had to bestow, and it was a distinct honor to be called to fill it. The Warren family was rising in its immediate world, and this little world of Roxbury farmers provided an example of self-government which the boy who was to lead the fight against British government of the colony was never to forget.

Some insight into the personality of Joseph Warren, selectman, may be gained from the fact that he was single as he approached the age of forty-five. A number of the Warrens were men of sociability and rather extroverted. Another side of the family exhibited the characteristics of the reticent farmer, rather uneasy in social intercourse, somewhat shy of women, and as solid as the granite hills of New England. Samuel Warren, a brother of Joseph, the Roxbury selectman, and the selectman's son, who also was named Samuel, were farmers and bachelors until death. The younger Samuel was bashful of company generally and of women in particular.[15] The late marriage of Selectman Warren suggests that he was of this shy, quiet temper.

Joseph Warren's marriage on May 29, 1740, was to a woman

[14] Roxbury, Town Records, II (1730-90), 105-106, 112, 116 (Archives, Boston City Hall); Roxbury Selectmen to the Committee of the [Mass. Bay Council] Board, Roxbury, Jan. 24, 1752, Massachusetts Archives, XXXII, Indian Papers for 1750-57 (State House, Boston). Joseph's brother, Ebenezer Warren, was one of two sealers of leather annually from 1753 to 1755.

[15] Edward Warren, *Life of John Warren*, p. 8.

seventeen years his junior. Mary Stevens was the daughter of Dr. Samuel and Mary Calef Stevens and the granddaughter of Robert Calef, who had fought the witchcraft hysteria in the seventeenth century. These traditions of medicine and rationalism were reflected in the life of her son Joseph. With his mother's encouragement, the boy studied medicine and turned the Warren family from farming to the profession in which its members were to achieve national distinction. Joseph was formally a church member, but displayed that easy tolerance of all religious opinions which was characteristic of eighteenth-century deists. Mary Stevens had been admitted to full communion in the Roxbury First Church in 1720 and to church fellowship in 1732. Thus, Selectman Warren had known her long, though at first it was as a man of some twenty years knows a child of seven. Yet the difference seemed less great in later years, and the affection of maturity, if not the love of the spring of life, suggested marriage quite as much as did mere convenience. Besides, a man who was described—in his obituary to be sure—as of "good understanding, industrious, upright honest and faithful; a serious exemplary Christian; a useful member of society," was not a bad choice. Mary was a handsome woman and a good cook who loved children and might challenge her husband as a serious Christian.[16]

As summer heat changed into the beauty of a New England fall in 1740, Mary Warren told her husband that a child might be expected in late spring. The cycle of nature—birth, life, and death—was to begin again, and for it preparations must be made. This child must have advantages which Joseph II had not had, just as Joseph had started life with better prospects than had his father and his father's father. Certainly, if a son, he would go to the new school which there was talk of building in Roxbury and, perhaps, even to the college at Cambridge. But the birth itself was the immediate concern. On May 29, 1741, Joseph and Mary Warren observed their first anniversary; the following day a son was born whom they named Joseph.

At the birth of Joseph Warren III, the family had been established on its Roxbury land for two generations and had been in America for nearly a century. The Warrens were not yet prominent in the Bay Colony, having given Massachusetts neither great

---

[16] *Ibid.*, pp. 5, 7; *Boston Gazette*, Oct. 27, 1755, for obituary of Joseph Warren, Selectman.

divines nor distinguished statesmen. Still, since crossing the Atlantic, they had achieved much, including their neighbors' respect as honest officeholders, hard-working farmers, and good Christian men. Young Joseph Warren owed tribute to his ancestors for this heritage and for other things as well. Most important, certainly, was the American orientation which the family passed on to this boy, who was to become the very personification of the nationalism of the revolutionary generation. Having no relatives in England, the Warrens had no more ties with the mother country than many another American who had been born the subject of an empire, the capital of which he had never visited and the laws of which seldom touched his personal life. Largely it was the Warrens' agrarian, middle-class background which resulted in their having fewer British connections than some more aristocratic colonials. None of the Warren boys returned to England for schooling, as did the sons of some southern planters, or made business trips home, as did young John Hancock; nor did they hold appointments from the crown. Developing wholly on American soil, Joseph Warren's family was American in thought and in culture by the time of his birth.

A farm in an eighteenth-century town a few miles from Boston was by no means an unfavorable environment for a boy's growth. Before young Joseph could feel any lack of youthful companionship, a brother, Samuel, was born on October 10, 1743. Father Warren had part of the land in apple orchards, trees which a boy could climb easily enough, and there were acres of meadow and marsh to range across. At the barn was the warm smell of cattle, several milk cows and a yoke of oxen, and a small, black horse with bobbed tail. When this horse strayed from home in 1756, the children must have felt as much anxiety as Mrs. Warren, who advertised a reward of three dollars for its return.[17]

Farm life provided a healthy environment for the growth of the body, and Joseph, blessed with a fine physique, was in good health most of his life. He was equally fortunate in the opportunity he had of going to one of the best schools in New England, Roxbury Latin School. Cotton Mather, in noting that "God so blessed his endeavors, that Roxbury could not live quietly without a free school in the town," wrote that it "afforded more schol-

[17] *Boston News-Letter*, Sept. 9, 1756.

ars, first for the college and then for the public, than any town of its bigness, or if I mistake not, of twice its bigness in all New England."[18] Dr. Joseph Warren, his brother John, who attained distinction as a surgeon and Harvard professor, the Anglican "bishop of Boston" Samuel Parker, Massachusetts' Governor Increase Sumner, and Judge William Cushing were students or teachers at the school within twenty years. As the historian of the school points out, "It is to the credit of the school that it had as masters both Whigs and Tories, Revolutionaries and Loyalists, who had in common, not their political ideas but the quality of their minds."[19]

Roxbury had collected a subscription and erected a new school building in 1742, one year after Joseph Warren's birth. The Honorable Paul Dudley was "pleased to bestow for the use of the said school a good handsome bell."[20] When Joseph Warren answered that bell as a student, William Cushing, later a United States Supreme Court justice, was one of the school's teachers and helped prepare the lad for college. By then, Roxbury Latin was becoming exclusively college preparatory, and Joseph's course of study emphasized classical languages and literature. In Bayley's *English and Latine Exercises for School Boys,* published in Boston in 1720, Joseph studied the present indicative tense by such stirring sentences as, "I do study, while thou dost play. James doth cough, but we do sneeze. Fishes do swim." Like the *McGuffey Readers* of a later generation, the book included exhortations to godliness, proverbs to ponder, and statements on good government, tyranny, and the value of being a studious boy. Young Joseph's mind flitted from the exercises to such things as the doggerel verse he penned on the reverse of the title page:

> Wine will make us Red as Roses
> And our Sorrows Quite Forgett
> Come lett us Fudell all our Noses
> And Drink ourselves Quite out of Debt.

Still, Father Warren bought 200 shillings worth of Latin books

[18] Quoted in J. Evarts Greene, "The Roxbury Latin School: An Outline of Its History," American Antiquarian Society, *Proceedings,* n.s., IV, Part 4 (April, 1887), 360.

[19] Richard W. Hale, Jr., *History of the Roxbury Latin School* (Cambridge, Mass., 1946), pp. 70-71.

[20] The Old School Book, quoted in *ibid.,* p. 68.

for the boy, and Joseph's later knowledge of the language indicates the investment was sound.[21]

The weekends brought something of a holiday from school, though not from thought. The Sabbath, observed from Saturday sundown, was devoted largely to attendance at church meetings and family readings of scripture. Listening to his parents read the scriptures, Joseph gained a knowledge of the Bible, which, like so many of his contemporaries, he found convenient years later for use in his political writings. The new meeting house, which father Warren had helped plan, was built in 1741, and the Warrens purchased pew number 6 for £30 7*s.* 7*d.* Young Joseph, not yet three years old, may have watched the flames that destroyed the building in March, 1744. A new church was soon erected and it was this building, which stood until 1804, that the Warren children remembered as they grew older. The seats of some of the pews folded up as the people stood to pray, then would "come down with a clatter, fun for the boys, who thus responded to the amen."[22]

Through the years, the Warren family continued to grow. A third son, Ebenezer, was born on September 13, 1748. He was to become a landholder at Foxborough, selectman of that town, member of the General Court and of the state convention which ratified the U.S. Constitution, and a judge of Norfolk County. John, the fourth son, was born July 14, 1753. It was this youngest brother, whom he trained in his own profession, to whom Dr. Joseph Warren was to feel closest. The family, in the broad sense, was increased by the purchase of an old Negro manservant and a young Negro girl for housework, the two of whom were valued at four shillings less than the cattle in the appraisal of the estate.[23]

Young Joseph's father, the Roxbury selectman, developed a new strain of apples, the Warren russet. He remained an active farmer

---

[21] Nathan Bayley, *English and Latine Exercises for School-Boys*, 5th ed. (Boston, 1720); Suffolk County Probate Records, LI (May 24, 1756), 633. Joseph Warren's copy of Bayley is in the Massachusetts Historical Society Library.

[22] Edward Warren, *Life of John Warren*, p. 7; Thwing, *First Church in Roxbury*, pp. 139-140, 151; William Tudor, ed., *Deacon Tudor's Diary* (Boston, 1896), p. 3.

[23] Roxbury. *Vital Records*, I, 352; Suffolk County Probate Records, LI (May 24, 1756), 630-633.

until his death on October 22, 1755, when he fell from a ladder while gathering apples in the orchard and broke his neck.[24]

Joseph, now fourteen years old and just entering college, was able to appreciate the tragedy and its significance for the family. As a barelegged boy, he had peddled milk to the Boston market; now there were harder jobs that needed doing about the place whenever he was home from school. Also, he would have to be more careful with money than would many another college freshman. At fourteen he was the man of the family, and he was fortunate in the heritage which he received from his sober, hard-working, and civic-minded father.

The father died intestate and his wife Mary was appointed administratrix. It is a tribute to her ability that she was able to keep the farm together and send two of her sons to college. For Joseph's education she claimed to have spent more than £266. Peter Oliver, a political if not a personal enemy of Dr. Warren, admitted that as a boy Joseph was "possessed of a genius which promised distinction" and "his friends educated him at the college in Cambridge." This is the only evidence that the lad, like Alexander Hamilton, was so outstanding that a subscription was taken to educate him. Joseph's consent to allow his mother the expenses for his education, which she claimed from her husband's estate, indicates that she was his primary financial support.[25]

Joseph entered Harvard College at the age of fourteen, with the freshman class of 1755. By this time the school had become something more than a theological seminary, but was yet less than a university. The training of New England doctors and lawyers was by reading and the apprentice method in the colonies, or attendance in the inns of court and the medical schools of Europe. A large share of the nearly 5,000 volumes in the Harvard Library when Joseph Warren attended college consisted of the Holy Scriptures, scriptural commentaries, writings of the Greek and Latin fathers, sermons, and theological treatises. But the library also held some of the Greek and Roman classics, works on political theory, ancient and modern history, and biography. There was even plenty to interest the young man intending to become a doctor of medicine, though it would be several decades before Joseph

[24] *Boston Gazette,* Oct. 27, 1755; Edward Warren, *Life of John Warren,* p. 4.

[25] Suffolk County Probate Records, LXIV (July 13, 1765), 471; Peter Oliver, The Origins and Progress of the American Rebellion, p. 186, Gay Transcripts (Mass. Hist. Soc. Library).

Warren's brother John would serve as the driving force behind the founding of Harvard Medical School. In Joseph's student days, the library owned the transactions of the scientific societies of England and France, a "collection of the most approved medical authors," and two skeletons, one of each sex.[26] A chair in mathematics and natural philosophy had been endowed in 1727, and John Winthrop, one of the few significant colonial scientists, occupied it while Joseph Warren was at Harvard.

In July, 1755, Joseph Warren, with the training of Roxbury Latin School behind him, passed the entrance examinations, which covered the classical writers "such as Tully, Virgil, The New-Testament, Xenophon," the rules of grammar, and Latin composition. Class rank was based upon social standing, and four years later this son of the Roxbury selectman graduated twenty-fifth in a class of thirty-five. In the fall of 1755, young Joseph obtained a Hebrew grammar and began his college work with the group that the college records name "Mr. Symmes's pupils afterwards Mr. Kneeland's."[27] Neither of the tutors who guided Joseph Warren through his four-year curriculum established a lasting reputation as a notable scholar or a great teacher. But the duties of Symmes and Kneeland ran as much toward keeping order among their charges as toward instruction. The entry of October 10, 1760, in Nathaniel Ames's diary of his Harvard years reads, "Kneelands and Thayers windows broke last night."[28]

The rules which the tutors were supposed to enforce were not much different from college regulations of today, except for Sabbath observance and prohibitions of cursing, lewd conversations, obscene songs, and stage plays. These official laws brought occasional fines upon the offenders, but generally were observed about as much in the breach as in the practice, and Joseph Warren got into little trouble on matters of student conduct. One provision of the laws forbade the frequenting of taverns or "victualling houses" in Cambridge. Noon dinner was eaten in Commons, while breakfast and supper could be taken in one's room. Warren took

[26] "The Fire at Harvard College," *The Magazine of History with Notes and Queries,* Extra No. 175, pp. 60-61.

[27] MS Admissions Book, 1725-1828 (Harvard College Archives); "The Laws of Harvard College [1767]," Colonial Society of Massachusetts, *Publications,* XXXI (*Collections: Harvard College Records,* Part III), 347; MSS Harvard Faculty Records, II (1752-66), 37, 46-47 (Harvard College Archives); *Boston Evening-Post,* June 30, 1755, for announcement of the entrance examinations.

[28] Sarah B. Baker, ed., "Extracts from the Ames Diary," *Dedham Historical Register,* I, No. 3 (July, 1890), 113.

at least some of his meals out of college, owing at his death some twelve pounds for "dyat from May 1757 to July 6 1759." During Warren's junior year, the undergraduates produced several plays, and Joseph seems to have been among the leaders of this illicit drama guild. In July, 1758, Nathaniel Ames wrote in his diary, "Cato a play acted at Warren's cham." Joseph incurred his only fines for being absent on four occasions, ranging from three days to nearly two weeks. Perhaps a lark in Boston was responsible, but it might well have been work on the farm which kept him home.[29]

In his freshman year, Joseph Warren shared a bed with a classmate in the freshman dormitory. As a sophomore, a student shared a room in one of two dormitories, usually on the ground floor where everyone going in or out could stop to lounge and chat. In 1756 Warren shared room 20 in Massachusetts Hall with Josiah Bridge of the class of '58. As a junior, he moved to room 3 in Stoughton Hall with Abiel Leonard, and in his senior year shared room 8 in Massachusetts, a choice room free from disturbances on an upper floor, with Samuel Cotton.[30] About the dormitories shuffled the widow Abdy, the aged sweeper and bedmaker who passed her ninetieth year when Joseph was a Harvard senior. Aiding her in these chores was the college character of that generation, Dan Barrett. The succinct epitaph which Warren penned for him is recorded in Jeremy Belknap's diary:[31] "1760, Mar. 15. Mr. Daniel Barrett sweeper and bedmaker to the college died, his inwards being almost consumed with drinking RUM, his summum bonum."

Danl Barrett's epitaph
Under this Stone there lies the Trunk
Of one who lived and died Drunk.
J. Warren.

It was in the rooms that college life centered. Drinking bouts were organized in the chambers and the latest pranks planned. One of the favorites was climbing the roof of Old Harvard to rip

[29] "Laws of Harvard College," pp. 349-350, 356-358; Baker, ed., "Extracts from the Ames Diary," *Dedham Historical Register*, I, No. 1 (Jan., 1890), 13; MS Account of Estate of Zachariah Boardman v. Estate of Joseph Warren, April 6, 1784, Chamberlain Collection of Autographs: The Miscellaneous Papers, V (1777-97), 949 (Boston Public Library); Harvard Faculty Records, II, 67, 75, 83.

[30] MSS Room Assignment Records (Harvard College Archives).

[31] Quoted in Samuel F. Batchelder, *Bits of Harvard History* (Cambridge, Mass., 1924), pp. 276-277.

off lead. One of the few personal anecdotes of Joseph Warren's Harvard career likely is associated with this prank. The story, as related by an early biographer who heard it from a witness forty years after the event, is that several students, intent on arranging college affairs in a way contrary to Warren's ideas, barred the door of their room against him. He climbed the roof, seized a rain spout, lowered himself as far as the open window of the room and threw himself in. "At that instant the spout, which was decayed and weak, gave way and fell to the ground. He looked at it without emotion, said it had served his purpose, and began to take his part in the business."[32] If the incident happened at all, it was probably connected with a prank to trap Warren on the roof, there to be caught cutting lead by the tutors. Whatever the motive, the action reflects a measure of youthful daring and courage that was characteristic of Warren.

Joseph Warren's Harvard years held something more than the round of studies and pranks of the average undergraduate career. These were the years of the struggle of France and Britain for half of the North American continent. News of the official declaration of war by the mother country reached Boston as Joseph was about to start his sophomore year. During the next three years, the Boston newspapers printed page after page of battle reports from the widespread war fronts. Joseph could read the exciting accounts of the guerrilla activities of Rogers' Rangers behind the French lines and, perhaps, was already dreaming that dream of personal military glory which was to lead him to an early death. Major victories, such as the capture of Louisburg, were celebrated in Boston by bell ringing, artillery fire, bonfires, and rejoicing. In April, 1759, during Joseph Warren's senior year, the undergraduates received permission to form the college's first military company. This "Marti-Mercurian" band was allowed to exercise at certain hours, providing that arms were not kept in the dormitories.[33]

As the summer of 1759 and graduation ceremonies approached, the seniors paid more heed to college affairs and less to war news. On June 29, Jonathan Trumbull, later a Federalist governor of Connecticut, stood before his classmates and delivered the oration

[32] Samuel L. Knapp, *Biographical Sketches of Eminent Lawyers, Statesmen, and Men of Letters* (Boston, 1821), pp. 108-109, was perhaps the most widely read of many works in which the story appeared.

[33] *Boston Weekly Advertiser*, May 29, Aug. 21, 1758; Batchelder, *Bits of Harvard History*, pp. 51-52.

at the valedictory ceremonies. In July, Warren and his friends, who had shared four years of college experiences together, received their degrees and said farewell. Most of them would receive master's degrees, but there was little formal work in Cambridge required for this. Following graduation, young Warren served a term as master of Roxbury Latin School in 1760, for a salary of £43 9*s*. 4*d*., most of which was turned over to his mother.[34]

The thesis that a master's candidate argued was still primarily an exercise in logical reasoning on an abstract question. For this purpose one question served about as well as another, with the possibility of discovering a "scientific" answer based on experiment or historical evidence being of little moment. Joseph Warren's thesis in medicine was nearly as abstract as that of the student who tried to answer the question of whether or not Adam had an umbilical cord. Warren was one of the candidates who had to be prepared to speak at the 1762 graduation exercises on the master's question he had chosen. During the years since 1760, he had read and thought about whether or not all diseases arose from obstruction. In an age in which universal causes and laws were sought in all fields of mental activity, his negative answer reflects that regard for individual treatment of the sick which is a part of every good practitioner of medicine and which was not notably widespread in his day.[35] The fact that Warren's thesis was in the field of medicine suggests that Harvard recognized the need to prepare students in their professions, though no formal classes in medicine were as yet offered.

More important than a Harvard thesis in the training of a colonial doctor was his apprenticeship to an established practitioner. The fortunate youths who could afford a European medical education were few indeed; by far the majority of American doctors of the Revolution were trained in the colonies. By the time of Warren's graduation from Harvard, Zabdiel Boylston had retired from practice and William Douglass was dead. Only two physicians of their stature were active in Boston. Silvester Gardiner had been trained in London, established the first apothecary shop in Boston in 1741, and was as competent a doctor as he was

---

[34] *Boston Evening-Post*, July 23, 1759; Hale, *Roxbury Latin School*, p. 68.

[35] In the Latin: "An omnes Morbi oriantur ab Obstructionibus. Negat Respondens Josephus Warren." MS Book of *Theses* and *Quaestiones* (Harvard College Archives). A full list for the colonial period is in Edward J. Young, "Subjects for Master's Degree in Harvard College from 1655 to 1791," Mass. His. Soc., *Proceedings*, XVIII (1880-81), 119-151.

a businessman. Doctor James Lloyd, however, took a larger number of students into his home, and it was to him that Warren applied for his training. After a five-year apprenticeship to a Boston doctor, Lloyd had gone to England, where he studied with William Cheselden, one of Europe's great surgeons, heard William Smellie's lectures on midwifery, met William and John Hunter, and served as a dresser at Guy's Hospital. Returning to Boston in 1752, he quickly built a large practice in obstetrics and general medicine. He introduced to the colonies the use of ligatures in place of the searing of wounds, and he followed some of Cheselden's techniques in amputation. To his credit, he carried on the work of Boylston in smallpox inoculation. Lloyd was able to pass on to Joseph Warren both the most advanced knowledge of the European medical schools and the information he had acquired during his years as an apprentice.

Lloyd and other leading Boston physicians were often men of culture and high position in society. Douglass, for example, had been interested in such diverse subjects as earthquakes, eclipses, historical writing, and free schools. At his master's home and beautiful garden, young Warren found one of Boston's centers of social life; Lloyd's friends and patients included many colonial aristocrats, as well as Sir William Howe and Lord Percy. Though fashionably dressed and driving in coaches to visit their patients, the Boston doctors did not affect the long wigs, gold-headed canes, and foppish costumes of French physicians. And they had somewhat less to do with medical fads and quackery, such as "celestial beds" to bring youth to the senile, than did their English colleagues.[36] Joseph Warren was fortunate in being able to serve his apprenticeship with a man of much common sense, excellent medical training, and a good deal of wisdom. Also, in Lloyd's home he made deep friendships that survived the period's political animosities, such as that with John Jeffries, a student of Lloyd who was to become well known for his balloon ascensions.

As an apprentice to Lloyd, Warren learned the technical aspects of his profession primarily by practicing it. Most doctors were their own apothecaries and the compounding of drugs for Lloyd's patients was valuable experience. Clinical experience came from doing dressings and substituting on calls occasionally,

[36] Henry R. Viets, *A Brief History of Medicine in Massachusetts* (Boston and New York, 1930), pp. 68-73, 80-81, is the source of material in the two preceding paragraphs.

and Joseph learned diagnosis and treatment as he accompanied Lloyd on his rounds. The study of anatomy was the one lack in the apprentice system. Few doctors owned as much as a skeleton, and actual dissection was usually possible only by nocturnal and highly illegal body snatching. Warren studied the subject by charts and such printed words as those in a 1664 English translation of *A Description of the Body of Man: Being a Practical Anatomy* by J. Berengarius.[37] Despite his lack of academic training in medicine, and with the peculiar advantages afforded by the apprentice method, Warren was able to become one of the outstanding physicians in Boston and to carry systematic instruction of students beyond that of any predecessor in Massachusetts. Lloyd's influence was reflected in Warren's attention to obstetrics as an important part of medical practice and in his general skill as a physician.

Technically, Warren was a candidate for the master's degree at Harvard while serving his apprenticeship with Lloyd. This was relatively easier than it would be today, since the requirements for the degree were largely formal—little more than paying a few pounds tuition and staying out of jail. Nevertheless, there were expenses—for the apprentice training as well as the college tuition. Mother Warren again helped, taking on a fifty-pound debt to Lloyd in order to support her eldest son in training for the profession which had been her father's. On August 3, 1763, Joseph deeded two-fifths of the Roxbury farm to Lloyd, the deed to be canceled if £100 were paid. This sum, the remainder of Lloyd's fee for his medical education, Warren was able to pay within two years.[38]

The young man thus had a good start in life. His father and mother had done well by him, in both natural endowments and in character. Young, daring, and courageous, he yet had a sense of responsibility and of civic duty. At Roxbury Latin School and Harvard College he had received as good an education as New England could provide, and James Lloyd gave him a fine medical training. Now all he needed was patients and a chance to prove his genius.

[37] Warren's signed copy of Berengarius' *Anatomy* is in Harvard Medical Library.

[38] MS James Lloyd, Ledger, 1758-78 (Boston Medical Society Library); Warren to Lloyd, executed and entered Aug. 3, 1763, Suffolk Deeds, C, 111-112.

# Doctor of Colonial Boston

CHAPTER II

The great epidemic disease of eighteenth-century Boston was smallpox. A large number of children died of measles in 1772, and occasionally scarlet fever took its toll. Yet no single contagious disease had a higher death rate or instilled greater fear in the people of any colony than did the pox. The first medical publication on this continent was Thomas Thacher's "Brief Rule to Guide the Common People of New England. How to Order Themselves and Theirs in the Small Pocks, or Measels." It was entirely appropriate that it was written by a citizen of Boston, where the scourge struck often and hard. Other colonies had their taste of it. The ship that brought William Penn to visit his colony in 1682 lost thirty of its company to the disease, and Jonathan Edwards was the most famous of thousands of colonists who died of it.[1]

Two theories as to the transmission of epidemic diseases were current in the colonies. One held that transmission was by air, food, and water, and that prevention should emphasize sanitary controls; the other taught that contagion was the cause, and iso-

[1] Francis R. Packard, *The History of Medicine in the United States* (Philadelphia, Pa., 1901), pp. 66, 75.

lation of victims the control. On the latter theory, Boston enacted laws which required the quarantine of incoming ships, notification of town officials when a family was infected, and the placing of fences, red flags, and guards about the homes of such families. Such legislation helped limit the number of smallpox epidemics to five between 1701 and 1775, but the death rate in each was high. The average death rate due to the disease during this period was 35 per 1,000, climbing as high as 105 in 1721.[2]

Cotton Mather read reports of the use of smallpox inoculation in England, and tried to get Boston physicians to experiment during the epidemic of 1721. Only Zabdiel Boylston had the courage to do so, inoculating his own son and causing a conflict within the colony. His book on the disease, published first in London, was reprinted in Boston in 1730, the year after another epidemic had hit that town. But it was the successful practice of inoculation rather than the pamphlet warfare which really won the day. In 1729 there were only twelve deaths among nearly 400 persons who were inoculated, as compared to 500 deaths among some 3,600 natural cases. Nevertheless, town officials usually were reluctant to allow inoculation until the number of cases reached twenty or more, when they were forced to recognize the ineffectiveness of their efforts to stop the spread of the disease by isolation of the victims. Actually, inoculation may have spread the disease among those who had not had it previously, yet refused inoculation. But its relative success in keeping down the death rate of those inoculated, as compared to the rate among natural cases, did prove its value. In the epidemic of 1752, only 28 per cent of the victims were those who bared themselves to the needle, while 87 per cent of all cases of smallpox were from inoculations in the epidemic which hit Boston during Joseph Warren's first year of practice.[3]

The epidemic of 1763 broke out in the North End of Boston late in the year. "Of the first 12 or 13 persons seizd with it, ten or eleven of them died. . . . A great panick seizd every body, either for themselves, their children, or relations that had not had

[2] Richard H. Shryock, "Eighteenth Century Medicine in America," Amer. Antiq. Soc., *Proceedings*, n.s., LIX, Part 2 (Oct. 19, 1949), 278; John B. Blake, "Smallpox Inoculation in Colonial Boston," *Journal of the History of Medicine and Allied Sciences*, VIII, No. 3 (July, 1953), 284.

[3] Blake, "Smallpox Inoculation," pp. 288, 291. See also Viets, *Medicine in Massachusetts*, pp. 55-65.

the distemper before."[4] Those who could, packed their goods and furniture in wagons and moved to the country. Joseph Warren, the youngest of Boston's doctors, didn't wait for older and wiser heads to lay plans for fighting the scourge. He was convinced of the value of inoculation, and saw in the epidemic an opportunity for his first business venture, the operation of a pox hospital. Some months before the government opened an inoculation hospital, Warren agreed with Drs. Thomas Bulfinch and Joseph Gardner to establish a private one.[5] This plan, though never executed, may have prodded the authorities to act. Years later, shortly before the war broke out, Warren revived his plan for a private hospital, which he intended to operate with a British army surgeon. In 1763 the larger body of public opinion agreed with Warren on the need for immediate inoculation. A number of Bostonians invited William Barnett, a New Jersey doctor who had gained a reputation as an inoculator in Philadelphia, to come to Boston. And, when inoculation was authorized in Boston, Warren and his colleagues were swamped with patients.

The lower house of the General Court, in which towns other than Boston were able to control a majority, refused to support an inoculation hospital in town. However, the governor and Council cooperated with the selectmen of Boston in arranging to have several doctors open one on Point Shirley in Chelsea in February and another shortly thereafter at Castle William in Boston Harbor. At the Castle, Joseph Warren was one of two resident physicians. The other, Samuel Gelston, came up from Nantucket, having operated a pox hospital at Martha's Vineyard. Warren purchased two featherbeds, pillows, and three blankets from Dr. Lloyd on credit, and he and Gelston stayed at their posts day and night.[6] Drs. Nathaniel Perkins, Miles Whitworth, and Lloyd treated their patients at the Castle, and most of the other doctors used the Point Shirley hospital, where the New Jersey doctor, Barnett, was in charge. Busy as the few doctors of Boston were, a slight accident to one of them during the peak of the epidemic assumed exaggerated importance. Warren's master, Lloyd, fell down a cellar

[4] James Gordon to William Martin, Boston, March 9, 1764, Mass. Hist. Soc., *Proceedings,* XXXIII (1899, 1900), 389.

[5] Viets, *Medicine in Massachusetts,* p. 79.

[6] *Boston Post-Boy,* Feb. 20, March 5, 1764; James Lloyd, Ledger, Feb. 25, 1764; Viets, *Medicine in Massachusetts,* pp. 75-76.

stairway and broke a finger, which had to be amputated. This for some time prevented him from treating his 300 patients, and threw an added burden upon the other doctors. "The ablest physitians had undertook so many patients that it seemed impossible they could properly attend so many, as every body [was] striveing who should be first inoculated lest they should take it the natural way."[7]

On March 12, 1764, the *Boston Post-Boy* printed a statement of the Boston selectmen admitting that they had *"no hope to stop the progress of the smallpox.* But notwithstanding we will keep up guards at the infected houses until next Saturday night." A week later the newspaper encouraged inoculation, pointing out that not one who had been inoculated so far had died. The people of Boston responded in numbers difficult to handle. Two factors other than the success of inoculation in earlier epidemics accounted for the flood of patients in 1764. The town officials set April 20 as the final date for inoculation, so that the treatment of 5,000 cases was condensed into two months. And, more important, on March 13 the physicians agreed to inoculate the poor free of charge. The established fees of £1 5*s.* 4*d.* for medicine and treatment and three dollars for a week of food and nursing prevented many from submitting themselves before this. Conditions dictated an extension of the time allowed for inoculation at the Castle until mid-May. By August 13, 1764, the selectmen could announce "that no one person in the town is now sick of the smallpox."[8] Warren and his colleagues had proved most conclusively the value of inoculation: of 699 Bostonians who took the disease naturally, 124 died, while the deaths among the 4,977 persons inoculated numbered only 46.[9]

It is difficult to conceive of a more rugged initiation into medical practice than that received by Joseph Warren in this epidemic crisis. Castle William's barracks had forty-eight rooms with accommodations for ten persons in each. Quarantined there for several months, Warren treated several hundred patients, many with other ailments besides the smallpox. From his success as an inoculator, he gained a reputation in Boston that any young physi-

[7] Gordon to Martin, Boston, March 9, 1764, Mass. Hist. Soc., *Proceedings*, XXXIII (1899, 1900), 390-391.

[8] *Boston Post-Boy*, Aug. 13, 1764; Blake, "Smallpox Inoculation," p. 291.

[9] *Ibid.*

cian in a town of comparable size today might envy. Actually, he had begun practice a short time before the epidemic, many of his patients being Roxbury people who had known him as a boy. On June 15, 1763, he wrote the name of his first patient, Samuel Sumner, Jr., of Roxbury, in his new ledger. Before the year was out, his practice extended to forty other patients, ranging from Mr. John Fowle in jail to "Mrs. Mary Collins, school mistress," as well as several relatives of the Stevens and Williams families. But it was the epidemic that brought him patients from the Boston aristocracy and expanded his practice considerably. Among those who came to him for treatment were the merchant Richard Clarke (later a key figure in the tea incident), the customs official Benjamin Hallowell, Thomas Flucker of the Governor's Council, Foster Hutchinson, and Andrew Oliver. And there were also patients from the poorer North End of Boston, where the Sons of Liberty were to establish their stronghold—men like "Mr. Wm. Dawes carpenter," who was to ride express to Lexington on April 18, 1775, at Joseph Warren's direction.[10]

The smallpox epidemic had disrupted life in Boston for nearly eight months, during most of which time Warren had viewed the town's spires from the confinement of Castle William. Once the disease was stamped out, Warren gladly returned across the bay to town and to the respite of normal activities. Twenty-three years old and with some promise of success in his profession, he now turned his thoughts to marriage. Portraits and engravings of Warren, depicting him as he appeared in 1775, make clear the handsome features to which the ladies of Boston testified. In Copley's portrait (see frontispiece), Joseph tends toward heaviness; yet, the fine figure he cut in the streets of Boston as a young man is revealed. Of medium height (five feet, eight to ten inches, perhaps), he has broader shoulders, a more barreled chest, and heavier calves than Copley's Hancock, but none of the paunch of Sam Adams in that Copley portrait. His dress of ruffled cuffs, half-buttoned vest, and well-cut coat is more elegant yet more casual than Adams', and stops quite short of Hancock's foppishness. The head is almost a perfect oval, with high forehead, classic Greek nose, full lips, and eyes so gentle as to belie the courage which lay behind them. Every stroke of Copley's brush attests to the same

[10] MS Joseph Warren, Ledger, 1763-68 (Mass. Hist. Soc. Library, permission for the use of which was kindly granted by Dr. Richard Warren of Boston).

qualities which contemporaries noted in their word portraits of Warren. Joseph's open, frank countenance reveals his true modesty, even temper, and acute sensibility to human suffering. Understanding of human frailty in others, he was a man of character himself, without, however, being prudish. Engaging, affable, and easy in manner, he also had a taste for philosophy and belles-lettres that made him welcome in many drawing rooms and gained the esteem of enemies as well as friends.[11]

During the summer of 1764, this promising young doctor fell in love with Elizabeth Hooton. At eighteen years of age she was acknowledged to be one of the most beautiful young women of Boston. In addition she possessed a "handsome fortune," being the only daughter of Richard Hooton, a deceased merchant. On Thursday evening, September 6, 1764, the young couple was married in the Brattle Square Church by that outstanding Whig clergyman Samuel Cooper. The Portuguese coin that Joseph paid the minister for the service did nothing to insure against the misspelling of his bride's name as Horton in the church records.[12] Three months later another marriage was solemnized on a Thursday evening in Boston, Samuel Adams being married to Elizabeth Wells. It was not long before the two men were to be deeply involved in politics, but at the moment Warren thought most about advancing in his profession and supporting his newly established household.

If Warren's financial condition was not of the best on the eve of the American Revolution, it was because of prodigal spending

[11] Copley's portrait of Warren is in the Museum of Fine Arts, Boston, and a copy of it by a later artist hangs in Faneuil Hall. Descriptions of Warren by contemporaries who knew him well include: Mercy Warren, *History of the Rise, Progress and Termination of the American Revolution* (Boston, 1805), I, 222-223; John Eliot, *A Biographical Dictionary* (Salem, Mass., 1809), p. 471; Perez Morton, "An Oration Delivered at the King's Chapel in Boston, April 8, 1776," in *Orations Delivered at the Request of the Inhabitants of the Town of Boston to Commemorate the Evening of the Fifth of March, 1770* (Boston, [1785]), p. 188; William Gordon, *The History of the Rise, Progress, and Establishment, of the Independence of the United States* (London, 1788), II, 49-50; Catherine B. Mayo, ed., "Additions to Thomas Hutchinson's 'History of Massachusetts Bay,'" Amer. Antiq. Soc., *Proceedings*, LIX, Part 1 (April, 1949), 45.

[12] *Boston Post-Boy*, Sept. 10, 1764; Ellis L. Motte *et al.*, eds., *Records of the Church in Brattle Square, Boston* (Boston, 1902), p. 443; Frederick Tuckerman, "Notes from the Rev. Samuel Cooper's Inter-leaved Almanacs of 1764 and 1769," New Eng. Hist. and Geneal. Soc., *Register*, LV, No. 2 (April, 1901), 147-148.

and careless business methods rather than failure in his profession. For a youth of his age, his first year and a half in practice, through December, 1764, was encouragingly successful. And from that time forward his business, if not his fortune, steadily rose. During the first years of practice, Warren charged one shilling, four pence for the extraction of teeth, one of his most common medical services. Patients who needed false teeth were sent off to the silversmiths, Warren himself patronizing his friend Paul Revere, who made two teeth for the doctor.

Warren's standard fee for an office visit and medicine or dressing was three shillings, while house calls brought four shillings, four pence. Calling the doctor out at night cost six shillings, and delivery of a baby one pound, eight shillings. Many colonial doctors left the latter service in the hands of midwives. James Lloyd, however, had studied midwifery in England, and Warren profited from his teacher's experience in this field. Occasionally he had to do surgery, his one recorded fee for an amputation being four pounds. One patient made remittance of his fee in flour, while others paid with knee buckles, locks, blankets, and pairs of shoes. John Morley, a Boston merchant, paid one hamper of beer, and Warren canceled the remaining two pounds out of sympathy for the man's misfortune. In the months from May through December, 1764, Warren recorded fees of about sixty-five pounds in his ledger. Ten years later, during the same eight months of 1774, he was charging, if not collecting, over £292.[13] Actually Warren's advancement to the front rank of the Boston medical profession took less than a decade. As early as 1769, a colleague described him as being "now first in business in this town," and eagerly sought Warren's approval in order to advance himself.[14]

Other evidence of Warren's progress in his profession is the number of patients he treated. During the first years of practice he steadily gained new patients, 275 people coming to his office between 1765 and 1768 for their first visits. By 1774 he was treating twenty-five to fifty new patients each month. These new patients, with Warren's regular clientele, meant that he was seeing as many as twenty patients on busy days. During the peak of his

[13] This paragraph is based on Joseph Warren, Ledgers, 1763-68 and 1774-75 (Mass. Hist. Soc. Library).

[14] Thomas Young to ———, [Boston, Sept., 1769], printed in Henry H. Edes, "Memoir of Dr. Thomas Young, 1731-1777," Col. Soc. of Mass., *Publications*, XI (*Trans.*, 1906-07), 8.

practice, the summer of 1774, he averaged 225 visits per month. In this growth there was a deeper significance than the expansion of business of a young Boston doctor, for as Boston's busiest physician, Warren was in an excellent political position. Unlike the newspaper editors, lawyers, merchants, and professional politicians of the colony, Warren appeared to his contemporaries to be a disinterested, civic-minded man who did not enter public affairs because of selfish motives. Also, few Bostonians were able to meet as many townsmen, from all ranks of society and every political party, in so intimate a way, as did Warren in making his rounds. While it might not be fair to charge him with using the consulting room as a political forum, the gentleness, charm, and persuasiveness of his personality must have won many friends while bandaging wounds who turned into political supporters when he mounted the rostrum.

Hundreds of pewterers, ropemakers, saddlers, wigmakers, sailors, and slaves came to Joseph Warren as patients. Many of their names survive only in the pages of their doctor's ledger, a neatly penned number of shillings and pence standing behind each name. These long lists of laborers and artisans provide adequate proof of Joseph Warren's popularity as a doctor among the lower classes. A tribute to his skill is found in the number of intelligent, wealthy clients, many of whom were to become political enemies, who visited him during his first years of practice. Thomas Hutchinson, lieutenant governor of the colony, was the most prominent of them. The number of government supporters who sought his services dropped off, however, as Warren became more deeply involved in politics, while new Whig patients were added to his practice. In Massachusetts, at least, political loyalties of the period ran so deep as to extend to the choice of one's doctor, as well as to the newspaper that one read.

There is no question but that members of the Whig party took Warren to heart as a doctor as well as in his role of political leader. Some consulted him only once; others, like John Adams, who was a close personal friend of Warren, made him their family doctor. James Otis and Thomas Cushing, Justice Edmund Quincy and Josiah Quincy, Jr., Benjamin Edes and John Gill, Samuel Adams and John Hancock were just a few of his political allies who called upon him in his professional capacity. And political friends proved to be useful in an even more remunerative respect. In 1769, Warren received the commission to treat the sick in the Boston almshouse. Benjamin Church and Miles Whitworth, the one a questionable Whig and the other a declared supporter of the governor's party, had had this commission in earlier years. The doctor who obtained this rather sizable practice was assured of the payment of fees by the Massachusetts Council. The Boston selectmen who recommended to the Council the payment of Joseph Warren's bill of £198 2*s*. 4*d*., for services from May, 1769, to May, 1770, were political friends of Warren. Two of them, John Hancock and Samuel Pemberton, were patients as well. Joseph Warren received £213 16*s*. and £252 16*s*. 5*d*. for his work at the almshouse during the next two years. In May, 1773, however, the commission went to Samuel Danforth, an outstanding Loyalist doctor.[15] It hardly seems credible that Warren's position was such that he no longer needed this additional income. Nor is there evidence of a consistent policy of rotating the commission at regular intervals among various Boston physicians. Possibly the strong political conservatism of 1773 played a part in Warren's loss of this commission.

In the mid-eighteenth century in several of the colonies, the use of mineral water for drinking and baths became something of a medical fad among the upper classes. An interest in springs developed at Boston about 1765, and was doubtless quickened considerably as the wife of Governor Bernard set the social pattern by traveling ninety miles to "take the waters."[16] The story was told of a number of people who hired a man to go to Stafford, Connecticut, to bring back mineral water. He filled a thirty-gallon cask, sold the water all the way back to Massachusetts at one dollar per gallon, and by refilling it at each brook along the route, managed to dispose of 160 gallons. The newspaper account of the

[15] Mass. Archives, Council Records, XVI (1765-74), 523, 600, 661, 667, 756, for the action of the Council on the bills of Warren and Danforth; MSS bills of Warren, with names of patients and fees, dated Jan. 2, 1771, and Nov. 20, 1771, Warren MSS, II, and Alexander Washburn MSS, XXII (Mass. Hist. Soc. Library).

[16] Bernard to Barrington, Boston, Aug. 27, 1768, Edward Channing and Archibald Coolidge, eds., *The Barrington-Bernard Correspondence and Illustrative Material, 1760-1770*, vol. 17 in *Harvard Historical Studies* (Cambridge, Mass., 1912), 172. On the general subject, see Carl Bridenbaugh, "Baths and Watering Places of Colonial America," *William and Mary Quarterly*, 3rd ser., III, No. 2 (April, 1946), 151-181.

fraud sagely concluded that "the people *believing* it genuine, soon found the salutary effects thereof."[17]

Joseph Warren's attitude toward such springs seems to have been somewhat skeptical. He did investigate the waters at Stafford with a view of taking up residence there as a consulting physician. His decision not to carry out this venture may have been due to skepticism as to the curative powers of the waters. It was less than a week after the *Boston Gazette* printed the story of the man with the cask of brook water that Warren visited Connecticut. He planned "to examine the waters that have been lately so much the subject of conversation, in order to ascertain their qualities and uses. Such examination (for which the Dr. is well qualified) by proper experiments, will enable him to determine in what distempers they are proper or improper. . . ."[18] Incidental evidence of Warren's contempt for doctors who put too much faith in elixirs is found in a newspaper article written less than one year later, during a heated dispute with a professional colleague.

The Young-Whitworth controversy developed out of the treatment of a Mrs. Davis, whose death was charged to Dr. Thomas Young. Miles Whitworth, whose patient she originally was, wrote a letter to the public prints in which he accused Young of incompetence, of treating Mrs. Davis without informing Whitworth of it, and of causing her death by bleeding. Thomas Young was well known in his day as a freethinker and something of an intellectual. By some people he was viewed with alarm as a vulgar demagogue. His letter in reply to Whitworth indicates little of learning and less of nobility of mind. Arguing that the patient had been progressing satisfactorily until she stopped taking his medicines, he closed the article by challenging Whitworth to a public debate on the arts, sciences, languages, and medicine, so that he could expose Whitworth as a "blockhead."[19] Both men shortly appealed to other members of the profession for their opinions, and Joseph Warren entered the lists under Whitworth's banner.

Warren's several letters to the *Boston Gazette* in this dispute display much professional learning, viewed of course in the light of the medical knowledge of that day. His analysis of the facts of

---

[17] *Boston Gazette,* Aug. 4, 1766.

[18] *Ibid.,* Aug. 11, 1766.

[19] *Ibid.,* April 27, May 4, 1767. The dispute came to such a pass that a son of Dr. Whitworth assaulted Young when they met in the street.

the case and his argument that bloodletting should be used with discretion and only in certain cases showed a judiciousness of mind quite in contrast with the attitudes of some physicians of the period. These letters also reveal, however, some of the less-elevated characteristics of political propaganda. Here one finds the felicitous choice of words and clever turn of phrase of the Suffolk Resolves, the blunt irony of Warren's political journalism, and the character assassination (as scurrilous as it is witty) that is found in his attack upon Governor Bernard. Though Warren's first letter declared that Mrs. Davis' death "was hastened by that ill-timed evacuation" of blood by Dr. Young, it was relatively temperate in tone. He expressed surprise that Young had never read anything on the subject of bloodletting and suggested that he refrain from quoting authors whom he did not understand or had not read carefully. But Warren concluded with the wise admonition to both parties of the quarrel "that (instead of boasting of their present attainments) the gentlemen of the faculty would apply themselves to such studies as may qualify them for being truly useful to mankind."[20]

This letter took his side of the dispute out of the hands of Miles Whitworth, and turned Young's wrath full upon Warren. It initiated a series of letters by Warren and replies by Young, under the pseudonym of "Misophlauros," in which the two men became successively more abusive. As to the medical aspects of the case, Warren denied that bleeding was a remedy for all patients with abdominal pains and respiratory difficulties. He argued that any general principle of medicine must be applied with good judgment and reference to individual circumstances, and, to illustrate the danger of bloodletting as a panacea, told a story of events aboard a warship after the surgeon had died. A seaman with a smashed leg was brought to the ill-qualified surgeon's mate for treatment. The apprentice doctor decided to amputate, but having done so was unable to tie off the arteries. Taking knife in hand, he cut off the sailor's nose, and the patient soon died of a hemorrhage. When he was asked to explain such conduct, he said he had seen his master stop a bleeding nose by taking blood from

[20] *Ibid.*, May 25, 1767. Warren wrote this and other letters in the series under the pseudonym "Philo Physic." Not only does the style suggest Warren as the author, but he is so identified by his contemporary, Harbottle Dorr, in the margin of the Dorr file of the *Gazette* (Mass. Hist. Soc. Library).

the foot, and hoped the system would work as well in reverse. In the last letters of the series, Warren attacked Young on points other than the treatment of the deceased Mrs. Davis. He discussed the supposed appearance of the new word "Youngism" in the language. Feigning interest in his native tongue, Warren pleaded that Young stop encouraging the growth of a word that was destroying the precision of English. "If in the public papers, inaccuracy, malevolence, bad grammar and nonsense, are found, they are immediately pronounced Youngisms. Self-conceit, vain-boasting, and invincible impudence are frequently expressed by the word Youngism." When Young threatened to sue for loss of reputation, Warren suggested he would have to prove he had a reputation to lose. He advised Young that the search for mineral waters would occupy his time more profitably than would court action. This was a reference to a mineral spring which Young had discovered and which, according to Warren, turned out to be common water springing when "a little gutter from a cow-yard," which emptied into the well, was blocked off.[21]

The outcome of this public dispute seems to have been a deep contempt for his opponent on the part of Joseph Warren and an impotent rage on the part of Thomas Young. Considering the heat of this quarrel and the damage to Young's reputation, it is a bit surprising to find the breach healed in two years. In September, 1769, Warren called upon Young and said, "Sir, I now wait upon you to signify my high satisfaction that your character, interest and business rises fast in this town and I now assure you sir that whatever may heretofore have happened I have now a real esteem of you and hearty friendship for you which I desire you may henceforth credit on the honor of a gentleman." These words were recorded with glee just one day later by Thomas Young. The style of them, stilted even for the eighteenth century, raises a doubt as to Warren's sincerity. This, one suspects, was the young political leader as much as the professional colleague speaking. Hopeful of gaining aid for the Whig party, Warren made his peace and Young accepted the proffered friendship gratefully. With the friendship of both Joseph Warren and Benjamin Church, Thomas Young fancied himself "as well settled respecting medical friendship" as he could wish.[22] It was not long

[21] The letters of the series on which this paragraph is based were printed in the *Boston Gazette,* June 8–July 27, 1767.

[22] Edes, "Memoir of Dr. Thomas Young," p. 8.

before Young's important role in the Whig faction was to become clear.

Perhaps the most significant aspect of Joseph Warren's medical career was his role as a teacher. Generally Warren's importance in the history of medicine has been obscured because of his prominence as a political figure. Warren, to be sure, introduced no significant innovations in medical practice, nor did he devote his efforts to original research. His influence was quite marked, however, upon the generation of students whom he trained. His teaching naturally emphasized the apprentice method by which he had learned the art of healing. Going beyond this, however, Warren attempted to give some systematic instruction in surgery, anatomy, and general medicine, resembling the more formal academic training of the European schools. The student lived in Warren's home for two years, studying and serving the eighteenth-century version of an internship at the same time. He dressed wounds, acted as a nurse in the office, and answered night calls in uncomplicated cases. Thus was established an intimacy, as friends as well as colleagues, between teacher and student that was rare in a college.[23]

A number of Warren's students attended Harvard together during the early 1770's, and there formed a club for the study of anatomy, very probably at Joseph's suggestion. The membership of the Spunks or Spunkers Club, in which Warren's younger brother John was the leading spirit, included Jonathan Norwood, William Eustis, and David Townsend. Some of Warren's other students, among whom were Samuel Adams, Jr., Lemuel Hayward, Robert Williams, and David Jones, may have been members of the club. Meeting secretly, they dissected animals and, possibly, an occasional cadaver obtained by a midnight excursion to the cemetery. At one time, they organized an expedition to try to steal the body of a criminal between the gallows and the grave.[24] John Warren, of course, decided to study medicine with his brother Joseph, and many of his classmates at Harvard followed

[23] Brief mention of Warren's role as a teacher is found in Thomas F. Harrington, *The Harvard Medical School: A History, Narrative and Documentary, 1782-1905* (New York, 1905), I, 47, and in Viets, *Medicine in Massachusetts*, p. 86.

[24] Albert Matthews, "Notes on Early Autopsies and Anatomical Lectures," Col. Soc. of Mass., *Publications*, XIX (*Trans.*, 1916-17), 285-289; Samuel F. Batchelder, "Harvard Hospital-Surgeons of 1775: A Study in the Medical History of the American Revolution," *Harvard Alumni Bulletin*, XXII, No. 22 (Feb. 26, 1920), 501; Batchelder, *Bits of Harvard History*, pp. 157-158.

his example. The bond thus established among them continued for several years after they had dispersed to the towns of Massachusetts and established their own practices. When John Warren settled at Salem, Eustis wrote that the Spunks "often speak of the loss of their last member with sorrow which can only be felt among themselves." Two years later, as revolution broke out, Norwood wrote to John suggesting that they enter the army together, where a Spunks Club "might again exert itself for the benefit of mankind."[25]

The influence of Joseph Warren, both professionally and politically, is discernible in the careers of his students. No charge of medical incompetence was made against any of them, and only one had his patriotism questioned. Many of these men served in the army medical department during the war, and William Eustis, governor of Massachusetts and United States' secretary of war, followed the example of his teacher in turning from medicine to public affairs. John Warren, the outstanding member of the group, was to surpass his brother Joseph in medical skill. One of the great surgeons of his day, he engaged in original research and was the most important single figure in the founding of Harvard medical school. John Warren's interest in improving medical education and his own learned lectures in anatomy and surgery bespeak the success of the efforts of Joseph Warren and James Lloyd to systematize the instruction given to medical apprentices.

Joseph Warren, though not engaged in research himself, was the lifelong student of his subject that any good teacher must be. His letters in the Young-Whitworth dispute indicate an acquaintance with the professional literature of his day, as his knowledge of classical languages displays the interest in polite learning that was characteristic of educated contemporaries. There was little resembling a professional society in Boston until the end of the eighteenth century, except for a short-lived body organized in 1735, and Warren was largely dependent upon his own resources for extending his knowledge and skill. Seldom were doctors any

[25] William Eustis to John Warren, Boston, Nov. 17, 1773, and Jonathan Norwood to *id.*, Falmouth, Casco Bay, Mass., June 5, 1775, Warren MSS, II. Both of these letters mention a "Sp——rs Club," and historians of Massachusetts medicine have long been interested in finding verification of the full name of the club. The present author found such evidence in a third letter, signed "A Lamb of the Spunks Club." D. N. Bond to [John Warren], Marblehead, Mass., April 18, 1774, Warren MSS, II.

more successful in getting a cadaver than were Harvard undergraduates. During Warren's first year of practice, however, Benjamin Church and William Perkins did get a subject from the authorities. Very likely Warren accepted the invitation to be present at the lectures on anatomy that accompanied the secluded dissection.[26] During these years, the members of the profession also joined together in supporting a bill in the General Court, "preventing any person from practising physic or surgery, until he has undergone a proper examination."[27] Joseph Warren's letters to Thomas Young, and his request that a Salem doctor examine his brother carefully on his medical knowledge, suggest his support of high standards for the medical profession.

Warren had been educated by the best method available on this side of the Atlantic, and studied his profession with the penetrating intelligence and good judgment which were his as long as he practiced medicine. And, so doing, he became one of the outstanding doctors of Boston. Combining a high degree of skill with a charming personality and sympathy for suffering, he acquired a larger practice than any of his colleagues. Further, he gave a more systematic instruction to more students of medicine than any Boston doctor before the American Revolution. This is not to deny that Warren might have remained in obscurity had it not been for his political activities. In a history of American medicine, Joseph Warren's place does not loom large in comparison to that of his brother John or of Benjamin Rush. It was the course of political affairs in Massachusetts and the movement toward independence from Great Britain that brought the name of this young physician to the attention of two continents. It is in the rise of an obscure Boston doctor to leadership of the American Revolution in Massachusetts that Joseph Warren's most important story is to be found. And the story of his political leadership is closely interwoven with the development of Massachusetts parties which began about 1760.

[26] *Boston Gazette,* Dec. 5, 1763. Perkins announced another series of lectures in the *Boston Gazette,* Nov. 25, 1765, as noted by Albert Matthews, "Note on Dr. William Lee Perkins (1737-1797)," Col. Soc. of Mass., *Publications,* XX (*Trans.,* 1917-19), 12. On the early medical society, see Viets, *Medicine in Massachusetts,* pp. 65-68.

[27] *Boston Chronicle,* Jan. 7-11, 1768.

# Politics and Taxes

## CHAPTER III

Massachusetts depended upon the sea, and it was through the port of Boston, her cultural and political capital, that most of her economic lifeblood flowed. And in Boston, young Warren might have seen many an apparent paradox in the year 1760. Part seventeenth-century Puritan town and part eighteenth-century cosmopolitan city, Boston also had one foot in Europe and one in the New World. As late as 1759, a court would sentence a woman to walk the streets with a letter sewn on her garments for having committed incest; as early as 1769, Warren could attend a reading of "The Beggar's Opera," a "grand concert of vocal and instrumental music," or even horse racing with a hundred-dollar purse. Warren could see much in the street and tavern names (King Street and Cromwell's Head), even in the social customs, of Boston that was an American echo of Old England. The merchants met daily at one o'clock to walk on the Royal Exchange, in imitation of those in London, and, in the Boston Common, Warren and his friends had their own mall where "after drinking tea, the gentlemen and ladies walk[ed]."[1] Yet the contrasts between

[1] *Boston Post-Boy,* Aug. 20, 1759; *Boston Chronicle,* Sept. 25-28, 1769; *Massachusetts Gazette,* Jan. 12, Sept. 21, 1769; "Bennett's *History of New England,*" Mass. Hist. Soc., *Proceedings,* V (1860-62), 110-112, 125.

mother country and colony in Joseph Warren's youth were quite as marked as were the similarities. In nothing, perhaps, does the Boston of his day seem to present more of a paradox than in its political life.

In 1760, when Joseph Warren adopted Boston as the city of his future, the British Empire was in the sixth year of a war with France. Professing their glory in the name of Britons, many New Englanders died in that war under the British flag. Others, their fathers and brothers perhaps, smuggled enough goods to the enemy under that same flag to prolong the struggle. And there were few in the colonies who would condemn them for doing so. Acknowledging the supremacy of Parliament, many Bostonians ignored or defied the laws that body made; pledging to defend their king at the cost of their lives, many were to die in overthrowing him.

As to internal politics, two factions had long existed in Massachusetts. By 1760 leadership of the opposition had come into the hands of a closely knit group of Boston politicians, and the Court or Prerogative party now looked to the Massachusetts back country for much of its support. Served in large part by the Connecticut River, and to some extent isolated from the seaboard by ranges of hills, the western counties had developed an independent economic life and strongly conservative political sentiments. Several important political leaders of that section could be counted upon to support the colonial administration.

In 1760, however, factional dispute was largely suspended, partly because of the war, partly because of Thomas Pownall, the remarkable politician who occupied the governor's chair. There were two important changes in that year, but Bostonians saw no evil forebodings in either of them. On June 3, Pownall left the Province, entrusting the government to Thomas Hutchinson, acting governor until the arrival of Francis Bernard from New Jersey. The year ended with news reaching Boston of the death of George II. Both of these events seemed minor compared to the French war and the great fire of March, which had destroyed 350 homes and warehouses, with an estimated property damage of £100,000 to £300,000 sterling.[2] Yet the political changes of 1760 were to have grave consequences for many who lived to see the decade out.

Of the change in England a few words may suffice. Insofar as

---

[2] *Boston Post-Boy*, March 24, 1760.

Bostonians had thought of him at all, they had considered George II a good king. They had rejoiced at royal births and weddings and now they sincerely mourned the King's death. Joseph Warren reputedly contributed to a volume of memorial poems, but his verse has never been identified. A man like Warren might have followed the London advices in the newspapers closely enough to know that a group of politicians had gathered about the heir apparent, hoping to come to power when he did. But of the structure and principles of English political parties most Bostonians might well have had no more than vague ideas. In fact, such parties as there were had little in the way of grand principles by which they could be easily distinguished. By 1760 everyone in English public life was a Whig, if by that was meant a supporter of the principles of the Revolution of 1688. George III did, to be sure, try to be king, but a king who would gain his power through Parliament, rather than over it. Opposed to his court party were Rockingham Whigs, Pittites, and others—diverse groups which could not be welded into a unified party. Important as English politics were to become to the American colonist, Bostonians expressed no alarm upon the accession of George III.[3]

The arrival of the Bay Colony's new governor in August, 1760, was an occasion for festivities and rejoicing. Joseph Warren was now studying with Lloyd in Boston and may well have seen Francis Bernard as he was met on the road to Boston by a cavalry guard, the members of the governor's Council, and a procession of coaches of Boston's first gentlemen. Escorted through cheering crowds to the courthouse, the governor received the salute of the militia and cadet companies, took his oath of office, and attended "an elegant dinner" at Faneuil Hall. Some months later, Bernard addressed the General Court, praying that parties and factions would be dissolved in Massachusetts as they had been in Britain. "For my own part," he told the legislature, "I shall follow the example of my royal master, at a distance indeed, but as near as I can;

[3] George H. Guttridge, *English Whiggism and the American Revolution*, vol. 28, in University of California, *Publications in History* (Berkeley and Los Angeles, 1942), 41-47, 50-55, and Charles R. Ritcheson, *British Politics and the American Revolution* (Norman, Okla., 1954), chaps. 1-5, for the development of English parties between 1760 and 1770. Both works reflect the abiding influence of the "Namier thesis." Succintly stated in Lewis B. Namier, *England in the Age of the American Revolution* (London, 1930), pp. 4, 94-95, 128, 175-177, its fully elaborated proof is in the same author's *The Structure of Politics at the Accession of George III* (London, 1929) 2 vols.

particularly I shall found my administration on as broad a bottom as may be. . . ."[4] So spoke Francis Bernard in his innocence of Massachusetts politics. Less than one year later he wrote rather ruefully that the people of his colony were divided into parties of nearly equal strength, and that they were "jealous of their liberties (of which they form high and sometimes unconstitutional ideas)."[5] By that time Francis Bernard was beginning to abandon his broad bottom, and to found his administration on one or the other of those parties. In assuming, with Thomas Hutchinson, the leadership of the Prerogative party, he made an obvious and a congenial choice.

The change from the halcyon days of 1760 to the stormy political weather of 1765 was due to two great issues, which determined the dividing lines of the colony's political factions and led Joseph Warren into political life. One of these issues, Parliament's right to legislate for the colonies, was the source of the modern terminology applied to the two parties, Patriot and Loyalist or Whig and Tory. Contemporaries, however, occasionally spoke of the Liberty and Prerogative parties, indicating a greater awareness of the other issue—the attempt of the governor and his administration to control colonial patronage and dominate public affairs.[6] If detached from modern connotations of social or economic leveling, "Conservative" and "Radical" are also useful, for when used with "Moderate" they provide a terminology which includes all three political forces in Massachusetts.

Whatever the labels, it was one of these groups that Warren had to join if he wished to align himself with an organized body of public opinion. In the early 1760's the political force which he

---

[4] *Boston Evening-Post,* June 1, 1761. On Bernard's arrival in Boston, see *Boston Post-Boy,* Aug. 4, 1760.

[5] Channing and Coolidge, eds., *Barrington-Bernard Correspondence,* p. 53.

[6] Thomas Hutchinson uses the term "Liberty party" to mean the opposition to the government or the Prerogative party, not simply to designate the revolutionary organization known as the Sons of Liberty. He also seems to be referring to a political party in speaking of Samuel Adams as being "always on the side of liberty" and of several politicians as being "friends of liberty." Further, he applies the terms "privilege" and "prerogative" to the Country and Court parties. Francis Bernard usually referred to the opposition as "the Faction," but occasionally called it the "Party of the People." Thomas Hutchinson, *The History of the Colony and Province of Massachusetts-Bay,* ed. by Lawrence S. Mayo (Cambridge, Mass., 1936), III, 72, 96, 98, 211-214; [Francis Bernard, Thomas Gage, and Samuel Hood], *Letters to the Ministry* (Boston, 1769), p. 52.

was later to head was just a loose coalition of men with varied interests, who worked unitedly only rarely and on certain issues. This remained true until 1773, when an organized, colony-wide party was finally formed. In Boston young Warren found a disciplined political machine which he might join; on the province-wide level, however, the opposition to the administration had neither party structure nor party discipline. Such support as the Boston politicians got from outside of Boston came from members of the Assembly who owed their election to the voters of their towns, rather than to any colony-wide political party. These representatives might be persuaded to support Warren and Samuel Adams, but they could not be compelled to do so, and insofar as they were interested in patronage, they were natural allies of the governor's party. The governor distributed jobs and favors, with consent of the lower house being unnecessary. Of 113 members of the General Court in 1764, 60 were justices of the peace, 15 were judges of common pleas courts, 14 were captains, 4 were registers of probate, and 3 were sheriffs.[7] In their capacity of legislators, these men would be likely to support the governor who had appointed them. So long as it upheld English policy, the colonial administration was virtually assured of continuance in office during good behavior and of the right to this patronage. By discriminating use of the appointment power, Bernard and Hutchinson were able to form a political party with loyal members in many counties and to maintain discipline until the eve of the Revolution, when threats and violence by the opposition destroyed the Prerogative party. By late 1774, there was scarcely a man in Massachusetts who dared accept a royal appointment.

Despite the resources of the governor's party, the Warren-Adams faction defeated the administration in nearly every battle between 1765 and 1775. In part this was due to the important position of Boston in the life of the colony. It was to Boston that the news of changing British policy first came, and among its population that the initial reactions to such changes were expressed. Samuel Adams and Joseph Warren came to head a corps of lawyers, editors, and other articulate leaders which, by judicious use of mass rallies and the Boston press, was able to shape public opin-

[7] Ellen E. Brennan, *Plural Office-Holding in Massachusetts, 1760-1780: Its Relation to the "Separation" of Departments of Government* (Chapel Hill, N.C., 1945), pp. 72-73.

ion in all parts of the colony. The actions of Boston mobs in the Stamp Act crisis, the Boston Massacre, and the tea incident illustrate how the decision of the capital city might almost perforce be that of Massachusetts. Towns outside of Boston issued no united repudiation of such violence, and this led to the equation of Massachusetts with Boston in the minds of ministers at home. At least as important, however, in the success of the Liberty party was its skill in making use of the growing demand of many people for independence from parliamentary legislation. When questions of commerce and imperial taxation arose, an appeal was made to businessmen like John Hancock and John Rowe, natural conservatives who found no sympathy on these issues in the organized Prerogative party. During the *Liberty* incident, Hancock turned to Joseph Warren for advice; and during the tea crisis, John Rowe, who owned one of the tea ships, was visited by Warren, who urged him to stand by the policy of the Sons of Liberty. Other men, like Warren's close friend John Adams, who detested mob violence, nevertheless found a home in the Liberty party on constitutional issues. In short, Joseph Warren and Samuel Adams were able to shape their program to capture public opinion in Massachusetts. The Conservatives, who had their program planned in England, with little regard to colonial views, became a party of politicians without a foundation among the mass of the people.

Warren might, of course, have aligned himself with the third force in Massachusetts politics, the Moderates, who represented the least-organized body of public opinion in Massachusetts. Never forming a political party, they were as significant as either of the two which did exist, because their support was essential to both. Accepting the leadership of Warren and Adams for many years, they revealed their moderation when they rejected this leadership in the period from 1768 to 1773. Most of these men were concerned with the redress of specific grievances and the repeal of specific laws by Parliament. For an intense nationalist like Warren, these things were only steps toward complete self-government for his colony. Also, Warren would not have been happy with the Moderates, because they never took the issue of colonial patronage as seriously as did the Liberty party. During the period of conservatism following 1768, the moderate politicians, John Hancock, Thomas Cushing, and John Adams among them, deserted Warren's party. They were willing to lay down the cudgels as soon as the Townshend Acts were repealed, and some of them found it in themselves to cooperate with Hutchinson. The Warren-Adams faction, however, persisted in fighting the Conservatives when imperial grievances were as scarce as hens' teeth.

Before Joseph Warren's entry into politics during the Stamp Act crisis, some of the issues which divided the political forces of Massachusetts were becoming well defined, and a basis had been laid for the development of the Liberty party. Opposition had been voiced to British laws, questions had been raised as to Parliament's taxing powers, and the fight had commenced against the Conservatives' domination of the administration and the judiciary. These developments, however, could be attributed largely to one man, James Otis. And Otis, time was to discover, was a moderate at heart. Such support as he received was largely personal, rather than that of an organized party. It was left to Samuel Adams and Joseph Warren to bring the remaining elements to provincial politics: the creation of a political party to promote their aims; an amoral view of means, including the use of force, to carry out their policies; the demand for complete independence from parliamentary legislation; and an unflagging opposition to the aristocratic Prerogative party which went beyond the nature of James Otis' personal feud against Hutchinson.

The issue of Conservative control of colony politics, which was to draw Warren into politics, was being agitated by Otis, Adams, and others during Joseph's first years in Boston. As a young doctor in a town of fewer than 20,000 people, Warren quickly became acquainted with the leading political figures and heard much of this issue. While Warren was still a medical student, James Otis had fought the use of writs of assistance with his advanced argument that a law in conflict with the Constitution is no law. Warren, being an acquaintance of John Adams, probably knew of the role that the appointment of Thomas Hutchinson to the chief justiceship played in Otis' opposition. In 1762 Warren might have read *Considerations on the Election of Councellors,* a pamphlet protesting plural officeholding, and he could hardly have been unaware of the fight in the General Court to reduce Superior Court judges' salaries and to exclude these Conservative officials from legislative seats. Two years later, Warren's friend Samuel Adams drafted instructions which warned the Boston members of the General Court to guard the balance of the three branches of government and suggested a law barring from the legislature any member who accepted a post from the governor or crown.[8] These early years in Boston provided Warren with a lively schooling in colony politics, and it was the Conservative party's domination of offices which was to be one of his central targets from the Stamp Act crisis to the removal of Thomas Hutchinson.

The other issue which led Warren into politics, Parliament's right to legislate for the colonies, was also becoming bitterly contested in these years. In 1764 the Grenville Ministry lowered the molasses tax, hoping to make smuggling unprofitable and the collection of duties more reliable. All parties in Massachusetts opposed this law; Governor Bernard said he "could write a volume" against the act, and James Otis did write one. However, young Warren would not have had to study the arguments very thoroughly to perceive a difference of attitude. While Bernard protested against the size of the tax, Otis denied Parliament's right to tax at all. The Massachusetts House drafted a petition to Parliament which rejected the English legislature's authority, but Hutchinson and the Conservatives in the Council revised it, praying exemption from the taxes as a privilege, rather than demanding it as a right.[9] The Sugar Act of 1764 led many men in many colonies to think seriously of the relationship of their colonial governments to the British Parliament, and, by the time of the Stamp Act crisis, Joseph Warren's ideas were becoming well matured.

The Stamp Act of 1765 was similar to one which the Massachusetts General Court had enacted, without violent opposition, in 1755. The earlier law had imposed taxes on skin, vellum, parchment, and paper used for newspapers, mortgages, deeds, and other legal documents. A stamp commissioner was to swear to "faithfully execute the trust" reposed in him.[10] In view of this, the reasons for the vehement protests against the act of 1765 and the forced resignation of the stamp commissioner become even more

[8] *Ibid.*, pp. 41-45, 49-50; Boston. *A Report of the Record Commissioners of the City of Boston, Containing the Boston Town Records, 1758 to 1769* (Boston, 1886), p. 120, hereafter cited as *Boston Town Records, 1758 to 1769*.

[9] Francis Bernard to John Pownall, Castle William, Oct. 30, 1763, Bernard MSS, III, 105; Edmund S. and Helen M. Morgan, *The Stamp Act Crisis: Prologue to Revolution* (Chapel Hill, N.C., 1953), pp. 34-35. The important provisions of the Revenue Act of 1764, usually known as the Sugar Act, and other important laws are easily available in Merrill Jensen, ed., *English Historical Documents: American Colonial Documents to 1776* (London, 1955), hereafter cited as Jensen, *Colonial Documents*.

[10] *Boston Weekly News-Letter*, Jan. 16, 1755. Lawrence H. Gipson, *The Coming of the Revolution, 1763-1775* (New York, 1954), p. 70, discusses proposals of 1732 and later for a parliamentary stamp tax.

intriguing. Joseph Warren's letters and the hardships he faced as a young doctor during 1765 and 1766 provide interesting clues to these reasons, for it was the events of these years that determined he would earn his fame in politics rather than medicine. The passage of the Stamp Act carried an implicit challenge to that self-government of the colonies with which Joseph Warren had grown up. In Roxbury his neighbors had elected his own father as a selectman, and the town had been governed well without interference from abroad. Why should the colony not be allowed to govern itself, as it had very largely done in the past? Why should the people of the Bay Colony not choose their own officials, as Roxbury did its selectmen, rather than pay taxes for the salaries of men appointed in London or by Governor Bernard and his Council? With a family background and education that was more American than British, Warren was genuinely agitated by the levying of stamp duties, and turned increasingly from the quiet duties of treating the sick to the turbulence of the political arena.

One of Warren's closest friends, Edmund Dana, was in London at this time, too busy courting a noblewoman to write home. Joseph sent a letter of congratulation upon Dana's marriage, with a long account of political affairs in America. Engaged as he was, Dana may well have taken Warren's words lightly, but they reveal a young mind which had given thoughtful consideration to the subject of colonial rights and the causes of opposition to the Stamp Act. He called the levying of stamp taxes a "strange project" which had all of the colonies "inflamed to the highest degree." Americans, he felt, were a people who loved liberty zealously and believed that they would lose it if they lost the power to tax themselves. They were closer to the state of nature than were people of older countries, where through the years "some particular families have been able to acquire a very large share of property, from which must arise a kind of aristocracy."[11] Warren's realization of the danger of such an aristocracy arising in Massachusetts was one thing which led him into political opposition. While many colonists viewed with alarm the use of tax money to support a standing army, Warren warned that the revenue would be "perverted to enrich a set of corrupt individuals" at the colonists' expense.

[11] Copy, Joseph Warren to Edmund Dana, Boston, March 19, 1766, Miscellaneous MSS (Mass. Hist. Soc. Library), also printed in Richard Frothingham, *Life and Times of Joseph Warren* (Boston, 1865), pp. 20-22.

Royal salaries payed with these taxes would make some colonial officials independent of the people and increase "the number of mercenary placemen" who would trample upon colonial liberties.[12]

Thus, aside from the implications of the Stamp Act for the imperial relationship, Warren saw a danger in the use of the new revenue to interfere in colony politics. The struggle for office of the Liberty party, with which Warren was aligning himself, would be made more difficult, the Prerogative party would be strengthened, and a small clique might acquire further offices independent of popular control. To understand his alarm, one need do little but read the appointments to office in the Boston newspapers which he followed. The political machine created by Francis Bernard and Thomas Hutchinson was beginning to take on the appearance of an aristocracy. By appointment and marriage, three families were coming to control a number of offices in the administration and judiciary, which was little short of amazing. While the strength of the opposition grew in the General Court, the Conservatives' control of the executive and higher courts of law was unimpaired, and there their strength was impressive indeed. Among the officeholders are found the names of Francis, Francis, Jr., and John Bernard; Andrew and Peter Oliver; and Thomas,

[12] "B. W.," in *Boston Gazette,* Oct. 7, 1765. Few of Warren's pseudonymous letters have been identified, and a few words may be said here about the basis of my identification. Most helpful is the Harbottle Dorr file of newspapers (Mass. Hist. Soc. Library), in the margins of which this contemporary of Warren gives his opinion as to the authorship of articles and letters. Some stylistic characteristics aid in identifying Warren's prose. Most articles with citation of statutes and legal arguments may be dismissed as the work of John Adams or Josiah Quincy. In comparison with other contemporaries such as Samuel Adams, who might have written the articles that I ascribe to Warren, Warren's style is more personal, bombastic, and emotional. He uses the personal pronoun "I" more frequently and an inordinate number of imperative sentences charging the people to action. In many of his articles there is a sense of the judgment of history and of future generations upon his own times. Certain phrases, such as "that Liberty wherewith Christ has made you free," occur several times in different pieces. Finally, some peculiarities of punctuation and orthography found in his manuscripts are found in these printed writings. Thus, his use of a dash rather than a period as the full stop is found in his manuscript letters, in the newspapers, and in printed and manuscript texts of official documents attributed to him, but is rare in the writings of most contemporaries. A striking contrast to Warren's style is that of Samuel Adams, whose writings are easily identifiable by his extraordinary number of long sentences and extensive use of the semicolon.

Thomas, Jr., Foster, Elisha, and Edward Hutchinson.[13] Aside from such wholesale nepotism, not uncommon in the period, the members of these families often filled two or more posts at the same time. A few of the offices occupied by Thomas Hutchinson at one time included the lieutenant governorship, the chief justiceship of the Superior Court, and a seat in the Council.

If there was danger of the growth of a permanent aristocracy, Warren nevertheless felt that it did not yet exist on the scale that it did in Europe. America was a new country with "a more equal division of property," which gave more men an interest in preserving liberty.[14] Here was an unconscious statement of one of the dominant themes in American thought—the virtue and superiority of the New World compared with the vice and decay of Europe. Also interesting is Warren's belief that men with some property would have a special concern with protecting free government. If Joseph Warren ever led a revolution, it would, in his mind, be to preserve political liberties from English encroachment and to prevent the growth of a politically powerful colonial aristocracy, rather than a movement for economic leveling or to attain political privileges for a disfranchised people.

One of the English liberties which Americans fought to preserve was the right of trial by jury. Anticipating trouble in convicting offenders whose fate depended upon a sympathetic jury, the Ministry had provided for trial in either a court of record or a vice-admiralty court, where juries were unnecessary. Warren wrote Dana that this suspension of jury trial for the colonists "had roused their jealousy and resentment." Being nearer the state of nature, the colonists looked upon their liberties "not merely as arbitrary grants, but as their unalienable, eternal rights, purchased by the blood and treasure of their ancestors."[15] In our own age, we have come to look with suspicion upon talk of consti-

---

[13] *Boston Post-Boy*, June 23, 1766, Feb. 5, 1770, Sept. 2, 1771; *Boston Gazette*, July 8, 1771; Transcripts of Instructions to the Provincial Governors of Massachusetts, VIII, 2465-66 (Mass. Hist. Soc. Library); Mass. Archives, Council Records, XVI, 244, 402, 405, 433, 536, 601, 649, 676. During his governorship, Thomas Hutchinson was encouraged to obtain "a place in the customs at a port distant from Boston" for Andrew Oliver's son. The boy's only qualification urged as a reason for his appointment was his failure in business, including an illicit trading venture. ——— to Thomas Hutchinson, Boston, Sept. 20, 1771, Mass. Archives, Hutchinson MSS, XXV.

[14] Warren to Dana, Boston, March 19, 1766, Miscellaneous MSS (Mass. Hist. Soc. Library).

[15] *Ibid.*

tutional rights and sacred liberties, because we have so often found such language to be a cloak for baser motives, as the history of the states' rights argument makes clear. Certainly some revolutionists used the natural rights philosophy as it best suited their purposes. But the fact that some men were motivated by economic self-interest, or other things, does not mean that all men were insincere in speaking about their rights or preserving that measure of self-government that the colonies had achieved. The nationalism that characterized Warren's life and thought, combined though it may have been with other motives, was one impulse which led him to oppose the Stamp Act.

No one can say with assurance precisely how influential among the mass of Americans the constitutional issues of taxation only through representatives and trial by jury were. The incidence of the taxation was wide, and many people doubtless did oppose the tax simply because they would have to pay it. And paying taxes at this particular time, during the difficult economic conditions of 1765, was in no wise popular. The effects of the depression which followed the French and Indian War may have played a part in shaping the attitude of many colonists toward the Stamp Act. In Massachusetts its role is quite clear, and in that colony Joseph Warren's experiences are most illuminating.

Massachusetts was in an unhappy economic relationship with the mother country because of her unfavorable balance of trade. The Stamp Act ordered that the taxes imposed be collected in hard money, in the eyes of the colonists a most alarming further drain upon the specie left in America. Though the act did provide that the revenue would be used within the colonies to support the army, most colonists seem to have ignored, or been unaware of, this fact. In enumerating the evils of the act, Warren wrote, "Add to this, that it will drain the province of the little cash left among us, which at present barely serves for a medium of trade."[16] A traveler in Massachusetts noted that the people there had "no sort of coin among them,—nothing but paper bills," which were discounted at about five and one-half pounds of paper to one of sterling.[17]

Coupled with this difficult monetary situation was the recession following the Peace of Paris, which affected the colonies in varying

[16] "B. W.," in *Boston Gazette*, Oct. 7, 1765. On the general trade balance, see Gipson, *Coming of the Revolution*, p. 107; Jensen, *Colonial Documents*, p. 392.
[17] "Bennett's *History of New England*," p. 123.

degrees. In Massachusetts one of the richest businessmen in America failed, inaugurating a period of bankruptcy with reverberations far beyond the borders of the Bay Colony. John Hancock wrote that trade received "a most prodigious shock and the greatest losses to some people thro' Mr. Wheelwright's failure ever known in this part of the world." He advised his London correspondent to be careful in trusting anyone, as it was impossible to tell who would fail next. Within days other merchants were closing their doors and the General Court was debating a new bankruptcy bill. John Rowe, that pious New England merchant, provided another gauge of the seriousness of the crisis in his remark, "Did not go to church, my mind too much disturbed."[18]

James Otis wrote most vividly of the crash. The episode has been so ignored in considering Massachusetts' opposition to the Stamp Act that Otis' words deserve careful consideration:

> ... the failing of Mr. Wheelwright which happened here last week ... has given as great a shock to credit here as the South Sea Bubble did in England some years ago.... [He] acquired such an undue credit that he became next to the Treasurer, Banker General for the province and almost for the continent.... Nay to such a madness had people arrived that they took their money by thousands from the Treasury to trust it with this man, but last week, I say, the bubble broke, some say for £10000 sterling, and I can compare it to nothing but the late earthquake at Lisbon, such was the consternation for some little time that people appeared with pale horror and dread, and when a little recovered run about the city. Widows and orphans that are ruined can only bewail their fate. . . . This bankruptcy of Wheelwright and the difficulties and restrictions of our trade here has brought on divers others, and they are increasing daily.

Joseph Warren was appointed administrator of Nathaniel Wheelwright's estate and the complexity of the financier's business transactions is indicated by the suits in which Warren was engaged as late as 1772 against creditors and agents to whom the estate had been made over.[19]

[18] Abram E. Brown, *John Hancock: His Book* (Boston, 1898), p. 61; Anne R. Cunningham, ed., *Letters and Diary of John Rowe* (Boston, 1903), pp. 74-75.

[19] James Otis to George Johnstone and others, Boston, Jan. 25, 1765, Mass. Hist. Soc., *Proceedings*, XLIII (1909-10), 205. Wheelwright owed his partner alone more than £92,000. His total indebtedness exceeded £175,000. He had considerable assets, but after years of litigation there were more than £32,000 in unpaid claims against the estate. Deposition of William Phillips, Feb. 7, 1771, Chamberlain MSS: Samuel Adams and Joseph Warren, p. 170 (Boston Public Library); Suffolk County, Inferior Court of Common Pleas, Files, Document No. 102031, DIC, 83 (Suffolk County Courthouse, Boston).

It is clear that this depression of 1765 led to a long train of bankruptcies and seriously affected the merchants and financial community. The effect upon one not engaged in trade is revealed by Joseph Warren's difficulties in retaining the family farm in Roxbury. Joseph's mother and his brother Samuel had been running the farm since the young doctor's removal to Boston. By April, 1765, three months after the depression hit Boston, they were turning to Joseph for aid. Several times during the spring and summer he managed to send two to five pounds to pay debts and keep the household operating. In March and May, Joseph Warren and his wife deeded small lots of land in Roxbury and West Boston for some twenty-nine pounds. On July 22, Joseph and Samuel were forced to deed the entire farm to Nicholas Bowes for £666 13*s.* 4*d.*, the deed to be void if the debt were paid. Three months later, Joseph received £133 6*s.* 8*d.* from John Hancock on a mortgage. Ten years later Warren's estate owed twenty-four pounds for office rent which he had been unable to meet during the depression of 1765.[20] The statement of Otis which has been quoted would lead one to believe that Warren's difficulties were no isolated instance. Probably it was the economic condition of the Bay Colony, more than anything else, which made the opposition to additional taxes so widespread and which gave such a hand to the radical leadership of Adams, Warren, and the Sons of Liberty.

Whether radical, moderate, or conservative, Massachusetts men did oppose the Stamp Act. Governor Bernard felt that it was unwise to pass such an act without means of enforcement. Thomas Hutchinson argued against the proposal in 1764, not in this case claiming exemption as a privilege, but asserting colonial rights as firmly as had James Otis on the Sugar Act issue. Hutchinson, in fact, was more consistent in his opposition to the Stamp Act than was James Otis. Reversing a stand taken one year before, Otis wrote in 1765 that Parliament virtually, if not literally, represented the whole Empire and had the power to impose taxes on the colonists, "internal and external, on lands, as well as trade." Hutchinson rejected the distinction between external and internal

[20] Joseph Warren, Ledger, 1763-68, particularly April 11, 15, May 18, 29, June 7, 11, July 27, Aug. 13, 27, Dec. 18, 1765; all deeds in Suffolk Deeds as follows: Warren to Campbell, Oct. 18, 1765, CVI, 61; *id.* to Cheesman, May 22, 1766, CVIII, 212-213; *id.* to Bowes, July 24, 1765, CV, 18-19; *id.* to Hancock, Oct. 30, 1765, CVII, 86-87; bill of Oliver Wendell v. Estate of Warren, Chamberlain MSS.

taxes and dismissed the deceptive argument of the colonists' virtual representation in Parliament. Otis apologized for any offense given in previous pamphlets, said he was "heartily sorry," and begged humble pardon "for the least iota that may have displeased his superiors." John Adams condemned Otis for his reversal, Bernard noted that he was now repenting "in sackcloth and ashes," and a customs official satirically explained his conduct in a doggerel song:[21]

> So Jemmy rail'd at upper folks, while Jemmy's dad was out,
> But Jemmy's dad has now a place, so Jemmy's turned about.

Joseph Warren, twenty-four years old in 1765, showed no such equivocation as Otis did on the Stamp Act issue. Despite the personal stands of Hutchinson and Otis, Warren cast his political fortunes with the Liberty party. Doubtless he saw things as did the Boston mob which took Otis for its idol and made a shambles of Thomas Hutchinson's mansion. Otis' retreat was only a temporary one, founded upon fear of displeasure from the Ministry and the satisfaction which Bernard offered to the political ambitions of the Otis family. With the Stamp Act riots, Otis switched again, denying his authorship of the pamphlets in support of parliamentary power and declaring that he had always been a patriot. Perhaps Warren already detected some of the mental instability which was to incapacitate the Liberty party chief. As to Thomas Hutchinson, he was more important than Bernard in the leadership of the Prerogative party, and that party represented a growth of the very type of aristocracy which Warren feared. Also, Hutchinson believed in obedience to all British laws, even those which he felt were unwise. If the issue of parliamentary authority or independence should eventuate in violence, Warren could have little doubt on which side of the barricades Thomas Hutchinson would be. Warren considered death, "with all its tortures, preferable to slavery," and he as naturally joined the Radical party as Hutchinson did the Conservative.[22]

Warren already saw the possibility of war between America and

[21] Morgan, *Stamp Act Crisis*, pp. 100, 211-213; Edmund S. Morgan, "Thomas Hutchinson and the Stamp Act," *New England Quarterly*, XXI, No. 4 (Dec., 1948), 459-492; Ellen E. Brennan, "James Otis: Recreant and Patriot," *New England Quarterly*, XII, No. 4 (Dec., 1939), 701-711, 713-714.

[22] Warren to Dana, Boston, March 19, 1766, Miscellaneous MSS (Mass. Hist. Soc. Library).

England over some issue like the Stamp Act, since this law embodied the ultimate question of whether the colonies would be independent and self-governing or completely controlled by Britain. He felt that at best the act exhibited "an uncommon want of policy" by the home government. If the real motive were simply to raise money, no more unpopular method could have been found. If, on the other hand, the act were aimed at making the colonies more dependent upon England, it was equally ill conceived. Following the Stamp Act Congress, Warren argued that the tax act had united the colonies as they had never been before, a poor way to secure their dependence. He saw the colonies as having been foolishly jealous of each other before; now that they were united, they would not soon forget the power they were able to exercise by standing together. He was not yet thinking of a single government for all of the colonies, but Warren was speaking of American grievances rather than those of Massachusetts alone, and he thought of the American people as constituting a country with political sentiments and culture distinct from England. With some prescience, he predicted that if a war did come France would not stand idle when presented with a chance to regain her empire.[23]

In feeling that the Stamp Act embodied the ultimate issue of self-government or complete dependence upon England, Joseph Warren was expressing not the alarm of a young idealist, but the mature political wisdom of many men in both political parties. Governor Francis Bernard told the Assembly that unwise though the act might be, it must be obeyed now that it was law. In an Empire as diversified as Britain's "there must be a supreme legislature, to which all other powers must be subordinate."[24] He viewed all of the political evils in America as stemming from the vagueness of the relationship of Great Britain and her colonies. Britain viewed the colonies as corporations existing at Parliament's pleasure; the colonists even at this time saw them as separate kingdoms, not dependent upon England except by having the same king. The important question, Bernard felt, was not the Stamp Act, "but whether America shall or shall not be subject to the legislature of Great Britain."[25]

[23] *Ibid.*

[24] *Boston Evening-Post,* June 3, 1765.

[25] Channing and Coolidge, eds., *Barrington-Bernard Correspondence,* p. 96.

In studying the stand of Warren and other opposition leaders toward dependence on Britain, it is well to remember that it is doing no more than stating the obvious to say that there are few frank admissions before 1775 that complete independence was their aim. They were, after all, clever politicians who knew that they might lose moderate support by such declarations; and, what is more, they were wise revolutionaries who knew the danger of a premature stroke. Their stopping point, short of a complete denial of parliamentary authority, even in 1765, was but a single step. The Massachusetts House refuted claims for such authority in taxing the colonists and in regulating their internal affairs as well. And, if internal affairs, why not foreign policy? That the colonists would one day differ from Britain on imperial matters, such as trade policy, would be a conclusion hard to escape, even as early as 1765, for a mind as perceptive as Joseph Warren's.

Warren's most important early political activities were in the period of the Stamp Act's repeal, though his first public opposition to this law was made at the height of agitation against it. The Radical newspaper printed several articles by party leaders, and Warren's particular task was to raise the emotional temperature of the people. In an article well-designed to do this, he denied Parliament's power to tax the colonies in any way. He frankly admitted aiming at the passions of the people, leaving the appeal to reason to other writers. As an example of his style and ability as a propagandist, portions of this first letter to the press may be quoted:[26]

> Awake! Awake, my countrymen, and, by a regular and legal opposition, defeat the designs of those who would enslave us and our posterity. Nothing is wanting but your own resolution—For great is the authority, exalted the dignity, and powerful the majesty of the People. . . . Ages remote, mortals yet unborn, will bless your generous efforts, and revere the memory of the saviours of their country.
>
> Start, O start from your trance! By the unconquerable spirit of the ancient Britons;—by the genious of that constitution which abhors every species of vassallage;—by the august title of Englishmen;—by the grand prerogatives of human nature; the lovely image of the Infinite Deity;—and what is more than all, by the liberty wherewith Christ has made you free; I exhort you to instruct your representatives against promoting by any ways or means whatsoever, the operation of this grievous and burdensome law.

Boston gave official expression of its opinion of the act not only in its instructions as Warren had suggested, but also in its election

[26] "B. W.," in *Boston Gazette*, Oct. 7, 1765.

of Samuel Adams to a seat in the House of Representatives. The representatives were told that taxation by a body in which the people were not represented and the abolition of trial by jury were violations of the rights of British subjects. The town of Braintree, in a paper drafted by John Adams, gave similar instructions to its members.[27] When the House did meet, it followed Virginia's lead and passed fourteen resolves, which asserted that the colonists had rights under the British Constitution which were common to mankind and based on "the law of God and Nature." Among these rights were protection of property, jury trial, and the right to be taxed only by the general assembly of their colony.[28]

More ominous than newspaper propaganda and General Court resolves was the rioting which broke out in August, 1765, in Boston. Mobs were no new phenomena in the capital city. When Joseph Warren was a boy selling milk in the town's streets, crowds from South and North Boston had celebrated Pope's Day, commemorating the Gunpowder Plot, by laying open skulls. Justices of the peace, sheriffs, and militia were helpless in stopping these brawls, even in 1764 when a child's head was smashed by one of the wagon wheels. It was the Pope's Day mob which was responsible for most of the damage in the Stamp Act rioting.

The gutting of Lieutenant Governor Hutchinson's mansion on August 26 seems to have been related to smuggling and other factors than the Stamp Act. Samuel Adams condemned this action as being "of a truly mobbish nature," and Joseph Warren expressed his respect for the lieutenant governor and his regret at the attack upon him.[29] The earlier attack of August 14, against Andrew Oliver, was due to Oliver's appointment as stamp commissioner, and it is clear that political intimates of Warren and Adams were behind this affair. This first riot was led by Ebenezer Mackintosh, captain of one of the Pope's Day mobs, and from November, 1765, this force worked as a disciplined arm of the Sons of Liberty. In a letter describing the forced resignation in December of Andrew Oliver from his stamp post, a writer mentioned a supper the leaders of the Sons of Liberty had following the resignation, to which

[27] *Boston Post-Boy*, Sept. 30, 1765; *Boston Town Records, 1758 to 1769*, p. 155; *Boston Gazette*, Oct. 14, 1765.

[28] Seventy-Six Society, *Papers Relating to Public Events in Massachusetts Preceding the Revolution* (Philadelphia, Pa., 1856), pp. 1-4, hereafter cited as *Massachusetts Papers.*

[29] Harry A. Cushing, ed., *The Writings of Samuel Adams* (New York, 1904), I, 60; "Paskalos," *Boston Gazette*, June 2, 1766.

Samuel Adams, Benjamin Edes, and John Gill, the printers of the Radical newspaper, were invited. He asked that his correspondent keep this secret, adding, "We do every thing in order to keep this and the first affair private: and are not a little pleas'd to hear that Mc Intosh has the credit of the whole affair."[30] The "first affair" was doubtless the August riot against Oliver. Three or four others were invited to the December supper, and Joseph Warren likely was among them, for John Avery, the foremost of the "Loyal Nine" who sponsored the supper, had been a Harvard classmate of Warren, and Thomas Crafts, another of them, was Warren's masonic brother. The close connection in politics of this group with Warren and Adams suggests that the orders which Mackintosh received from Avery may have come from a still higher level of the party.

The Boston riots played little part in gaining repeal of the Stamp Act, but they did set a pattern for other violence, both at this time and in subsequent crises. If Warren had no hand in the riots of 1765, he did direct some of those which followed. From August, 1765, the destruction of property, tarring and feathering, and intimidation became standard political techniques. Massachusetts' Conservatives had stark evidence of the power of their opposition. To the timorous among them, it was enough to make them lose heart; to the strong, it became proof of the need of a reconstituted, and less democratic, government for the Bay Colony. The next demonstrations would lead to the stationing of troops in Boston to support the civil officers. In their immediate effects, the August riots gave control of Massachusetts politics to the Radical politicians and prevented the enforcement of the Stamp Act. In accomplishing the latter, it served as a precedent for the tea parties of 1773 and 1774 out of which war was to come.

If the Radical politicians approved of violence, there were some Boston merchants who did not. As a class, they fought the Stamp Act by joining with merchants in other port towns and re-

---

[30] [Henry Bass] to Samuel P. Savage, Boston, Dec. 19, 1765, Mass. Hist. Soc., *Proceedings*, XLIV (1910-11), 688-689. The original leaders of the Boston Sons of Liberty are suggested in George P. Anderson, "A Note on Ebenezer Mackintosh," Col. Soc. of Mass., *Publications*, XXVI (*Trans.*, 1924-26), 355-359. For the attacks upon Oliver, see Clifford K. Shipton, ed., *Biographical Sketches of Those Who Attended Harvard College*, 1722-25 VII (Boston, 1945), 393-399, hereafter cited by its familiar title, *Sibley's Harvard Graduates*, with volume and dates.

fusing to import goods from Britain until the act was repealed. This, again, set a pattern for methods used in later struggles with Britain, such as that of 1774, when Joseph Warren drafted the most comprehensive agreement that had been written until that time. The agreement of 1765 was made during a depression, goods essential to the fisheries and manufacturing were exempt from the boycott, and Massachusetts managed to put ships to sea without stamped ships' papers to carry on her export trade. Thus, Boston was able to continue her economic pursuits and attempt to adjust her trade balance while contributing pressure toward the repeal of the Stamp Act.

The Stamp Act crisis had crystallized the organization of the Radical party in Boston, and the battle lines had been drawn between that party and the Conservatives and between the colonies and Britain. The issues, which were to recur again and again until they were resolved by war, had been clearly formulated. The Radicals had tested their political techniques, including nonimportation, violence, mass disobedience of Parliament's laws, and an intercolonial congress, and had found them effective in preventing enforcement of the act and in obtaining its repeal. As Warren predicted, this lesson of 1765 was not to be forgotten. By posing the ultimate issue of independence or parliamentary supremacy, the crisis had provided Joseph Warren and many another American with an opportunity of thinking through his political ideas. It was the Stamp Act which led Warren into active political work, casting his lot with the popular Liberty party, of which he was soon to be an important leader. Almost unbelievably, the Radicals were able to find ammunition for their battle against the Conservatives in the repeal of the Stamp Act, and it was this which brought Warren to the fore as one of the Radicals' major propagandists and chief policy planners.

# A Pen for Propaganda

CHAPTER IV

During the Stamp Act crisis of 1765, Joseph Warren was just an average young doctor exhibiting the interest of any well-educated man of twenty-four in the political issues of the day. Within three years he had become one of the outstanding spokesmen and political organizers of the opposition to the Bernard administration. For two years he conducted a vigorous attack upon the governor, which was to play a part in Bernard's removal from the colony, and it was he who led the resistance to the commissioners of customs who attempted the enforcement of the Townshend Acts. During the summer of 1768, he directed the attack against British authority in the *Liberty* affair, which was to result in the stationing of royal troops in Boston. By then he stood at the head of the Boston medical profession and ranked with Samuel Adams as one of the two most important leaders of the Liberty party. Naturally well spoken, charming, and handsome, he was now tried, mature, and self-confident enough to become the most attractive political leader in Massachusetts.

Warren's political power coursed through several channels. Through the columns of the *Boston Gazette,* he conducted the attack upon Bernard which did so much to enhance his personal prestige and strengthen the Radical party. After the long round of visiting patients, he spent many evenings with the political clubs which were becoming so numerous in Boston. The membership and exact role of each of these groups is still obscure. Very likely Warren attended meetings of the "Monday Night Club," for Samuel Adams, James Otis, Thomas Cushing, Samuel Pemberton, Henderson Inches, and the other known members were his closest political associates. As politicians will, they told anecdotes about governors, legislators, and important merchants. The atmosphere of their meetings was relaxed, friendly, and familiar, and visitors were always welcomed.[1] Warren's attendance at meetings of the Sons of Liberty, who met in a distillery a few doors from Warren's home, is also quite probable. His classmate John Avery was one leader of this group, and Thomas Crafts, Warren's masonic brother, was another. Quite as important as these groups was the mechanics caucus in the North End of Boston, of which Warren was a chief director. Paul Revere, a leader of this body, wrote of the respect accorded to Warren's advice and of the trust the artisans placed in him. Yet Warren and the other Radical leaders formulated many of their policies in the course of their informal social relations, rather than in such organizations. And Warren's own influence stemmed as much from his leadership of Boston Masons as from his activity in the political clubs.

Of the several organizations with rather indirect connections with politics, the masonic lodges were the most important and have left the fullest records. Joseph Warren achieved the highest position in masonry in America, and his activities in this society were closely related to his political interests. There were two branches of masonry in the colonies, roughly divided along political lines. The modern freemasons had founded the first lodges, but by 1760 efforts were being made to establish ancient societies. In that year, St. Andrew's lodge of Boston received approval of its organization from the Grand Lodge in Scotland. This Boston body, like most ancient lodges, was dominated by men active in the revolutionary movement and had a more democratic membership than the older modern lodge of Boston. Membership of many modern lodges in the colonies included a large number of royal

[1] Charles F. Adams, ed., *The Works of John Adams, Second President of the United States, with a Life of the Author* (Boston, 1856), II, 162-163.

officials, British army and navy officers, and conservative, wealthy colonists. John Rowe, a conservative merchant, was grand master of Boston's modern lodge, St. John's.[2]

Joseph Warren joined St. Andrew's in September, 1761, as a young man of twenty, presumably for the same social and professional reasons that most doctors join such organizations. In November he attained the rank of fellow craft, and attended occasional meetings through August, 1762. From then until 1765, Warren's name is not found in the minutes as being present at lodge nights. On November 14, 1765, St. Andrew's voted to readmit him, and from then until the Revolution Warren was one of the most active masons in North America.[3] His resumption of interest in masonry, at the height of agitation against the Stamp Act, may have been coincidental with the political activities in Massachusetts. If it was, the membership in this lodge of Paul Revere, John Hancock, John Pulling, Thomas Crafts, and many another who played a role in the revolutionary movement makes the coincidence striking indeed. What, other than their political sentiments, could have led John Hancock, one of the most fashionable merchant princes in Boston, and a young doctor like Warren, to join St. Andrew's in the North End, rather than the aristocratic St. John's, which met at one of the best taverns in Boston? It was Thomas Crafts, one of the nine original leaders of the Sons of Liberty, who proposed Hancock for membership.[4] Possibly Samuel Adams was not the only force in turning John Hancock's fortune into the treasury of the Liberty party, as cousin John Adams believed.

The building of political sentiment among members of this powerful society was the work of years and was closely associated with masonic social activities. In 1765 St. Andrew's purchased as a meeting hall the Green Dragon Tavern, located on a little lane of Union Street near the Mill Pond. Despite attempts to rechristen it "The Freemasons' Arms," the more colorful name clung to the old two-story building in North Boston. Here on the second

[2] Harry L. Haywood and James E. Craig, *A History of Freemasonry* (New York, 1927), pp. 311-313; Sidney Morse, *Freemasonry in the American Revolution* (Washington, 1924), p. 18.

[3] MSS St. Andrew's Lodge, Records, I (1756-75), minutes of meetings for Sept. 30, Nov. 2, 1761, Nov. 14, 1765 (Mass. Grand Lodge Library, Boston).

[4] *Ibid.*, Sept. 9, Oct. 14, 1762; Morse, *Freemasonry*, p. 41.

Thursday evening of each month, from six to ten o'clock in the summer and five until nine in the winter, St. Andrew's met. The official meeting was often preceded or followed by supper and refreshments. Gathering about the fireplace in the long room, they lighted pipes and cemented the bonds of brotherhood with hot punch, port, and madeira:[5]

> But what I've said, I'll say again,
> Tis *Love,* pure *Love,* cements the whole,
> *Love*—of the Bottle and the Bowl.

It was here, more than in the meetings, that talk turned to politics, and to the members of St. Andrew's such talk was congenial indeed. Men in all walks of life began to look to Joseph Warren as a political leader, and it was among his masonic brothers that Warren found his most devoted followers. Crafts, Pulling, Revere, and other members of St. Andrew's lodge were to do good work for Warren in the revolutionary movement. His magnetic personality and sincere friendship gained a personal loyalty from these men, who accorded to other Radical leaders only a grudging political obedience.

Warren's attendance at lodges after his readmittance in 1765 was conscientious, and his personal charm and leadership, with his willingness to serve on committees, carried him rapidly to the most honored positions among the craft. The very evening on which he was welcomed back to membership, the masons appointed him to a committee to examine the treasurer's accounts. Early in 1766, they named Warren to help shape new regulations on charity, and in December elected him senior warden and to a committee to revise the bylaws. Upon the death of Jeremy Gridley, the grand master of Boston's modern lodge, he waited upon that group at the British Coffee House and sought permission for the members of St. Andrew's to attend the funeral. With Revere and other members of his own lodge, Warren marched behind the bier, following the steps of John Rowe, James Otis, and other masons of St. John's. On November 30, 1768, St. Andrew's chose Warren to succeed William Brubeck as master of the lodge.[6]

[5] St. Andrew's Lodge, Records, I, minutes for Feb. 12, 1767; poem by Joseph Green, quoted in Morse, *Freemasonry*, p. 29; Mass. Grand Lodge, *Proceedings, 1733-1792* (Boston, 1795), p. 253, for the liquor consumption at one feast.

[6] St. Andrew's Lodge, Records, I, minutes for Nov. 14, 1765, Feb. 18, Dec. 1, 1766, Nov. 30, 1768; Mass. Grand Lodge, *Proceedings, 1733-1792*, pp. 120, 123.

In the decades before the American Revolution, the establishment of a separate province of ancient masons in the colonies was the most significant development in American masonry. For a number of years, the necessity of obtaining charters from the Grand Master of Ancient Masons in Scotland had hindered the growth of this group. A grand master at Boston, who could authorize the creation of new lodges in the colonies, headed modern masonry, and its growth was correspondingly rapid. The commissioning of a grand master of ancient masons developed out of a struggle between St. Andrew's and St. John's, the grand lodge of moderns in Boston.

The conflict between the two Boston societies began within three months of Joseph Warren's re-entry into masonry. He assumed leadership of the ancients from the beginning, and probably conceived the plan to establish a grand master of ancient freemasons in the colonies. If a grand master were appointed, he would be able to create lodges in other towns, which in some cases might serve as focal points of revolutionary sentiment. As one of a committee, Warren waited upon St. John's to invite them to attend St. Andrew's lodge so there might be "a happy coalition." The grand lodge not only refused the invitation, but also denied that the members of St. Andrew's were free and accepted masons, and ordered their own members not to visit the irregular lodge. Warren's society accepted the challenge, voted the answer of the grand lodge "by no means satisfactory," and renewed a long-interrupted correspondence with the Grand Lodge in Scotland. In April, 1766, John Rowe, deputy grand master of St. John's, visited St. Andrew's. Possibly the moderns had reconsidered their position, and were trying to forestall the creation of an ancient grand master in the colonies by suggesting a *rapprochement;* possibly it was another instance of John Rowe keeping a foot in both camps of factional disputes, whether masonic or political. In any case, the hair was up on the necks of the members of St. Andrew's, and Warren persisted in his efforts to get a commission for an ancient grand master in America. Before the year was out, the members of St. Andrew's had resolved against attending any modern meetings until the offensive vote of St. John's was rescinded. On November 30, 1768, the same day that he was chosen master of St. Andrew's, Joseph Warren was appointed one of a committee to make application to Scotland for an ancient grand master in the colonies.[7]

Warren's committee met with other lodges of ancients in Boston to draft a joint petition to Scotland, requesting the appointment of Joseph Warren as grand master. In May, 1769, the Grand Lodge in Scotland named Warren to this post, though at first his jurisdiction was limited to the area within 100 miles of Boston. He acquired a grand master's apron and the articles necessary, and two days after Christmas his brothers installed him in his new post "in ample form." Some years later his jurisdiction was extended to all ancient masons in North America.[8] In his new position, Warren attended meetings of the new grand lodge of ancient masons through March 3, 1775, a month and a half before the Battle of Lexington, missing only three meetings in those years. For both political and social reasons, he continued to attend St. Andrew's as well. Warren exercised much of his political leadership through St. Andrew's lodge, the members often adjourning meetings to play their roles in such crises as the Boston Tea Party. And in their political as in their masonic activities, Warren provided a daring, courageous leadership for them.

Warren's political writings, another important element in his leadership, first attracted wide attention in 1766, as Boston rejoiced in the repeal of the Stamp Act. George Grenville's ministry had lost the support of George III long before news of the Boston riots, the Stamp Act Congress, and the nonimportation agreements reached royal ears. In July, 1765, the Marquis of Rockingham formed the administration which Charles Townshend described as a lutestring ministry that would serve well for summer wear.[9] Still, it was to be eight months before the Stamp Act was repealed on March 18, 1766. When repeal did come, it was accompanied by the Declaratory Act, asserting Parliament's authority over the colonies, and a few weeks later, Parliament approved a uniform

[7] Documents in St. Andrew's Lodge, Records, I, are as follows: St. Andrew's to St. John's Grand Lodge, Boston, Jan. 24, 1766; vote of St. John's, Jan. 27, 1766; minutes of St. Andrew's, Jan. 22, Feb. 6, April 10, 1766, June 12, Nov. 30, 1767, Nov. 30, Dec. 8, 1768; St. Andrew's to Grand Master in Scotland, Boston, Feb. 13, 1766. Portions of them have been printed, in some cases inaccurately, in Mass. Grand Lodge, *Proceedings, 1733-1792*, pp. 101-102, and *Proceedings of the Most Worshipful Grand Lodge of . . . Massachusetts* (Boston, n.d.), pp. 495, 497-498.

[8] Mass. Grand Lodge, *Proceedings, 1733-1792*, pp. 226, 456-457.

[9] Horace Walpole, *Memoirs of the Reign of King George the Third*, ed. by Denis le Marchànt (London, 1845), I, 210.

tax of one penny per gallon on foreign and British molasses imported into the colonies. Francis Bernard had suggested this rate in 1763, arguing that Britain would increase its revenue by a low tax, whereas Americans would never pay the higher duties on foreign molasses of the Sugar Act.[10]

Bostonians ignored the acts to assert British supremacy and increase the revenue; the repeal of the Stamp Act they celebrated even before authentic news came from England. As early as January, the Sons of Liberty appointed a committee to plan "grand rejoicing" when news of repeal should come. After premature rejoicing in April, a reliable account of the repeal arrived on May 16. Spontaneous demonstrations broke out, only to be surpassed three days later on the date appointed by the selectmen for the official celebration. Artillery was fired, debtors released from jail, and a pyramid, illuminated with 280 lamps, erected on the Common.[11] Despite such happiness, harmony was not to be the lot of Massachusetts politics if Joseph Warren could prevent it. Within two weeks he had fired the first guns of an intensive campaign to drive the governor from the Bay Colony.

On June 2, 1766, the *Boston Gazette* printed a letter by Warren, signed "Paskalos," and addressed "to him whose guilty conscience tells him, he is the man."[12] The letter was a slashing attack upon Governor Bernard, in which Warren called him a beggar and a coward, who had "wantonly sacrificed the happiness of this Province" to his foolish passions. The occasion was Bernard's recent veto of James Otis as speaker of the House and of six councilors, but the dissension referred to was the governor's presentation of a "requisition" for paying damages to victims of the Stamp Act riots. Warren suggested that Bernard had ordered that his letters urging repeal of the Stamp Act be circulated only if this would be likely to help him; if it had appeared that the act would not be repealed, another set of letters would have been published. Unsubstantiated though the charge was, it was good propaganda, and the duplicity and insincerity which some contemporaries pro-

---

[10] Bernard to John Pownall, Castle William, Mass., Oct. 30, 1763, Bernard MSS, III, 105; John R. Alden, *General Gage in America, Being Principally a History of His Role in the American Revolution* (Baton Rouge, La., 1948), pp. 152-153.

[11] Tudor, ed., *Deacon Tudor's Diary*, pp. 21-22; Samuel A. Green, *Ten Fac-simile Reproductions Relating to New-England* (Boston, 1902), pp. 38-40; Charles F. Adams, ed., *Works of John Adams*, II, 179.

[12] The Dorr file of the newspaper identifies Warren as the writer of the series of letters, and the style is characteristic of his known writings.

fessed to see in Bernard made the argument doubly telling. "Paskalos" closes by pledging the governor that he will continue the assault upon "your vices and follies (which you know are many and great) unless you immediately desist from your barbarous attempt to spread dissention and ruin through this my native country."

Francis Bernard had faced newspaper opposition before. In 1764 he had recommended the prosecution of writers against the administration in Massachusetts, but had been cautioned to tread softly by Lord Shelburne.[13] Warren's attack, however, was from a pen dipped in gall and wielded by a hand that knew few restraints. A week after the initial attack, "Paskalos" answered those who had protested his lack of respect toward the governor. He vowed that he could no more allow his country to be harmed than to stand by and see his parents stabbed by a ruffian. The only alternative, he said, to his charge that Bernard was a liar was that he was insane, and in that case he should certainly be removed from office. In this and other letters, Warren expressed his regret at the attack upon Hutchinson's home. He said he honored the lieutenant governor, who had served the public with integrity from his youth, and Warren clearly distinguished between Hutchinson and the villainous Bernard.[14]

One more letter appeared in June and others irregularly through February, 1767. In the *Gazette* of June 16, Warren made clear the intent of his attack, as he told Bernard, "And now Sir, if you are not too angry to hear my friendly advice, I counsel you to depart from this province in as honorable a manner as you can." Warren vowed to do everything possible to effect the governor's removal, preferring to see "one worthless treacherous man reduced to his native insignificancy" than to see thousands of innocent men hurt. Warren also dubbed the governor "Verres," and again accused him of duplicity in pretending that the Stamp Act's repeal was largely due to his efforts, while charging the colonists with disloyalty and blaming all of them for the crimes of a few. Later letters were answers to those appearing in defense of Bernard over the signature "Philanthrop."[15]

This administration writer had called Warren a public enemy

---

[13] Shelburne to Bernard, Whitehall, England, Nov. 14, 1764, Transcripts of Instructions to Provincial Governors, VII, 2386-87.

[14] *Boston Gazette*, June 9, 1766.

[15] *Ibid.*, Nov. 10, Dec. 8, 1766.

for attempting to destroy the established government, and generally defended Bernard. Warren turned the charge against himself into one against Bernard, arguing that he was the real public enemy for attempting to destroy the separation of powers in the government. The governor had denied the right of election of the Council, drawn upon the treasury without the Assembly's consent, and punished members of the General Court who voted against his wishes.[16] The accusation that the governor had undermined the separation of powers was the only charge with any substance, and indicates the real motive behind the entire campaign. The series of letters could scarcely be considered a serious protest against British policies. The ultimate aims were to drive Bernard from Massachusetts and to bring the Radical party to power. The former was accomplished by the close of the decade; the latter awaited the Revolution to achieve complete success. Warren's propaganda played an important role in preparing public opinion for both.

Joseph Warren's activities as a propagandist were those of a popular leader appealing for mass support, rather than of a lawyer or a political theorist concerned with fine constitutional points. In his "Paskalos" letters he subordinated reasoned arguments to name calling and other smear techniques, and it is in this very emphasis that his significance is to be found. For bitterness, lack of restraint, and directness of attack, Warren's letters were hitherto unmatched; compared to them, the public criticisms of Stamp Commissioner Oliver had been moderate in the extreme, and most of the writings on the Stamp Act had dealt with policy or attacks upon the English Ministry. Warren's campaign against Francis Bernard inaugurated those unrestrained, libelous, personal attacks upon the royal officials who led the Conservative party which were to become common in the columns of the Radical newspapers. From this time, the supposedly villainous characters of royal officials were to play nearly as great a role as British policy in Radical propaganda.

The concern shown by the administration in replying to Warren reflects the impact which this propaganda was having upon the people of the colony. While the two factions used songs, plays, poems, parades, sermons, even funerals to gain support, newspapers played the major role in party propaganda. A good illus-

[16] *Ibid.*, Dec. 29, 1766, Feb. 2, 1767.

tration of their importance is the confusion in Radical ranks during the brief period when John Mein's *Boston Chronicle* was conducting a counterattack. This Conservative paper was so effective that breaks developed up and down the seaboard in the nonimportation agreements, and the Radicals drove Mein from the colony by threats and violence.

Propaganda was particularly important to the opposition, because it was their one hope of building a colony-wide political party to fight the administration. Such support as Warren and Adams gained outside of Boston was from politicians or their constituents who were of the same mind as the Liberty party. Having no patronage with which to discipline members of the General Court, Warren's faction tried to persuade colonial voters to approve their policies and, by instructions to their representatives in the House, compel members to vote with them. Their appeal was directly to the people of the individual towns in the colony, and, before the creation of committees of correspondence, public propaganda was the basic technique. Speeches of Adams and others in the House, as well as the petitions and protests of that body, were primarily propaganda and only secondarily intended for serious consideration by Britain or for aiding the General Court in shaping legislation. On one occasion James Otis protested Samuel Adams' publication of a letter from the House to Lord Hillsborough, so that the public would see it before the minister did. Adams' reputed reply was, "What signifies that? You know it was designed for the people, and not for the minister."[17] It was this vital role of propaganda in political organization which made the *Boston Gazette* and Warren's articles in that journal so important.

The *Gazette* scarcely fits the stereotype of the small colonial newspaper, written, edited, and printed by a single hand. Benjamin Edes and John Gill had a volunteer editorial staff of some size and extraordinary talent. Nearly every leader of the opposition, including Otis, the Adamses, Josiah Quincy, Jr., John Hancock, Benjamin Church, Thomas Cushing, and Warren, contributed to its columns. On Saturday afternoon and by lamplight in the evening, they worked amid the type cases, "cooking up para-

[17] Bernard to Hillsborough, Boston, July 9, 1768, Bernard MSS, VI, 339. A good evaluation of the importance of the media of propaganda in building revolutionary sentiment is Arthur M. Schlesinger, *Prelude to Independence: The Newspaper War on Britain, 1764-1776* (New York, 1958), chap. 2.

graphs, articles, occurences" for Monday's issue. Another Radical newspaperman, Isaiah Thomas, wrote, "It may be truly said, that in those meetings were concocted many of the measures of opposition to the British acts of parliament for taxing the colonies—measures which led to, and terminated in the independence of our country."[18]

Some of the Radicals spent most Saturdays there; others came around occasionally and at other times disassociated themselves from such "curious employment," as John Adams called it. Otis was to be found there often, even after insanity began to disable him, growing so talkative that nobody could find room for a word—most irritating to John Adams who rather liked to let others know that he too was a thinking fellow.[19] Samuel Adams, growing somewhat paunchy, appeared to be older than he was. Despite his graying hair and palsied hands, however, there was no doubt of the quiet magnetism of his personality. Among the younger men, Warren and his close friend Josiah Quincy complemented each other well. Warren was robust and healthy, Quincy frail, thin, and often coughing from the tuberculosis which Joseph unsuccessfully tried to cure. Joseph wrote the passionate, emotional appeals; Josiah wove constitutional arguments into his pieces, without, however, burdening them with quite as much legal learning as did John Adams. Adams, in fact, refused the invitation to do "scribbling in the newspaper," and wished to argue issues without "painting, pathos, rhetoric, or flourish."[20] Warren, one of John Adams' closest friends at this time, spent many an evening at the newspaper room doing just such scribbling. And John Adams did admit that Warren was often an animating force, persuading him to support the revolutionary movement more boldly.

Warren's sharpest attack upon Francis Bernard, the "True Patriot" articles which so stung the governor that he attempted to prosecute the printers, was a part of the struggle of the Radicals to capture the Massachusetts Council. This body, which was the upper house of the General Court and was advisory to the gov-

[18] Charles F. Adams, ed., *Works of John Adams*, II, 219; Isaiah Thomas, *The History of Printing in America*, 2nd ed. (Albany, N.Y., 1874), II, 54, note; Thomas Hutchinson to [John Cushing], Milton, Mass., Aug. 5, [1768], Mass. Hist. Soc., *Proceedings*, XL (1906-07), 536.

[19] Charles F. Adams, ed., *Works of John Adams*, II, 219.

[20] Quoted in Philip Davidson, *Propaganda and the American Revolution, 1763-1783* (Chapel Hill, N.C., 1941), p. 6.

ernor, was dominated by Conservatives, including the lieutenant governor, province secretary, and judges of the Superior Court. In Massachusetts, unlike other royal colonies, the legislature elected the Council, and the Radical attempt to capture more seats might well prove successful. The single obstacle was the governor's power of negativing councilors elected by the legislature. In 1766, Bernard had rejected James Otis as speaker-elect of the House. That body replied by refusing council seats to Secretary Andrew Oliver, Justice Peter Oliver, Attorney-General Trowbridge, and Bernard's most trusted advisor Thomas Hutchinson. Angered by this move, Bernard vetoed six councilors chosen by the House, which in turn refused to fill the seats thus vacated, despite the governor's request that they do so.[21]

This fight for the Council by the two Massachusetts parties, with no issues relevant to Britain involved, had led to the "Paskalos" letters. Warren's renewal of the attack followed Bernard's referral of the contest to the home government. The governor had long favored a change in the Massachusetts charter, but his appeal home was designed less to effect such an amendment than to justify his own conduct. In September, 1767, Lord Shelburne sent royal approval of his veto of councilors whose "private resentments" might induce them "to embarrass the administration and endanger the quiet of the province." Shelburne charged the House with misusing its power by refusing council seats to officials whose presence there would expedite business and who were such fine servants as the lieutenant governor and secretary.[22] This letter, which Bernard naively communicated to the General Court in confidence, provided the material for Warren's new attack.

Bernard might have assumed that the Radicals would make political capital of Shelburne's letter. However, the relative political peace of the winter session of the General Court so lulled him that he believed the opposition had experienced a change of heart. The Assembly enacted the provincial measures which he recommended without quibble. Early in February, 1768, he expressed his pleasure with "an evident disposition to restore the

[21] Francis C. Walett, "The Massachusetts Council, 1766-1774: The Transformation of a Conservative Institution," *William and Mary Quarterly*, 3rd ser., VI, No. 4 (Oct., 1949), 607.

[22] Shelburne to Bernard, Whitehall, England, Sept. 17, 1767, Transcripts of Instructions to Provincial Governors, VII, 2380-81; also printed in *Boston Gazette*, March 7, 1768.

peace of this government" and foresaw a reconciliation between himself and "the malcontents."[23] On February 29, the *Boston Gazette* printed Joseph Warren's letter signed "A True Patriot," which came as a dash of cold water to dispel the governor's dreams.

This letter, despite the consternation it caused in government circles, contained not one constitutional argument on the level of John Dickinson's *Farmer's Letters,* not one telling criticism of an administration such as is found in the writings of Benjamin Franklin. In part its significance lay in the proof afforded by the incident that Bernard could no longer depend upon the Council for advice or aid, could no longer win a crucial vote in the House, could no longer depend upon a Boston jury to indict a Radical. Also, the letter was deliberately designed to smear the character of the governor and destroy the remnants of public confidence in him. Warren declared that Bernard's actions provided the most glaring instance in world history of "obstinate perseverance in the path of malice." The governor had proved himself to be an enemy of the Province, and had displayed cruelty to its people, not from the hope of personal advantage, but solely because of his "diabolical thirst for mischief." The only concrete charge leveled against the governor was that his "jesuitical insinuations" caused Shelburne to form an unfavorable opinion of the colony. Having done what he could to arouse public emotion against Bernard, Warren concluded:[24]

> But I refrain, lest a full representation of the hardships suffered by this too long insulted people, should lead them to an unwarrantable revenge. We never can treat good and patriotic rulers with too great reverence— But it is certain that men totally abandoned to wickedness, can never merit our regard, be their stations ever so high.
>
> If such men are by God appointed.
> The devil may be the Lord's anointed.

The article verged upon slander, and many Moderates in Massachusetts questioned its truth and the wisdom of publishing it. Much of their concern, however, was because of the danger to government of such propaganda, and because of the final lines which some viewed as profanity. Bernard, of course, was justly incensed. Warren's use of Shelburne's letter, which Bernard had

[23] Channing and Coolidge, eds., *Barrington-Bernard Correspondence,* p. 143.

[24] *Boston Gazette,* Feb. 29, 1768. The author is identified as Warren in the Dorr file of the newspaper.

communicated to the General Court in confidence, was stinging enough; the malicious attack upon his character was unbearable. The day following publication, he called his Council to meet and referred the newspaper to it for advice. The members expressed abhorrence of the letter and advised the governor that they stood ready to do anything necessary to support the dignity of government. But Bernard soon discovered that they would not advise a prosecution of the printers and dropped his plan to ask their approval of this step.[25] Instead, Hutchinson, as chief justice of the Superior Court, was to bring the matter to the attention of the grand jury.

In the House the governor met with even less success. The representatives were unable to discover either libel or sedition in the article, since no person was named in it. Nor, they said, did they see anything in Warren's letter which might hurt "the majesty of the King, the dignity of the Government . . . or the true interest of the Province." They asserted their belief that liberty of the press, "a great bulwark of the liberty of the people," must be defended, and voted (56 to 18) to take no further notice of the paper. By a narrow 39 to 30 margin, they approved a message to the governor, another propaganda document designed to justify Warren's view and implicitly damn Bernard.[26] The next day Bernard prorogued the General Court.

The grand jury of Suffolk County assembled within a week of Bernard's failure to get action from his legislature. Hutchinson's "long and forcible" charge to the jurors, in which he warned them that they would violate their oaths if they did not present a bill against the printers, apparently came as a surprise tactic to Warren's party. The jury directed the attorney general to prepare a bill for the following morning, but Warren and his friends did yeoman work that night, if Bernard's account is to be credited. Certainly some "tampering with the jury" is the most plausible explanation of the jurors' vote of "ignoramus" when they reassembled.[27]

While these actions were proceeding against Edes and Gill, the

[25] Messages of Bernard and the Council are in *Boston Gazette*, March 7, 1768; Bernard's account to the home government is his letter to Shelburne, Boston, March 5, 1768, Bernard MSS, VI, 274.

[26] *Boston Gazette*, March 7, 1768.

[27] Hutchinson, *History*, III, 135; Bernard to Shelburne, Boston, March 12, 1768, Bernard MSS, VI, 278.

printers were setting type for further articles by Warren. One week after the initial letter, he succinctly told Bernard that if the hat fit he was welcome to wear it. Though adding "villain" and "monster" to the growing list of epithets which he applied to the governor, he felt constrained to deny that he had intended any profanity against God, a point which had alienated some people. This second article concluded with a condemnation of the divine-right theory of government. A third letter in the series appeared on March 14. Warren now complimented the House of Representatives and the grand jury for their courage and independence from the administration's influence. Having discovered some of those responsible for the misfortunes of the colony, he pledges to "deprive them of the power of injuring us hereafter."[28]

Joseph Warren's three short letters had political repercussions within the Conservative party and on public opinion in Massachusetts, probably beyond his own expectations. Among the most effective local pieces of propaganda published, they goaded the administration into its first positive action to combat the growing strength of the Radicals. Aside from the attempt to break the Radical newspaper by prosecuting its printers, it withdrew the advertising of the vice-admiralty court from its pages. And, to offset its influence, the Conservatives began publication of the *Massachusetts Gazette,* a political sheet inserted in issues of two established newspapers, the *Post-Boy* and the *News-Letter.* Without the journalistic talent of its rival, however, the administration paper failed by September, 1769.[29] That Warren's propaganda had its effect in arousing public opinion against the government became clear in the events of March 18. By this time, however, the issue of executive and judicial officials sitting in the Council had been lost sight of in the struggle against the enforcement of new revenue acts which had been passed in 1767.

The new acts were the work of Charles Townshend who, as chancellor of the exchequer, was given the most difficult job in

[28] *Boston Gazette,* March 7, 14, 1768. A final article by "T. N. Monument-Maker," March 27, 1769, may also be by Warren, but adds nothing to the "True Patriot" letters. The controversy is briefly examined in Arthur M. Schlesinger, "Propaganda and the Boston Newspaper Press, 1767-1770," Col. Soc. of Mass., *Publications,* XXXII (*Trans.,* 1933-37), 402-403.

[29] *Ibid.,* pp. 404-405. The "True Patriot" articles came to the notice of the English public when they were printed in [Thomas Hollis], *The True Sentiments of America* (London, 1768).

England in the Ministry of William Pitt, now Lord Chatham, which replaced Rockingham's short-lived rule. Having tried several expedients to augment revenue at home, Townshend would have been foolish indeed to have ignored the protests of English taxpayers that the colonists were doing nothing to help the Empire through its financial crisis. The Townshend Act of July 2, 1767, called for duties on glass, paper, paint, and tea imported by the colonies, rather than the internal taxes against which colonial agents had protested in 1765. The revenue would be used to pay for the defense of the colonies, the administration of justice, and the salaries of civil officers in some colonies. A second act established a board of five commissioners in place of the surveyors general of customs, who had been charged with enforcing such laws.

Bostonians sounded the alarm quite as much against the customs commissioners and the proposed civil list as against the new taxes. Thomas Cushing, speaker of the Massachusetts House, was unconcerned about trade regulation, but warned that any legislation intended to raise money for a colonial civil list would be opposed as unconstitutional. Such legislation, of course, would entrench the Conservative party even more firmly in office and threaten the power of the Warren-Adams faction. Rumors were blown with the wind as to the salaries to be provided Hutchinson, Andrew Oliver, and the justices of the Superior Court, and Warren concentrated much of his effort upon attacking the customs commissioners.[30]

The first response to the new taxes was a movement to encourage home manufacturing and economy among the people. The Boston town meeting of October 28, 1767, asked the colony to pledge nonconsumption of some forty articles of foreign manufacture, and local producers made proposals to supply the townspeople with starch, powder, glue, snuff, paper, and linen. Bostonians pledged not to buy lamb for three months, and the senior class at Harvard voted to receive their degrees dressed in clothes of American manufacture.[31] Actually, the Townshend Acts merely provided the excuse for these nonconsumption agreements, which

[30] Cushing to [Denis De Berdt], Boston, May 9, 1767, Miscellaneous MSS, XIII (Mass. Hist. Soc. Library); *Boston Post-Boy*, Aug. 10, 1767.

[31] *Boston Town Records, 1758 to 1769*, pp. 222-224, 230-232, 240; broadside minutes of the town meeting in Faneuil Hall, Oct. 28, 1767, "The town then took into consideration . . ." (Mass. Hist. Soc. Library); *Boston Post-Boy*, Jan. 11, 1768.

were set on foot for other reasons than forcing repeal of the British laws. The items taxed by the new act were not included in the nonconsumption lists, and the Boston town meeting admitted the movement was aimed at relieving the colony of its "insupportable debts and taxes." Any industry, however small, which was developed due to nonconsumption would aid an economy that was in a slough of depression. Once again, as in 1765, nonconsumption was sound economics as well as wise politics.[32]

Other measures were more directly designed to force repeal of the laws. The nonconsumption agreements were voluntary, and the supporters of the plan did not control the governmental machinery which might have been used to carry out the program. Thus, early in 1768, Boston adopted nonimportation, which required the regulation of only a few hundred shippers, rather than the persuasion of several thousand consumers. In the *Boston Gazette,* Warren and his friends pursued the propaganda campaign, Warren serving on a committee to thank John Dickinson for his *Farmer's Letters,* which the paper printed.[33] The Boston newspapers also carried pages of news concerning John Wilkes's trial for republishing issue number 45 of his *North Briton.* "Forty-five" became a Radical slogan at Boston, inscribed on doors and windows throughout the town, with some Whig rallies resolving themselves into awesome struggles to drink forty-five toasts to liberty and its defenders. Joseph Warren and his friend John Adams were members of a committee of the Sons of Liberty who addressed a letter to Wilkes in June, 1768. In the name of forty-five friends of liberty, they sent congratulations on his election to Parliament. This began an irregular correspondence of the committee and of Warren individually with the Englishman. From his room in King's Bench Prison, Wilkes assured the Boston politicians that he was opposed to the Townshend Acts.[34]

---

[32] *Boston Town Records, 1758 to 1769,* p. 227; Carl Bridenbaugh, *Cities in Revolt: Urban Life in America, 1743-1776* (New York, 1955), p. 254, on general economic conditions.

[33] Charles M. Andrews, "Boston Merchants and the Non-Importation Movement," Col. Soc. of Mass., *Publications,* XIX (*Trans.,* 1916-17), 201, 224; *Boston Town Records, 1759 to 1768,* pp. 241, 243-244. The *Boston Chronicle* of 1768 and the first half of 1769 carried more of the serious pamphlet literature than most newspapers, but see *Boston Gazette,* May 29, 1769, and *Boston Evening-Post,* Oct. 16, 1769.

[34] Worthington C. Ford, ed., "John Wilkes and Boston," Mass. Hist. Soc., *Proceedings,* XLVII (1913-14), 190-215. On pp. 199-200 is printed Warren's longest letter to Wilkes, a general attack upon the Ministry for deluding the King into oppressing the colonies, dated Boston, April 13, 1769.

Warren, who had favored the unity achieved by the Stamp Act Congress in 1765, doubtless favored the circular letter which the Massachusetts House sent to other assemblies in America. While admitting that Parliament was the supreme legislature in the Empire, the letter denied that body's power to tax the colonies, denounced independent salaries for colonial officials, and suggested that the colonies communicate their sentiments on the acts and stand together in their protests. This attempt to unify public opinion and exert a pressure on the mother country, which Massachusetts alone could not muster, was viewed with grave concern in England. It might have been preparatory to another congress of the colonies or result in a correspondence that would prove dangerous to England, as the committees of correspondence did some years later. Lord Hillsborough called the letter "most dangerous and factious . . . an open opposition to and denial of the authority of Parliament."[35] Governor Bernard received orders to dissolve the General Court if the House refused to rescind its vote. Faced with Hillsborough's alternative—rescind or be dissolved—the House voted against rescinding by 92 to 17, a smashing victory for the Radical party. Following the dissolution, the names of the seventeen members who voted to rescind were posted on Liberty Tree as public enemies, and a campaign was begun which retired twelve of them from the legislature. The "glorious ninety-two" became the toast of the Atlantic seaboard.[36]

The most significant protest against the Townshend Acts was the intimidation of crown officials by the Boston mob. The customs commissioners were not long in Boston before they discovered that they were likely to have trouble in their new posts. Since 1761, John Temple, a close associate of Warren and other Radical chiefs, had headed His Majesty's customs officers as surveyor general of the northern customs district. That he should have cheerfully yielded a post as chief of the northern service to become one of five commissioners is perhaps too much to expect of a civil serv-

[35] *Massachusetts Gazette*, June 27, 1768; Hillsborough to the Governor of Rhode Island, Whitehall, England, April 21, 1768, Miscellaneous MSS, XIII (Mass. Hist. Soc. Library), also printed in Jensen, *Colonial Documents*, pp. 716-717.

[36] Documents on the rescinding order are in [Alden E. Bradford, ed.], *Speeches of the Governors of Massachusetts from 1764 to 1775* (Boston, 1818), pp. 145-156, hereafter cited as Bradford, *Massachusetts State Papers; Massachusetts Gazette*, July 7, 1768. Robert J. Taylor, *Western Massachusetts in the Revolution* (Providence, R.I., 1954), pp. 58-59, contends that the vote on rescinding is evidence of back country opposition to the Townshend Acts.

ant. His fight against Francis Bernard, however, was of longer making, stemming from Temple's removal from office of one Cockle, collector of customs at Salem. Mutual allegations of customs corruption were exchanged, but equally important was the fact that Temple, a son-in-law of James Bowdoin who led the Radicals in the Council, was aiding the opposition faction against Francis Bernard. Joseph Warren well knew the friends and enemies of his own party, and Warren supported Temple in the public prints during the Cockle incident.[37] Now, as the threat developed of four commisisoners surrounding the one royal official upon whom they could count, the Radicals very literally prepared to take up cudgels against them.

Warren and Adams controlled the Boston town meeting and used it as the forum for the initial attack. This body had extraordinary importance in the revolutionary movement, because of the frequent proroguing and dissolving of the colony's General Court. Each time a governor refused to convene the legislature, Warren and his friends turned to the town meeting to rally opposition opinion. Thus, when they demanded a General Court meeting in October, 1767, and the governor temporized, the Radicals attacked the commissioners in the town meeting and in the newspapers. James Otis became frankly alarmed at the animosity which was being created against the commissioners. He spoke at length, denying that the commisisoners had to be attacked to be shed of the taxes, and suggesting that Bostonians should consider it a favor that Boston was the center of the customs service. Otis called upon the people to treat the officials with respect, and said that riots and disorders could not be justified regardless of how heavy one's burdens or great one's grievances.[38] This, of course, was merely Otis' very personal view, not that of Warren and the more extreme Sons of Liberty.

By March 18, 1768, the date for celebration of the Stamp Act

[37] John Temple to George Grenville, Boston, Oct. 3, 1764, *id.* to Richard Jackson, Boston, Sept. 10, 1764, and *id.* to Commissioners of the Customs, Boston, June 23, 1766, all in Transcripts of British-American Customs Records (Mass. Hist. Soc. Library); Benjamin Hallowell to John Pownall, Boston, Sept. 29, 1773, B. F. Stevens, *Facsimiles of Manuscripts in European Archives Relating to America, 1773-1783* (London, 1895), XXIV, No. 2029; Charles Paxton to George Townsend, Boston, Nov. 6, 1769, Mass. Hist. Soc., *Proceedings,* LVI (1922-23), 350; "Paskalos" in *Boston Gazette,* Feb. 23, 1767. Cockle was one of the customs officials who favored the use of writs of assistance.

[38] *Boston Evening-Post,* Nov. 23, 1767.

repeal, the commissioners had begun to fear for their safety. Actually, this day was peaceful compared to the Stamp Act riots of 1765. Yet the suggestion of Sam Adams and his biographer that the commissioners called for troops because of a few "disorderly boys" is hardly credible.[39] Royal officials might well be intimidated and the customs service hindered without houses being torn down. That feelings ran high on the evening of March 18 was partly due to Joseph Warren's "True Patriot" articles and the recent attempt to indict the printers of the *Gazette*. Warren's friends met at the British Coffee House, and toasted the newspaper and the Assembly which had refused Bernard's request to consider Warren's article. Effigies of Charles Paxton, one of the commissioners, and of Inspector Williams were hung on Liberty Tree for a time, and small groups were abroad, shouting about the houses of royal officials and breaking a few windows.[40]

March 18 did pass without serious violence, yet it was only three months until fighting was to be seen in the streets of Boston once again. The *Liberty* incident in June led the customs officials to seek refuge from an angry Boston populace aboard the King's ship-of-war *Romney*. It was also this event which was most responsible for the sending of those regiments of redcoats to Boston who were to clash with the townspeople on March 5, 1770. In both of these dramatic stories—the fight against the customs commissioners and the resistance to the British army—the figure of Joseph Warren strides large across the stage. Propaganda was now to be supplemented with threats and violence, and Warren showed equal daring and skill in the use of these weapons.

---

[39] Samuel Adams' *Appeal to the World*, printed as a committee report in *Boston Town Records, 1758 to 1769*, pp. 307, 315-316; John C. Miller, *Sam Adams, Pioneer in Propaganda* (Boston, 1936), pp. 141-142. On March 28, the commissioners wrote, "we must depend on the favour of the leaders of the mob for our protection and in such circumstances we cannot answer for our security for a day, much less will it be in our power to carry the revenue laws into effect." George G. Wolkins, "The Seizure of John Hancock's Sloop *Liberty*," Mass. Hist. Soc., *Proceedings*, LV (1921-22), 270-271.

[40] *Boston Town Records, 1758 to 1769*, pp. 305-307.

# Appeal to Force

CHAPTER V

The incident which drove the King's commissioners of the customs from Boston grew out of the confiscation of a sloop owned by that wealthy young merchant turned politician, John Hancock. The *Liberty* tied up at Hancock's wharf on May 9, 1768, with a cargo of wine, and rumor was that the duties would not be paid. Joseph Warren warned Benjamin Hallowell, comptroller of customs, that if the ship were seized there would be "a great uproar" and that he "could not be answerable for the consequences."[1] Warren and his friends seem to have planned a deliberate violation of the revenue acts to test the commissioners' power, and the royal officials were ready for such a challenge. Bernard and the customs officers might have profited by confiscating the ship, and they would have been delighted to have John Hancock as their target, since it was notorious that his wealth was supporting the political activities of the Liberty party. Throughout the affair Joseph Warren took the lead in shaping Radical policy and in negotiations, being the one man of the opposition whom the Conservatives genuinely respected. Hallowell felt that Warren was a

[1] Transcript of Examination of Mr. Hallowell at the Treasury Board, July 21, 1768, Arthur Lee MSS, I, 40 (Houghton Library).

man of integrity and of sufficient influence both to dissuade Samuel Adams from rash actions and to prevent the townspeople from using violence.

When the *Liberty* docked, a tidesman, Thomas Kirk, boarded her, and the next day he declared that nothing amiss had taken place during the night. On May 10 the part of the cargo which was Hancock's personal property was entered and the duties paid. Whether or not there was other wine aboard which had been illegally unloaded the night before was the disputable point. On June 9, Kirk swore that one month earlier, while aboard the *Liberty* as tidesman, he had been confined below deck by Hancock's men and had heard the cargo taken off. In seizing the vessel, the customs officials also alleged that Hancock had loaded a new cargo of tar and whale oil before filing the ship's cargo list and posting bond. This was a mere technicality, since for convenience's sake it was the accepted practice of the port to file lists and post bonds after loading. By waiting until June 10 to seize the vessel, with its new cargo in the hold, the royal officials would get additional profit from the condemnation.[2]

Yet the alleged smuggling of 100 pipes of wine was no such technical violation. It was publicly known before the *Liberty* arrived that the wines would be smuggled, and Hutchinson said that afterwards it was "the publick talk of the town, and became a common topick" that the duties had not been paid. Also, the Radical leaders did not denounce the seizure or defend Hancock against the charge of smuggling; rather, they criticized the way in which the seizure was made.[3] The practice was to post notice of the seizure of a vessel and paint the king's broad arrow on her, leaving the ship at the dock. The customs officials, however, cut the *Liberty* loose and carried her off under the protection of the *Romney's* guns. Never had this procedure been used before, and a crowd quickly collected about Hancock's wharf. People hurled stones at the collector and comptroller of customs, and later that

[2] Hutchinson, *History*, III, 137; Oliver M. Dickerson, "John Hancock: Notorious Smuggler or Near Victim of British Revenue Racketeers?" *Mississippi Valley Historical Review*, XXXII, No. 4 (March, 1946), 517-524, 526-528; Wolkins, "Hancock's Sloop *Liberty*," pp. 251-252.

[3] *Ibid.*, p. 273; Samuel Adams, in a document adopted by the Boston town meeting, wrote that "the opposition was made, not at all to the seizing of the vessel by the officers of the customs but wholly to the manner in which it was secured." *Boston Town Records, 1758 to 1769*, p. 309, and, in the same tenor, Cushing, ed., *Writings of Samuel Adams*, I, 314-315.

night an inspector barely escaped the wrath of a mob. Crowds surrounding the homes of several customs officials broke windows, and a small boat owned by the collector was burned on the Common.[4]

Of all the factors in this explosive situation, none was more important than the naval vessel to which the *Liberty* was moored. The *Romney* had hovered about Boston for some time, a symbol of royal authority and a potential aid in enforcing the trade laws. Further, she had been impressing seamen from ships entering Boston Harbor, and New England dislike of this practice was as intense at this time as in 1807. On June 10 it added fuel to the fiery emotions of the Boston populace.

The day following the seizure the commissioners fled to the *Romney,* there being talk of a general insurrection for the night of Saturday, June 11. Warren now began to act. The commissioners considered him to be "a person of credit" and he held a meeting with Hallowell out of which came a half-hearted agreement. Warren was simply interested in breaking the power of the customs officials, and tried to avoid excessive violence by promising to keep the townspeople peaceful until Monday night, if the royal officials would return the *Liberty* to Hancock's wharf, the owner posting bond for her. Harrison, the collector, sent a note to Hancock, agreeing to Warren's proposal. On Sunday, June 12, Hancock went to Warren's home for advice on the note, but the doctor was out. During the day Warren told Hallowell that all was settled; if the ship were returned Monday morning, bond would be posted. That evening, however, Warren, Samuel Adams, Otis, and other Radical leaders met at Hancock's home. Just what was said is unknown, but at midnight Sunday Warren called at Hallowell's house and told him the arrangement was off. His friends had advised Hancock to sign nothing and to refuse to have any part in an agreement with the customs officials.[5]

Warren and his friends decided upon a town meeting for June 14 as the initial step in organizing public opinion. When attendance overflowed Faneuil Hall, the meeting adjourned to the Old South Church. The town chose a twenty-one-man committee to

[4] *Boston Chronicle,* June 6-13, 1768.

[5] Transcript of Hallowell's Examination, Arthur Lee MSS, I, 40; *Boston Town Records, 1758 to 1769,* p. 309; Joseph Harrison and Benjamin Hallowell to John Robinson, Boston, June 12, 1768, Bernard *et al., Letters to the Ministry,* p. 97.

present to Governor Bernard a petition which declared that the town was virtually invested and in a state of war and prayed that Bernard would order the *Romney* out of the harbor. The committee, including Warren, was composed of the highest echelon of opposition leadership, including important Moderates like Speaker Thomas Cushing and the selectmen of Boston. John Rowe, Hancock, and Warren, a committee to discover when the governor would receive the petition, reported that Bernard was at his country estate. The larger committee met at John Hancock's home and formed a procession of carriages. Bernard received the members graciously, even charming some of them who had never met a royal governor before. But Warren, Adams, and Otis were seasoned politicians, and demanded an answer. Bernard promised to try to have impressment regulated to avoid inconveniences, but argued that he was bound by oath to protect the commissioners and that he had no command over the *Romney*.[6]

On June 15 another committee—Warren as chairman, Samuel Adams, and Benjamin Church—presented to the town meeting resolves that protested the way in which the *Liberty* had been seized and the invasion of the town by armed force. Warren, however, had made them a bit too strong, and "a lawyer a noted Son of Liberty," doubtless James Otis, opposed them. He argued that this was a colonial rather than a town affair, a point which seldom bothered the sensibilities of a Boston town meeting. The town named Warren one of a committee of twenty-one to report the recent occurrences to Denis De Berdt, the agent of the Massachusetts House in England, certainly a more irregular step for one town of the Province than would be the voting of a few resolves. Warren and his old medical foe, but now political ally, Thomas Young, seem to have authored this letter.[7]

In lieu of his spirited resolves, the town meeting placed Warren at the head of still another committee to draw up instructions for Boston's representatives to the General Court. This paper, in his characteristically florid prose, expressed concern at the cash being

[6] *Boston Town Records, 1758 to 1769,* pp. 253-257; Cunningham, ed., *Letters of John Rowe,* p. 165.

[7] Wolkins, "Hancock's Sloop *Liberty*," p. 284; *Boston Town Records, 1758 to 1769,* pp. 255-257. In the listing of the committee members, the names of the moderator and the selectmen are naturally placed first. Next, as the chief committee members, are Young and Warren, followed by the honorary listing of members of the General Court who served on the committee.

drained from the colony to support idle pensioners, and charged that the harmony following the Stamp Act's repeal was disrupted by unconstitutional acts of Parliament. Warren declared that the colonists would defend their "dear and invaluable rights and liberties, at the utmost hazard of our lives and fortunes." Here was the tone of Jefferson in 1776 sounding the keynote of Radical policy in the crisis of 1768. Warren presents no closely reasoned argument on the constitutionality of the revenue acts but an emotional call to colonists against an attempt "to dragoon" them and "to suck the life blood of the body politick, while it is streaming from the veins." Every word was propaganda designed to rally the Bay Colony to the leadership of the Radical party and to prepare the people for an insurrection. A spy in Warren's party told Bernard that the Radicals were merely awaiting a pretext to begin an insurrection against the crown officials. In September, 1768, with British troops on the way to Boston, the Radicals tried to implement Warren's policy of armed defense of colonial rights.[8]

Warren's specific instructions to Boston's representatives ordered them to try to prevent impressments and to initiate an investigation of whomever had misrepresented the town as being in a state of disorder and had called for military force. He also recommended that the General Court declare any person who solicited troops for Massachusetts "an enemy of the town and province, and a disturber of the peace and good order of both."[9] This last was virtually the same as Warren's earlier resolve, declaring such persons to be traitors, which the town meeting had rejected. The attack upon royal officials, particularly Francis Bernard, was one of the keystones of Warren's policy, and the adoption of this instruction gave town approval to his campaign to have the governor recalled. Actually, Bernard had refused to ask for troops, fearing that the town's animosity would turn from the commissioners to himself. This, however, was of little moment to Warren and the Sons of Liberty, who ascribed to him the introduction of armed force.

From the *Romney*, the commissioners professed to see a state

---

[8] *Ibid.*, pp. 258-259; Bernard to Barrington, Boston, May 9, 1768, Channing and Coolidge, eds., *Barrington-Bernard Correspondence*, pp. 157-158. The general style of the instructions is Warren's, and normally the man who was to write such a document was made committee chairman. The long quotation from a statute of Queen Anne likely was supplied by John Adams, a member of the committee.

[9] *Boston Town Records, 1758 to 1769*, pp. 257-259.

of insurrection rather than a riot in Boston, and asked Bernard's protection in returning to town. General Thomas Gage, stationed at New York as commander of British military forces in North America, offered to send troops to aid Bernard in restoring royal authority. The governor submitted the proposal to his Council, which unanimously advised against accepting the offer and denounced the commissioners for fleeing a town in which no insult or injury had been offered them, in order to misrepresent Boston as being riotous. Bernard wrote Gage that, in view of his Council's opposition, he was "well contented to wait till orders shall come from England."[10]

Such orders were already on the way. The complaints of the commissioners before the *Liberty* incident led Hillsborough to instruct Bernard to render them all support possible. When news of the June riot reached London, the government immediately dispatched two regiments from Ireland to Boston. Hillsborough ordered Bernard to prepare accommodations for them and to use them to support royal officials. Having received too many excuses of the governor's helplessness before the Boston mob, he added a warning: "Full responsibility thus rests with you and terror or danger in execution of your office will not be an excuse for remissness of duty."[11]

Actually, Joseph Warren knew that there were many people in Massachusetts, even some of his friends in Boston, who did not favor his policy of using violence to combat the Townshend Acts and harass the British army that was on its way. The Boston selectmen spoke against lawlessness, and one of his political allies, Thomas Cushing, condemned people like Warren and Adams who tried to make people believe that the Ministry was depriving them of their rights and pursuing a severe colonial policy. Their design, he told an English correspondent, seemed to be "to sett us at variance and engage us [in] hostilities with one another."[12]

Boston merchants did, to be sure, refuse to import goods from

[10] Commissioners of the Customs to Bernard, *H.M.S. Romney,* June 13, 1768, Transcripts of British-American Customs Records; *Massachusetts Gazette,* Oct. 10, 1768; Mass. Archives, Council Records, XVI (1765-74), 333-343; Bernard to Gage, Boston, July 30, 1768, Gay Transcripts: State Papers, XI, 49.

[11] Hillsborough to Bernard, Whitehall, England, July 11, 1768, Transcripts of Instructions to Provincial Governors, VIII, 2419; *id.* to *id.*, Whitehall, England, July 30, 1768, *ibid.*, 2423.

[12] Thomas Cushing to [Denis De Berdt], Boston, May 9, 1767, Miscellaneous MSS, XIII (Mass. Hist. Soc. Library); Arthur M. Schlesinger, *The Colonial Merchants and the American Revolution, 1763-1776* (New York, 1957), p. 96.

England, and the Liberty party was able to dominate the General Court for two more years. When Joseph Warren and Samuel Adams counseled armed resistance, however, their pleas fell upon deaf ears. The regrettable incident in King Street on March 5, 1770, which history has dignified as the Boston Massacre, stands out in bold relief as the single major crisis in a period of political moderation extending from the *Liberty* incident of 1768 to the Tea Party of 1773. The failure during these years of Warren's party to rally the people of Massachusetts to its standard until the passage of the East India Company Act is a measure of the importance of British policy and of the American merchant class in the making of the War for Independence. The unflagging zeal of Warren and Adams in the absence of imperial issues is, however, no less suggestive of the importance of domestic politics in their eyes.

Throughout 1768 Warren was working wholeheartedly for the Liberty party. Again and again he urged John Adams to attend town meetings and "harangue there." Adams pointed to the example of James Otis, already exhibiting signs of insanity, and replied, "That way madness lies." Warren smiled and grudgingly admitted this truth. When news arrived that British troops were being sent to Boston, Warren took a leading role in planning the Boston town meeting which called a Massachusetts convention that some hoped and others feared might resolve upon armed resistance. Thomas Hutchinson wrote that the freemasons, of whom Warren was master, had "a great secret," probably a reference to the plan for a convention of Massachusetts towns.[13]

The town meeting of September 12, 1768, was one of the most carefully planned and closely controlled of Boston's revolutionary period. On the evening of September 10, the Liberty party leaders gathered at Warren's home. Otis was still so important that he was invited, though Warren and Adams knew that their lawyer friend might steer a moderate course. The agenda for the town meeting was settled at this caucus. Those present discussed in detail the speakers, the order in which they would appear, and the subject matter of the meeting.[14] Warren assumed a position

[13] Charles F. Adams, ed., *Works of John Adams*, II, 214; Thomas Hutchinson to [John Cushing], Milton, Mass., Aug. 5, [1768], Mass. Hist. Soc., *Proceedings*, XL (1906-07), 536.

[14] John C. Miller, "The Massachusetts Convention, 1768," *New England Quarterly*, VII, No. 3 (Sept., 1934), 454-455; *Boston Town Records, 1758 to 1769*, p. 319.

upon every important committee to be appointed, while the regular Boston representatives to the General Court—Otis, Hancock, Adams, and Cushing—were proposed as the delegates to the planned convention.

Word of the secret conference at the doctor's house spread quickly in Boston, alarming both Moderates and Conservatives. Bernard and Hutchinson feared a plot to seize Castle William, which guarded the entrance to Boston Harbor. Other rumors had it that a tar barrel would be set afire as a beacon to call the countryfolks in to resist the landing of the troops.[15] September 11 was an anxious day for all supporters of the government as they waited for the Radicals to reveal their hand in Faneuil Hall the following morning.

The town meeting went precisely according to plan. Warren and others who could be counted upon were to present a petition to the governor requesting him to summon the General Court. A larger committee, also including Warren, was then assigned the task of suggesting further measures for the meeting's consideration. These measures, of course, had been planned two days before at Warren's home. Thus, when the first committee reported Bernard's refusal, the second was able to present immediately a set of resolves which were unanimously adopted. The townspeople asserted their right to be free of taxes and of standing armies in peacetime without their consent, and ominously pledged their "lives and fortunes," the phrase Warren had used in his June instructions, in defense of these rights. Then, after noting that the governor had refused to call the General Court into session, the meeting resolved to appoint its delegates to a provincial convention. Following the extreme leadership of the Radicals, the town meeting recommended that all inhabitants who did not own guns provide themselves with arms as quickly as possible.[16]

The invitation to the towns of Massachusetts to attend the convention in Faneuil Hall was coldly received in some parts of the colony. A few towns refused to vote on the Boston proposal for a convention, and Hatfield's selectmen said they did not believe conditions were so alarming as to make the proposal "either salutary or necessary." They argued that war was the only alternative to a loyal petition, and warned against being brought to this

---

[15] [Thomas Hutchinson], *Copy of Letters Sent to Great Britain* (Boston, 1773), pp. 10-11; *Boston Town Records, 1758 to 1769,* p. 318.

[16] *Ibid.*, pp. 259-264, 319-320; Bernard *et al.*, *Letters to the Ministry,* p. 54.

insane step by leaders who were dominated by "passion and disappointment and private resentment." No delegates attended the convention from Berkshire County and only one from Hampshire.[17] The Massachusetts back country was clearly a long way from being prepared to support rebellion.

Actually, the Massachusetts convention of 1768 was nothing but the House of Representatives, convened under a different name and without precept from the governor. Thomas Cushing, speaker of the last House, and Samuel Adams, clerk of that body, were chosen moderator and secretary of the convention. Here was the Liberty party's answer to the Conservatives' refusal to call the General Court. The first of many extralegal bodies created by Warren and Adams, it served as a pattern for the county conventions of 1774, assembled after town meetings were forbidden, and for the Provincial Congress, established when Thomas Gage refused to summon the House. Yet, in its immediate purpose the convention of 1768 was a failure. Called to gain back-country support in opposing the landing of the British troops, it proved to be the first step in a reaction against the policies that Joseph Warren represented.

The convention sent a petition to the governor requesting the calling of the General Court. Bernard refused to receive it, and, knowing he would soon have troops to support him, ordered the illegal meeting to dissolve. A second address by the convention pledged obedience to the king, and assured the governor that it was convened only to present the people's grievances and to learn the truth of the rumor that troops were coming. Bernard rejected this paper also, and, on the eve of the arrival of the troops, the convention appointed a committee to draw up a summary of its activities, preparatory to dispersing. This paper recited the colonial grievances, but timidly advised the people "to avoid any undue expressions of resentment, and to prevent, as much as in them lies, all tumults and disorders."[18]

Nothing could demonstrate more clearly the depth of the Radicals' failure. Without the support of lawyers like John Adams, James Otis, and Joseph Hawley and of merchants like John Rowe

[17] Broadside, Selectmen of Boston to the Selectmen of Stoughton, Boston, Sept. 14, 1768 (Boston Public Library); Hutchinson, *History*, III, 356-357, prints the Boston invitation; Selectmen of Hatfield to the Selectmen of Boston, *Massachusetts Gazette*, Oct. 6, 1768; Taylor, *Western Massachusetts*, p. 59.

[18] Hutchinson, *History*, III, 151-152; *Boston Gazette*, Sept. 26, 1768.

and John Hancock, Joseph Warren and Samuel Adams could influence few but the Boston laborers and artisans upon whom they depended for votes in the town meeting. The convention's resolutions were a far cry from Warren's June instructions to the Boston representatives, pledging that the colonists would defend their rights with their lives. The convention ended the day the troops arrived, some of its members fearing arrest and transportation to England. Irascible John Mein wrote that the delegates had intended to oppose the troops, but instead "broke up and rushed out of town like a herd of scalded hogs." Warren at this time took the precaution of burning his private papers. By late September four regiments of British regulars had been ordered to Boston. Speculation in London was that they would soon quell any insurrections, as "the American Wilkes," Sam Adams' current sobriquet in court circles, could not bear the smell of gunpowder and fainted at a drawn sword.[19]

Yet, before the ships carrying the first troops tied up in Boston Harbor, Warren and Adams were planning new steps in opposition to British policy. Unable to prevent the landing of the troops, they sought to obstruct the quartering of those which did land. If they could refuse the use of Faneuil Hall and the manufactory house as barracks, Lieutenant Colonel Dalrymple would have to lodge his men in private homes or in Castle William. The former might serve as grounds for "an insurrection of the people against the invaders of their property"; the latter would render the army useless in supporting Bernard and the commissioners.[20]

The governor considered the Council, upon which he might have once depended, as lost to Warren's party by this time. James Bowdoin, chief of the Liberty party in the Council, was a close friend of both Warren and Samuel Adams. He loaned Warren a large sum of money, and Warren worked closely with him in the propaganda campaign following the Boston Massacre. Bernard

[19] The holding of the convention led the House of Commons to resolve that the governor of Massachusetts should gather information on treasons committed in his colony and send the indicted to England for trial. In December, 1768, Bernard mentioned the officials involved in calling the convention as liable to prosecution, but omitted Warren, who held no official position as did the selectmen. [John Mein], *Sagittarius's Letters* (Boston, 1775), p. 81, note; Gipson, *Coming of the Revolution*, pp. 192-193; *Massachusetts Gazette*, Sept. 19, 22, 1768.

[20] Bernard *et al.*, *Letters to the Ministry*, pp. 57, 60.

claimed that the councilors met without being called and had "suffered so great a change" that they scarcely appeared to be the same men. Though "in their hearts friends to government," they had been intimidated by the Liberty party.[21] In answer to a request for quarters, the Council supported the Warren-Adams policy, declaring that none should be provided in the town until Castle William was filled. Upon applying to the Boston selectmen, Dalrymple received a similar rebuff. It was not until October 20 that a serious attempt was made to break the stalemate. Thomas Gage came up from New York and personally appealed to the Council for quarters. That body finally granted use of the manufactory building, and Sheriff Greenleaf tried to dispossess the Radical supporters who had leased it. Warren and Adams posted members of their party in the yard of the building to challenge the sheriff, but the latter had a guard of troops at his back. The two leaders met at Warren's home and drew affidavits to be signed by witnesses to the episode. If resistance could not be manufactured, propaganda could.[22]

Friction developed between the inhabitants and the soldiers, as might have been expected in any garrisoned town. One report from the Liberty party was that several officers were plotting to attack a physician, and a prominent doctor was jostled and struck in the street. Warren was the only doctor of the three in Radical circles who had as yet cut such a political figure that British officers would know of his activities and recognize him on sight. Two months after this encounter, Warren refused to answer the challenge of an off-duty officer and was seized by the collar. Having but one opponent now, Warren knocked the officer down and went on his way. There were other such scuffles, and, when the men of the Twenty-ninth Regiment had passes from their barracks, the blame did not lie wholly with the civilians. But such incidents could be exaggerated, as they were in the accounts which

---

[21] *Ibid.*, pp. 52, 65; Leonard W. Labaree, *Royal Government in America: A Study of the British Colonial System Before 1783* (New Haven, Conn., 1930), p. 159.

[22] Mass. Archives, Council Records, XVI, 356, 359-360, 362-363, 370; extracts of letters from Gage to Bernard, New York, Oct. 2, 1768, and Lt. Col. Dalrymple to Gage, Boston, Oct. 2, 1768, Gay Transcripts: State Papers, XI, 94, 96-98; depositions of Benjamin Church, Thomas Crafts, Adam Collson, Giles Brewer, John Beers, and one unsigned, in the hand of Samuel Adams, [April 14, 1769], Bowdoin-Temple MSS, II (Mass. Hist. Soc. Library); Samuel Adams to James Bowdoin, [Boston, April 15, 1769], in *ibid.*

the Radical leaders penned for circulation to newspapers in several colonies.[23]

Yet try as they might, the Liberty party was unable to disrupt the calm of the Bay Colony, to say nothing of all America. Such incidents as there were seemed as ripples on the smooth sea of political moderation. In November, 1768, Thomas Gage wrote that Boston had "the appearance of peace and quiet." Samuel Hood, commander of British naval forces, wrote in similar vein, "Everything here has been quite quiet ever since I came, and I am very confident will remain so. . . . The worst is certainly past here, and I hope and trust all will be well by-and-by." Thomas Cushing noted, "Our people behave with the greatest caution and prudence so that I am perswaded the commanders of the troops and men of war are not a little surprised at the errand they were sent upon. . . ." One of the most rabid of Warren's party members was cooperating with the British officers at the same time. William Molineux, realistic businessman that he was, leased a sugar house and stores on Wheelwright's wharf as barracks for the British troops at thirty pounds sterling per month.[24]

Transatlantic communications being slow, the British Ministry took a serious view of American affairs, despite the political quiescence of Massachusetts. George III spoke his concern with acts of violence and resistance to English laws at Boston in his speech at the opening of Parliament. In February, 1769, Hillsborough made several proposals to the Cabinet relating to Massachusetts. His belief that the Massachusetts Council must be appointed rather than elected stemmed from Francis Bernard. Further, if the Massachusetts House challenged Parliament's power to legislate for the colonies, the Bay Colony charter should

[23] Oliver M. Dickerson, ed., *Boston Under Military Rule, 1768-1769, as Revealed in "A Journal of the Times"* (Boston, 1936), pp. 15, 17, 34. This news sheet, published from Sept. 28, 1768, to Aug. 1, 1769, consisted principally of reports of alleged oppression by the troops and of propaganda against the Conservatives. Its editor emphasizes its reliability, though it seems to have been a particularly biased propaganda instrument. See Schlesinger, "Propaganda and the Boston Press," pp. 407-410.

[24] Samuel Hood to George Grenville, Boston, April 15, 1769, William J. Smith, ed., *The Grenville Papers* (London, 1853), IV, 420-421; Gipson, *Coming of the Revolution*, p. 191, for the Gage quotation; Cushing to Denis De Berdt, Boston, Jan. 19, [1769], Miscellaneous MSS, XIII (Mass. Hist. Soc. Library); John R. Alden, ed., "A Letter from William Molineux," *New England Quarterly*, XVII, No. 1 (March, 1944), 107-108.

be forfeited. At the same time, Hillsborough suggested that Governor Bernard be called home for advice and that a baronetcy be given him.[25]

Before the summer of 1769 had passed, Francis Bernard did, in fact, step aboard his majesty's ship *Rippon* bound out for England, never to return to the Province he had governed for eight crucial years. As the ship weighed anchor on August 1, he could have stood on deck and seen the bonfires and heard the guns which should have been fired in celebration of the anniversary of the accession of the House of Hanover. Actually, much of the rejoicing was because "the king had been graciously pleased to recall a very bad governor" and because "a worse cannot be found on this side."[26] Bernard well knew whom he could credit for this farewell and for the trouble of past years, which had caused the home government to question his ability to control his Province. He had had more than his fill of Adams and Otis. Both had been bitter political foes and had not scrupled to damn him personally. And, if Bernard had full knowledge of Joseph Warren's activities, he might well have reflected bitterly upon this younger opponent. Certainly nobody had done more to destroy his career as a royal governor.

Warren's "True Patriot" letter in March had set the tone of the year 1768. As late as October, Thomas Hutchinson wrote that this "infamous libel" had the people so aroused that he feared for his personal safety. Nearly two years later, the Lords of Council charged that seditious publications went unpunished, "manifesting a design to stir up the people to acts of violence and opposition to the laws." The reference was so clearly to Warren's attack upon Bernard that the Massachusetts Council felt compelled to explain its conduct in the episode.[27] Also, Warren had stage-managed the *Liberty* affair, which had convinced English authorities that Bernard could not maintain order in the capital city without military support.

Throughout the later months of 1768 and early 1769, Joseph Warren and the Sons of Liberty continued their harassment of

[25] *Massachusetts Gazette*, Jan. 12, 1769; John Fortescue, ed., *The Correspondence of King George the Third from 1760 to December 1783* (London, 1927), II, 82-84.

[26] *Boston Gazette*, Aug. 7, 1769.

[27] Hutchinson, *Copy of Letters*, p. 10; Mass. Council to William Bollan, Oct. 30, 1770, Bradford, ed., *Massachusetts State Papers*, pp. 273-274.

Bernard and his administration. Their influence extended to Harvard College, where vandals cut a heart-shaped piece from the breast of the governor's portrait hanging in College Hall. Warren served on town committees which drafted a petition to the king and instructions to the representatives in the General Court. When Bernard refused to act upon the legislature's demand that he remove the troops from Massachusetts, it refused to proceed to business for two weeks, and the governor adjourned the body to Cambridge, giving them new cause for attacking him. The Assembly finally did act, requesting that the king remove Francis Bernard from his office, and rejecting the governor's request for a salary during his leave in England. Two months after Bernard's departure from Massachusetts, Warren and Adams obtained copies of letters written to English officials by the governor, General Gage, Commodore Hood, and the customs commissioners. Warren served on a committee to vindicate Boston from the alleged libel of these letters. A commentary upon the letters was written and circulated in England, and the Suffolk County grand jury indicted the authors of the letters.[28]

Francis Bernard had been virtually driven from Massachusetts, and domestic party battles had played nearly as large a part as had his position as a royal agent. The first six charges in the complaint of the Assembly against Bernard were concerned with the struggle between the Prerogative and Liberty parties in Massachusetts. Aside from his having treated the House with contempt, all of these charges related to the governor's attempt to fill the Council with members of his own party and to displace officeholders who voted against his administration.[29] Bernard had been as interested in building party strength as in bulwarking British power in America when he proposed an appointed Council and accepted Gage's offer of troops. Joseph Warren and Samuel Adams saw this clearly and feared the destruction of their efforts to build a political organization which would extend to every county in the colony and to every office available. In their propaganda and in the violence which they approved or instigated, Warren and

[28] Tudor, ed., *Deacon Tudor's Diary*, p. 28; *Boston Town Records, 1758 to 1769*, pp. 272-273, 274, 279, 285-286, 297, 299; *Boston Gazette*, June 12, 1769; Bradford, ed., *Massachusetts State Papers*, pp. 175-176, 182, 188-191; Boston, Committee of the Town to Denis De Berdt, Oct. 23, 1769, *Massachusetts Papers*, p. 124.

[29] *Boston Chronicle*, May 3-7, 1770.

Adams were fighting for political survival, as well as home rule for Massachusetts.

Bernard left the government in the hands of Thomas Hutchinson, a more capable, if not more inveterate, foe of Radicalism. Hutchinson, whom Warren had once called a devoted public servant, now became the target of Liberty party attacks, as the new governor filled more offices with relatives and party men. Since the Radicals had captured a number of Council seats, there were fewer members of that body who held judicial or administrative posts. There was not, however, a serious curtailment of the patronage available to the Hutchinson and Oliver families, the heads of which now led the Conservative party. By 1771, as described by Samuel Adams, the grasp of the leading families upon offices was wondrous to behold:[30]

> Mr. Lynde is chiefe justice; his daughter is married to the son of Mr Oliver, the lt govr; Mr Oliver another of the judges is his brother; his son married Gov Hutchinsons daughter; and Judge Hutchinson lately appointed, who is also judge of the probate of wills for the first county, an important department, is the govrs brother. Besides which the young Mr Oliver is a justice of the common pleas for the County of Essex. Mr Cotton a brother in law of the govr is deputy secretary of the province and register in the probate office under Mr Hutchinson; a cousin german of the govr was sent for out of another province to fill up the place of clerk to the common pleas in this county; and the eldest son of the govr will probably soon be appointed a justice of the same court in the room of his uncle advanced to the superior bench. I should have first mentioned that the gov and lt gov are brothers by marriage.

Thus, the Conservatives held enough offices by appointment of the royal governor to make them strong supporters of British colonial policy. Political as well as economic motives induced the Hutchinson family to refuse to sign the nonimportation agreement adopted by Boston merchants in August, 1768, to force repeal of the Townshend Acts. Thomas Hutchinson played a behind-the-scenes role in the family business, and in view of his political position, could hardly condone smuggling or opposition to English policy. And there was also a difference of ideals between men like Warren and such men as Hutchinson—a natural split based upon temperament and their attitude toward democratic government.

Joseph Warren feared the growth of a colonial aristocracy, and

[30] Cushing, ed., *Writings of Samuel Adams,* II, 265-266.

until confronted with the daily problems of governing the ill-disciplined army that gathered about Boston after April 19, 1775, swore his faith in the ability of the people to govern themselves. Thomas Hutchinson, who had faced the responsibilities of office for years and shuddered at the thought of the financial and other policies the people might adopt, believed in government by the best men for the good of the entire society. Warren had seen the people of his town of Roxbury elect his own father to govern its affairs; Hutchinson had watched the people whom he tried to serve destroy his mansion. Warren, the young idealist, with his intense nationalism, dream of independence, and faith in democracy, rode the wave of the future. Thomas Hutchinson, the seasoned politician, believing that America must stay with Britain and that his own Conservative party came as close as could be to the disinterested governors of Plato's *Republic,* was swept into a backwater of history. Though one seldom finds a trace of it in their public propaganda, Joseph Warren and Thomas Hutchinson were men of large enough minds to ask whether or not they were entirely right and their opponents entirely wrong. In the privacy of their hearts, they asked searching questions about their widely divergent courses. After war broke out, Joseph Warren wrote Thomas Gage a letter in which he candidly admitted that he regretted not taking advantage of Gage's offer to talk frankly with him about the issues which were breaking up the Empire. Thomas Hutchinson privately recognized that his opponents might be as sincere as he was, and that both parties saw things "many times through a false medium and are biased though insensibly by one prejudice and another."[31]

In 1769, Hutchinson gained a powerful ally in the publisher of the *Boston Chronicle,* John Mein. By printing cargo manifestoes next to the nonimportation agreement, he tried to show that John Hancock in particular, and Boston merchants in general, were importing contrary to their pledge. Seeds of suspicion thus sowed found fertile ground—the minds of New York and Philadelphia merchants who had bound themselves to such agreements on the assurance that Boston would do so. Mein personally refused to sign the Boston agreement, and warned Massachusetts

[31] Hutchinson to [Israel Williams], Boston, April 26, 1765, Israel Williams MSS, II (Mass. Hist. Soc. Library).

retailers that the Committee of Inspection was giving permission to sell certain British goods to favored merchants.[32]

When the Conservatives had felt the sting of Joseph Warren's pen in 1768, they had had all of the executive and judicial machinery of the government to fight him, and had failed. Without such advantages and with Boston garrisoned by British troops, the Radical party was more successful. Counterpropaganda was used initially, but the final appeal was to force and intimidation. Merchants, including Hancock, printed letters denying any breach of faith, and Radical party writers castigated Mein in the *Boston Gazette*. The float in the Pope's Day parade of 1769 pilloried the *Chronicle* publisher in verse and effigy, a mob attacked him in the street, and he soon sought refuge in England.[33]

But threats and violence could be a two-way street. In September, 1769, John Robinson, one of the customs commissioners, fought James Otis in the British Coffee House. Canes were used and, if Joseph Warren's medical opinion in a political case is trustworthy, cutlasses as well. Taverns and coffeehouses, like newspapers, were now patronized by one or the other of the political parties. Royal officials and officers of the army and navy frequented the British Coffee House, and for Otis to go there was almost foolhardy in itself. Warren and other Radical doctors treated Otis, bleeding badly about the head and face, but he never permanently recovered his sanity. Some days after the fight, Warren sought out one of the assailants at the coffeehouse and demanded satisfaction on behalf of the injured lawyer, but the challenge was turned aside.[34]

By early 1770, street fights between townspeople and British troops had become commonplace. In October, 1769, Ensign John Ness was in charge of a guard which took much the same abuse as was handed out to Captain Preston's men five months later. Verbal taunting led to a shower of dirt and stones, and a mob

---

[32] Reports of meetings of merchants in Boston, New York, and Salem, relating to Mein's allegations, in *Massachusetts Gazette,* May 4, 11, 1769; *Boston Chronicle,* Aug. 14-28, 1769, Jan. 8-11, 1770.

[33] *Boston Gazette,* particularly issues of Aug.-Sept., 1769; *Boston Chronicle,* Nov. 6-9, 1769, for Mein's report of the Pope's Day float.

[34] The reports of both sides and the final judicial decision for Otis may be found in: *Boston Gazette,* Sept. 14, 25, 1769, July 29, 1771, Sept. 14, 1772; *Massachusetts Gazette,* Sept. 7, 11, 14, 1769; *Boston Chronicle,* Sept. 14-18, 1769; Thomas Young to———, [Boston, Sept., 1769], in Edes, "Memoir of Dr. Thomas Young," p. 7.

followed the guards through the streets. Ness appeared before Justice Dana to answer a warrant sworn by Robert Pierpont, leader of the crowd at the guardhouse. There another crowd rendered further abuse, which the justice ignored, claiming he was deaf. Depositions of other troops are extant relating to similar conflicts occurring as early as November, 1768, and frequently during 1769 and the first months of 1770.[35] Thus, the unfortunate clash of March 5, 1770, was but one of many which might have resulted in bloodshed.

Doubtless much of this fighting between soldiers and civilians was the kind that occurs in any garrisoned town, with no political significance whatsoever. Probably the British troops were more often to blame than were the Bostonians, but the contention that these conflicts were due to the oppression of a tyrannical king is another matter. Actually, the fight for survival of the Boston political organization was a key factor in this warfare. The arrival of the troops in 1768, rather than their removal in 1770, marks the beginning of the reaction in Massachusetts which lasted until 1773. Moderates had captured the convention of 1768, called to vote for resistance, and repudiated the extremist policies of Joseph Warren and Samuel Adams. The protection afforded by the British army enabled the Conservatives, under Hutchinson's vigorous leadership, to consolidate their position in office. As long as these troops remained in Boston, the dice were heavily loaded in favor of the Conservative party. If Warren and Adams could drive the army out, they might have a chance to play the political game against the Conservatives with more than equal odds once again. The careful organization in the Ness-Pierpont affair and in the Massacre itself suggests that these were well-planned political maneuvers, rather than accidental brawls.

Shortly before March 5, a demonstration before the shop of one of the merchants who was still importing goods from England resulted in Ebenezer Richardson, allegedly a customs informer, firing into the crowd and killing eleven-year-old Christopher Snider and wounding the son of John Gore. Possibly the demonstra-

[35] Depositions of officers and troops of the Fourteenth Regiment, including those of Ness and his men, are in Gay Transcripts: State Papers, XII, 40-97. All of these depositions are dated August 25, 1770, after the Boston Massacre, and are clearly designed to exonerate the troops of blame for that affair. Similar systematic taking of evidence was a standard technique of the Radicals, used after the Massacre and Battle of Lexington.

tion was planned by Warren and the Radicals; possibly it was spontaneous. In any case, Warren was called upon to cut the shot out of young Gore's thighs, and announced that he feared he would have to amputate the lad's finger. Warren headed the team of Radical physicians who opened Snider's body, and his testimony at the inquest led the jury to a finding of willful murder by Richardson. Warren also seems to have written the report of the shooting which appeared in the *Boston Gazette*. He and his friends encouraged everyone in Boston to attend the youngster's funeral which began from the boy's home near Liberty Tree. Hundreds of the inhabitants marched in the procession on February 26, just one week before the shooting in King Street.[36]

On Friday, March 2, tension was further heightened by a struggle between some men of the Twenty-ninth Regiment and the workers at Gray's ropewalk. Rumors quickly circulated that Monday was marked for a general engagement. The Radical leaders were determined to drive the redcoats out, and might themselves have been responsible for the posters which appeared on the morning of March 5. These notices, allegedly signed by the soldiers, informed the townspeople that the troops planned to defend themselves against any who opposed them. The speech of a mysterious figure in a red coat and white wig to a group in Dock Square that evening suggests an organized attack. Even stronger evidence was the fact that at least a score of men were seen carrying similar white sticks, to be used as weapons and marks of identification.[37]

There were fights in several parts of Boston on the evening of March 5. One group gathered about the red-coated speaker in Dock Square, and probably at his urging, huzzaed for the main guard and rushed off for King Street.[38] By shortly after nine o'clock

[36] Purdie and Dixon's *Virginia Gazette*, April 5, 1770; *Boston Post-Boy*, April 23, 1770; *Boston Gazette*, Feb. 26, 1770.

[37] Clarence E. Carter, ed., *The Correspondence of General Thomas Gage* (New Haven, Conn., 1931), I, 249; Albert Matthews, ed., "Documents Relating to Captain Thomas Preston and the Boston Massacre," Col. Soc. of Mass., *Publications*, VII (*Trans.*, 1900-1902), 7-8; Gordon, *History of the Independence of the United States*, I, 282-283; Cushing, ed., *Writings of Samuel Adams*, II, 126-128; Miller, *Sam Adams*, p. 178.

[38] This speaker was blamed by the Conservatives for the violence of the night. The intimation was that he was a public officeholder, since the red coat and white wig were common with eighteenth-century officials. Some evidence points to William Molineux as the speaker. A British officer blamed him for the affair, and Warren used him when threats and violence were required. One witness testified to being in a house with Molineux when the firing oc-

a menacing crowd was collected about the sentry posted before the door of the customhouse, a symbol as despised in Boston in 1770 as was the Paris Bastille in 1789. Captain Thomas Preston tried to restrain the party of soldiers he brought to rescue the lone guard. Taunts of "fire if you dare, G——d damn you, fire and be damn'd" were hurled, with snowballs and oyster shells following hard on them. In this confusion and against Preston's orders, one of his men fired when struck with a stick. A general fight began and the other soldiers fired their rounds. One of those who fired was Kilroy of the Twenty-ninth and one of the dead was Samuel Gray, leaders of the fight at the ropewalk three days before. As the crowd drew back and companies of British troops filed into King Street, three men were dead in the snow and several others lay wounded, two of whom died later. Thomas Hutchinson hurried to the townhouse at the head of the street, and by tact and courage persuaded the people to retire to their homes, the troops being ordered back to their barracks.[39]

At eleven in the morning, a town meeting gathered in Faneuil Hall and appointed a large committee to confer with the governor and Colonels Carr and Dalrymple. The afternoon meeting was so large that it adjourned to the Old South Church. At three o'clock the committee reported that Hutchinson denied he could give orders for the removal of the troops in accordance with the town's demand. Dalrymple, however, had suggested the transfer of one regiment to the Castle. The town voted the reply unsatisfactory, and Warren now entered the negotiations. The large committee was pared to seven men, Warren being the only one who had not served in the morning. He commanded as much respect among the Conservatives as any Radical leader, and had as much influ-

curred. Abigail Adams described Joyce Junior, whose name was often signed to threatening notes of the Sons of Liberty, as wearing a red coat and white wig. Depositions of Jeremiah Allen and Joseph Allen and Judge Oliver's charge to the jury in Frederic Kidder, *History of the Boston Massacre* (Albany, N.Y., 1870), pp. 86-87, 101, 281; Cushing, ed., *Writings of Samuel Adams,* II, 99-100, 124; Ronald S. Longley, "Mobs in Revolutionary Massachusetts," *New England Quarterly,* VI, No. 1 (March, 1933), 126; Esther Forbes, *Paul Revere and the World He Lived In* (Boston, 1942), p. 154.

[39] Much of the source material on the incident is in Kidder, *Boston Massacre,* to be supplemented by: Matthews, ed., "Documents Relating to Captain Preston," pp. 2-21; Randolph G. Adams, ed., "New Light on the Boston Massacre," Amer. Antiq. Soc., *Proceedings,* n.s., XLVII, Part 2 (Oct., 1937), 259-354. Besides these collections, the present account is based on: *Boston Post-Boy,* March 12, 1770; *Boston Chronicle,* March 5-8, 1770; *Boston Gazette,* March 12, 1770; Tudor, ed., *Deacon Tudor's Diary,* pp. 30-34.

ence among the townspeople as any man, except James Otis in his periods of sanity.

Returning to the Council chamber, several of the committee members assured the governor that if both regiments were not removed "all the neighboring towns were determined to unite and force the troops out of the town." In the *Liberty* affair, Benjamin Hallowell had realized that Warren had the power to bring on or to avert violence. Now, when Warren spoke in this new crisis, Hutchinson may well have had a similar premonition that this was no bluff. The governor warned that such action would constitute treason and his warning went unheeded. The Council advised the governor to urge the British officers to remove all troops, and Dalrymple finally agreed. That night, Warren and his fellow committeemen headed a citizens' guard to patrol the town. All men with arms were to report to a designated place if a general muster should be called by Warren's group.[40]

In the months following the King Street tragedy, Joseph Warren played a leading role in arranging the prosecution case against Preston and the soldiers and in directing propaganda. On March 12 the committee appointed a week earlier was instructed to tell Colonel Dalrymple that the town was uneasy because many of the troops were not removed and then to press for the fulfillment of his agreement. The same committee also wrote a report to the town, dated March 12, for propaganda purposes. It criticized the introduction of troops to Boston, condemned the conduct of the troops since their arrival, and declared that guns were fired from the customhouse during the March 5 shooting.[41] One week

[40] Boston. *A Report of the Record Commissioners of the City of Boston, Containing the Boston Town Records, 1770 Through 1777* (Boston, 1887), pp. 2-4, hereafter cited as *Boston Town Records, 1770 Through 1777;* Randolph G. Adams, ed., "New Light," p. 271; Mass. Hist. Soc., *Proceedings,* VI (1862-63), 484-487; Mass. Archives, Council Records, XVI, 457-460.

[41] *Boston Town Records, 1720 Through 1777,* pp. 8-9, 15; Kidder, *Boston Massacre,* pp. 21-23. Oliver M. Dickerson accepts the Radical contention that shots were fired from the customhouse, arguing that the soldiers could not have fired the number of shots discharged. However, his prime witness, later convicted of perjury on this subject, swore that his gun was loaded and fired twice, and that then his master fired a gun from the window. If civilians had time to load and fire several times, certainly professional soldiers would. Preston said they fired one after another, rather than in volley, thus giving the first men time to reload and fire again. Oliver M. Dickerson, "The Commissioners of Customs and the 'Boston Massacre'," *New England Quarterly,* XXVII, No. 3 (Sept., 1954), 314-320; Matthews, ed., "Documents Relating to Captain Preston," pp. 8-9.

after the event, Warren was named to a committee with James Bowdoin and Samuel Pemberton to draw up a full account of the Massacre. Their report, *A Short Narrative of the Horrid Massacre in Boston,* was the most important document in the propaganda battle.

Both parties rushed to get depositions from witnesses to the shooting. The Massachusetts Council warned against testimony collected by the Conservatives, which was designed to blame the town and prove that an attack upon the customhouse was planned. Warren's committee gathered testimony which Hutchinson felt was aimed at making the commissioners unpopular. This material was the basis of their report and was used extensively in the trials. The town meeting approved the Warren-Bowdoin report for publication and ordered that copies be sent to friends of America in England. The plan first adopted was to hire a vessel to carry dispatches home relating to the event, as Warren did after the Battle of Lexington, but the town abandoned this scheme.[42]

The narrative prepared by Bowdoin, Warren, and Pemberton traced events from the Stamp Act to March 5. It emphasized the coming of the commissioners and troops to Boston and their oppressive acts before the tragedy. Three points were made in relation to the Massacre itself: that there had been firing from the customhouse; that there was a deliberate plot by the troops to attack the inhabitants; and that townspeople were assaulted in several parts of Boston on that evening. Warren's committee sent copies of the pamphlet to Wilkes, Pownall, Barré, Franklin, and others in England. In the letters of enclosure, Warren and his friends emphasized that their opponents' depositions were taken secretly and misrepresented the facts. From London someone friendly to the Radicals wrote that the publication was considered "the most important one ever bro't from America."[43] During the

[42] Kidder, *Boston Massacre,* pp. 23-24; Mass. Council to William Bollan, March, 1770, Bradford, ed., *Massachusetts State Papers,* p. 235; Peter O. Hutchinson, ed., *The Diary and Letters of His Excellency Thomas Hutchinson, Esq.* (Boston, 1884), p. 25; *Boston Town Records, 1770 Through 1777,* pp. 13, 17-18.

[43] [James Bowdoin, Joseph Warren, and Samuel Pemberton], *A Short Narrative of the Horrid Massacre in Boston* (Boston, 1770); Committee of Boston to John Wilkes, Boston, March 23, 1770, Ford, ed., "John Wilkes and Boston," pp. 213-214; *id.* to Duke of Richmond, Boston, March 23, 1770, Bowdoin-Temple MSS, II (Mass. Hist. Soc. Library), which has a list of forty persons in England to whom the pamphlet was sent; *Boston Post-Boy,* June 18, 1770.

summer, copies of London papers printing Preston's account of the affray reached Massachusetts. The paper was designed primarily to exculpate himself, and the Sons of Liberty charged that it placed the responsibility for the Massacre upon the inhabitants of Boston. Warren, Adams, and others were appointed a committee to refute it. The town meeting approved their statement and ordered it sent to London.[44]

Besides its propaganda activities, the Bowdoin-Warren committee was to attempt to get indictments from the grand jury. If this were accomplished, they were to aid the king's attorney, attend the trials, "subpena all the witnesses, and do every thing necessary for bringing those murderers to that punishment for such crimes, as the laws of God and Man require." The court, meeting a week after the Massacre, decided to continue the trials to the next term. The Radical leaders dined together to discuss this move, which would make conviction less likely than while the heat of the crisis was still high. Warren led his committee to the courtroom and, with Samuel Adams, persuaded the judges to appoint a day later in the current term.[45]

Despite the aid of Bowdoin and Warren, the prosecution managed its case badly. Robert Auchmuty headed Preston's defense counsel and did an excellent job in gaining his acquittal. The other attorneys at the defense table, John Adams and Josiah Quincy, Jr., had little relish for the case, but served with honor. They had entered the case because their close friend Warren and several other Radicals, possibly hoping to ward off a vigorous cross-examination of the town's witnesses, had persuaded them to do so.[46]

The trials did not begin until October, 1770, and passions had abated in Boston during the interval. The English Ministry sent instructions to Hutchinson, ordering him to stay the sentences should convictions be voted. Only two of the soldiers were found guilty, however, and their sentences for manslaughter were limited

---

[44] Matthews, ed., "Documents Relating to Captain Preston," pp. 4-6.

[45] *Boston Town Records, 1770 Through 1777*, p. 13; Hutchinson, *History*, III, 205 and note.

[46] Preston to Gage, Boston, Oct. 31, 1770, Randolph G. Adams, ed., "New Light," pp. 338-339; Josiah Quincy, *Memoir of the Life of Josiah Quincy Junior of Massachusetts Bay, 1744-1775* (Boston, 1875), pp. 27-28; Miller, *Sam Adams*, p. 185.

to branding.[47] Doubtless there was an element of the fairness of the townspeople reflected in this outcome, as has often been contended. Such justice, however, was notably lacking on many another occasion in Boston's revolutionary history. Quite as important was the general character of the period. After the initial indignation in March, the political conservatism of Bostonians deepened and the verdicts in the trials were only reflections of this political mind. Those who did not go so far as to blame the Warren-Adams faction for the tragedy at least saw clearly that the members of the small British guard had little responsibility for it.[48] Here was no deliberate oppression by a tyrannical king, but a regrettable incident growing out of the increasingly bitter political wrangling of Massachusetts parties. By October, 1770, the troops had long been removed, and Bostonians were tired of political turmoils. If there were still some people outside of Boston who were loyal to Radical policy at the beginning of the year 1770, many of them fell away after the Boston Massacre and the conciliating repeal of the Townshend Acts. The Radical party had driven the British army from Boston and assured itself of a continued existence, but in its triumph it had unwittingly deepened the reaction against its leadership that had begun in 1768 when it had first counseled resistance to British troops. Joseph Warren and Samuel Adams never wavered in their devotion to their cause, but during the next three years their efforts were devoted to the dismaying task of keeping the remaining members of their party in the fold.

[47] Gage to Hutchinson, New York, April 30, 1770, Miscellaneous MSS, XIII (Mass. Hist. Soc. Library), also printed in Randolph G. Adams, ed., "New Light," pp. 306-307; Hillsborough to Hutchinson, April 20, 1770, Transcripts of Instructions to Provincial Governors, VIII, 2458-59; Hutchinson, *History*, III, 236.

[48] For example, William Palfrey to John Wilkes, [Oct. 23-30, 1770], Col. Soc. of Mass., *Publications*, XXXIV (*Trans.*, 1937-42), 423-425.

# Voice of the Minority

CHAPTER VI

The split in Radical ranks and the general increase of political conservatism did not come so soon after the Boston Massacre that more general causes may be ignored. Crucial to these political changes was the economic prosperity following the repeal of the Townshend Acts. During the period of nonimportation, newspapers were filled with comments on the hard times in New England. By July, 1769, there was word from high official sources in England that most of the duties would soon be lifted. Boston merchants declared that a limited repeal of the Townshend Acts would be unsatisfactory and voted to maintain nonimportation. Joseph Warren and some other Bostonians who were not engaged in commerce supported the merchants by signing nonconsumption agreements. They promised not to purchase boycotted goods from retailers and to refuse to purchase any goods whatsoever from merchants who imported any articles which were prohibited. This was the principle of nonconsumption which Warren was to embody in his proposals of 1774, and the wording of the agreement is so similar to his Solemn League and Covenant that there can be little doubt that he also authored this paper. As breaks developed over nonimportation in other cities, more and more

Bostonians clamored for ending all boycotts except that on tea. In October, 1770, a merchants' meeting at the British Coffee House voted to put an end to their agreements.[1]

The economy had begun to revive even before legal trade was resumed. In October, just before Thomas Preston's trial, Gage wrote that the Bostonians had quieted down a good deal, and Thomas Hutchinson could not remember a time "when the province was more free from real evils." Hutchinson, an astute observer of contemporary affairs, explained the reasons for this. "Commerce," he said, "never was in a more flourishing state. The Massachusetts province was, in this respect, the envy of all the other colonies . . . and had obtained the name of the silver money colony."[2] Such prosperity was in sharp contrast to conditions in 1765, and as surely laid a foundation for political conservatism as the depression of the earlier period had for radicalism. In every field Warren and his friends saw the conservatism deepen: in the press; in the governor's Council; in the breach within their own party; and among the people of Massachusetts in general.

Never since before the passage of the Stamp Act had the newspapers been so little concerned with political disputes as they were from 1770 to 1773. Dispatches from London seldom mentioned America and there was a decided decrease in the volume of letters on political subjects from readers. Thomas Hutchinson still had occasional difficulty in getting printers to insert Conservative essays, and Warren had a new outlet for his writings in the *Massachusetts Spy,* established as a Liberty party organ in 1770. The Conservatives, however, countered with a government sheet, the *Censor,* and the possibility of prosecuting Radical writers was substantially greater.[3]

When the *Spy* printed an exceptionally daring piece, the Massachusetts Council ordered the publisher and author to appear before them, and, upon their refusal, ordered the attorney general to prosecute the publisher and dismissed the author from his of-

[1] Schlesinger, *Colonial Merchants,* p. 106 and note 1; *Boston Chronicle,* Sept. 25-28, 1769; *Massachusetts Gazette,* July 27, 1769; MS Nonimportation Agreement, Boston, July 31, 1769 (Mass. Hist. Soc. Library); *Boston Post-Boy,* Oct. 15, 1770.

[2] Carter, ed., *Correspondence of Gage,* II, 561; Hutchinson, *History,* III, 252; Schlesinger, *Colonial Merchants,* p. 240.

[3] Hutchinson to Israel Williams, Boston, April 1, 1771, Israel Williams MSS, II; Schlesinger, *Prelude to Independence,* pp. 131, 143-144.

fice of justice of the peace.[4] Such actions had been unthinkable in 1768, when Joseph Warren published his "True Patriot" article. But the Massachusetts Council had changed since those days of Radical strength. Hutchinson was able to block a vote on an address presented by Bowdoin which expressed Radical sentiments, and persuaded the Council to condemn "Junius Americanus," the pen name Arthur Lee used for his newspaper letters in support of the American cause. The governor was developing to a fine art his technique of presenting such issues to the Council only when a Conservative majority was present, and made most appointments to office at such meetings.[5]

The defection from Radical ranks was gradual, and the party never lost its power in the streets and in the town meetings of Boston. Following the removal of the British troops, tarring and feathering was resumed as a choice pastime of the Boston mob. The instructions of 1770 to Boston's representatives to the General Court made clear the Liberty party's strength in the town meeting. Drawn by Joseph Warren and Josiah Quincy, Jr., these instructions posed the new issues between the two parties and sounded a new warning that the people might be called upon to go to war. Warren warned against the foreign luxuries and corruption which were sapping the colonists' military strength, and urged them to develop "the more martial virtues" against the time when they might have to "hazard all." Expressing once again the American nationalism which was the spark of his life, he urged the people to encourage the growth of population and manufactures, "the true riches of a people," and said the most important task before them was the creation of a "firm and lasting union of the colonies." Some men had used lies and fraud to cause jealousy and discord, but Warren saw the colonies' interests as being "so apparently inseparable" that the representatives should "keep up a cordial intercourse" with the other colonies. Warren had been delighted with the united action of the colonies in the Stamp Act Congress, Quincy was soon to travel through the South encouraging the establishment of correspondence committees, and Samuel Adams proposed this scheme again and again in the General Court. Thus, the instruction to maintain a correspondence

[4] *Ibid.*, pp. 140-142; *Boston Post-Boy*, Nov. 18, Dec. 16, 1771.

[5] William V. Wells, *The Life and Public Services of Samuel Adams* (Boston, 1865), I, 352; Cushing, ed., *Writings of Samuel Adams*, II, 264-265.

with the other colonies was entirely natural, but the "firm and lasting union" of the colonies which Warren recommended looked toward a much bolder program of an organized confederation.[6]

Warren urged this military preparation and colonial cooperation because of a "deep laid and desperate plan of imperial despotism." Particularly grievous was the removal of the General Court to Cambridge from its usual seat at Boston. Governor Bernard had removed the General Court from Boston in 1769, and the legislature had refused to conduct its business at Cambridge. Later instructions from home entrusted the place of its meeting to his discretion. When the body met at Cambridge for the session of March, 1770, it proceeded to business *"only from absolute necessity."* Hutchinson continued to tell the Court that he was meeting them there because of instructions and that he had no discretion in the matter. Thus, in their instructions to the representatives elected in May of that year, Warren and Quincy spoke out against such practices. Quincy wrote a long legal and historical argument against holding the Court outside of Boston, while Warren denounced the growing use of instructions. Though calling the practice unwarrantable, Warren criticized instructions on other grounds than unconstitutionality. He said that the colony was too distant for the English government to be able to send adequate orders, and it would be intolerable for the colony to obey instructions contrary to the sentiments of the people.[7] The implication was strong that, if the colonists did not like English policy, they would not obey it, regardless of where the law lay.

The sentiments expressed by the two young Radical leaders in these instructions proved to be those of a large majority of the House in the session which convened in May, 1770. The Assembly resolved to do no business until it was adjourned to Boston, and after a stalemate of nearly four weeks, the governor prorogued it. By the time of its next meeting in July, the House had reason to suspect that Hutchinson was playing party politics and acting upon his own decision, rather than upon instructions from home. The members sat for two more weeks without doing business, and

[6] *Boston Post-Boy,* May 21, 1770; *Boston Town Records, 1770 Through 1777,* pp. 22, 26-31.

[7] *Ibid.,* pp. 27-32. The important letters and official documents are in: Bradford, ed., *Massachusetts State Papers,* pp. 172, 195, 202; Transcripts of Instructions to Provincial Governors, VIII, 2439-40, 2469. On the constitutional significance of instructions, see Labaree, *Royal Government,* pp. 31-35, 198.

finally proceeded to it only out of sheer necessity. Here was one issue, at least, upon which many Moderates initially supported the Liberty party. But it was an issue left over from the Bernard administration, and James Otis, John Hancock, and other Moderates soon revealed their readiness to abandon it to Adams, Warren, and Quincy. Some actually believed that with native-born Thomas Hutchinson heading the government a genuine reconciliation of parties might be possible. By May of 1771, James Otis, his old bête noire, was declaring that he thought Governor Hutchinson was a good man, and vouched that the ministers, the justices, and the people generally felt the same as he did.[8]

Such political moderation, like the economic prosperity, was evident even before the repeal of the Townshend Acts. To be sure, a few of the Moderates continued to serve on town and province committees with the Radicals. In July, 1770, Hancock and Cushing accepted appointment to the committee with Samuel Adams and Joseph Warren which was to draft "a true state of the town, and the conduct of the commissioners since the 5th of March last." In November, the House followed the suggestion of Warren's instruction to Boston's representatives, and created a committee to correspond with people in Britain and other colonies.[9] Hancock, Cushing, and John Adams served on this committee, but it was evidence of the growing conservatism of all members of this group except Samuel Adams that they did nothing. It was left for Virginia to initiate an effective intercolonial correspondence system in 1773. To the minds of the Radicals, a clear instance of the new power of the Moderates was the choice of Benjamin Franklin, rather than Arthur Lee, as the agent of the Massachusetts House in England. Votes cast for Franklin were given in the face of the fact that he held a crown appointment and that his son was governor of the Jerseys. One man asked bitterly, "Can it be suppos'd such a person will promote the cause of Liberty?"[10]

By the spring of 1771, the Liberty party was in serious trouble. Under Thomas Hutchinson's strong leadership, the Prerogative

---

[8] Hutchinson, *History,* III, 210, 220-221, 244; Bradford, ed., *Massachusetts State Papers,* pp. 214-215, 236, 240-241, 254, 293; Charles F. Adams, ed., *Works of John Adams,* II, 266.

[9] *Boston Town Records, 1770 Through 1777,* p. 34; Wells, *Samuel Adams,* I, 373-374, 406.

[10] *Boston Post-Boy,* Oct. 29, 1770; William Palfrey to John Wilkes, [Oct. 23-30, 1770], Col. Soc. of Mass., *Publications,* XXXIV *(Trans.,* 1937-42), 424.

party had come a long way from the point at which Bernard had had to accept British troops to enforce law and protect the lives of administration men; it was now so strong that the Radicals were "afraid of a change of members in many towns." In Boston, Ezekiel Goldthwait defeated Samuel Adams in the race for the Suffolk registry of deeds by 1,123 to 467 votes.[11] Such a defeat for the Liberty party's chief indicates that a great many Bostonians took a very different attitude toward the Radicals in domestic politics from the vigorous support they gave on most imperial issues. Even on the latter question there was an important difference between the views of men like Joseph Warren and such Moderates as Thomas Cushing and John Adams. Several years of propaganda by Warren and others had made many people sincerely alarmed of a plot by the English Ministry to curtail their liberties and self-government. The breach among the leaders of the opposition was over the question of how far they should go. Extremists like Warren aimed at absolute home rule, while the Moderates desired only the return of British-American relations to their status before the Stamp Act's passage, and they were largely unconcerned with the Hutchinson-Oliver dominance in colony politics. Following the repeal of the Townshend Acts, most Moderates felt that the safe harbor of 1763 had been reached and were quite ready to rest upon their oars.[12]

Joseph Warren's close friend John Adams well represents the sentiments of many Moderates of this period. In May, 1771, the Braintree lawyer confided to his diary that he was done with sacrificing health, interest, and pleasure to the people. Speaking of the abandonment of the Liberty party by the people of Massachusetts Bay, he declared that he had "stood by their friends" longer than the people would themselves. For the future, he promised, "I shall certainly become more retired and cautious; I shall certainly mind my own farm and my own office." Adams did continue his friendship with Radical leaders, particularly Joseph Warren. A strong bond had grown between the two men—strong enough so that Joseph could frankly accuse John of being too cautious. Warren reassured him, however, that he wasn't a trimmer, for

[11] Hutchinson to Bernard, May 10, 1771, Mass. Archives: Hutchinson Correspondence, XXVII, 164; *Boston Post-Boy,* April 22, 1771.

[12] Hutchinson to Dartmouth, Oct. 9, 1770, quoted in Wells, *Samuel Adams,* II, 99-100.

when John Adams spoke he always spoke his true feelings. "This," Adams observed, "was a little soothing to my proud heart no doubt." Perhaps it was, but Warren, quite as honest, sincere, and outspoken as his lawyer friend, doubtless recognized in John Adams that blunt honesty which was to mark his entire career. And it was probably this honesty and frankness, qualities which Warren admired in Thomas Gage, that made Warren and Adams fast friends, differ though they might on political issues. Adams dined at Warren's home and even went to the political club occasionally. There, though Warren, Samuel Adams, Otis, and Samuel and William Cooper were often present, the conversation was less political than formerly. At Hancock's, Warren and John Adams drank tea, not being sure whether it was uprightly smuggled from Holland or some of the boycotted English goods. The company varied from house to house as John Adams made up for the years of pleasure he had sacrificed. But whether it was Captain Bradford's or Jeremiah Wheelwright's parlor, Warren was more than likely to be there, trying to persuade the Moderates that only extreme policies would be successful.[13]

Everyone in Boston was beginning to suspect that Thomas Cushing spoke out of a different side of his mouth to the Radicals than he did to Thomas Hutchinson. It was not long before John Adams told him that he had never known a wider-swinging pendulum. Unknown to the Radicals, Benjamin Church, a professional colleague of Warren and one of the few who appeared to be a firm Son of Liberty, was becoming an ally of the Conservatives. None of the defections from Radical ranks delighted the governor's party quite so much as that of John Hancock. Hancock's importance was not as a propagandist or political organizer but as a popular merchant who was wealthy enough to contribute large sums to Radical party coffers. To the Conservatives, however, this in itself made him a key figure to be won to their side. Thomas Hutchinson found him "pliable" and made "great use of him." It was all Samuel Adams could do to retain his friendship. Hutchinson named him commander of the governor's cadet company, suggested that he would approve his election to the Council, and encouraged Conservatives to try to make Hancock suspicious of Adams. By late 1771, Hancock refused to attend meetings of the

[13] Charles F. Adams, ed., *Works of John Adams,* II, 255, 260, 262, 289, 315; *Sibley's Harvard Graduates, 1736-1740,* X (Boston, 1958), 94.

Radical club, and, in the spring of 1772, supported a petition requesting that Hutchinson return the General Court to Boston because of the inconvenience of sitting at Cambridge, rather than because of charter right. When Hutchinson finally accepted Hancock's election to the Council, however, the latter refused the seat, still fearful of giving umbrage to the Boston Radicals.[14]

By 1772, Joseph Warren and Samuel Adams could find few unquestionable adherents of the Radical party in the taverns and newspaper rooms of Boston. Hutchinson was never able to win over James Bowdoin, "obstinate as a mule" and with "dark secret plottings," who continued to push opposition measures in the Council, while Samuel Adams fought to maintain his leadership in the House.[15] A few ministers, including Samuel Cooper, Warren's own minister at Brattle Street Church, could be counted upon to support Warren and Adams with chapter and verse. William Cooper and William Molineux were equally useful in town affairs.

As for Joseph Warren, there was absolutely no question of his devotion to the revolutionary crusade, and his position made him a more effective leader than some of the other Sons of Liberty. Despite his important role in the *Liberty* affair, the planning of the convention of 1768, and newspaper propaganda, he was on the surface less of a party man than were Adams and other public officeholders. During his life, there were few imputations upon his integrity and patriotism, though years later his political enemies did charge him with a political ambition from which they themselves were not entirely free. Thomas Hutchinson, who was not lightly given to falsehood, said that Warren had admitted to his intimates that nothing would satisfy him short of heading the political and military affairs of North America. Peter Oliver claimed that Warren's medical practice was so poor and his fi-

[14] Charles F. Adams, ed., *Works of John Adams,* II, 314; Hutchinson to Bernard, Jan. 29, 1772, and *id.* to James Gambier, May 7, 1772, Mass. Archives: Hutchinson Correspondence, XXVII, 285, 330. The most important sources on the Hancock-Adams breach are in: Cushing, ed., *Writings of Samuel Adams,* II, 9, 296-297, III, 23-24; Wells, *Samuel Adams,* I, 398, 438-439, 459, 465-466, 469, 472, 475; Mayo, ed., "Additions to Hutchinson's 'History'," p. 43; Gay Transcripts: Andrew Oliver Letter Book, I, 82-83. See further: Herbert S. Allan, *John Hancock, Patriot in Purple* (New York, 1948), pp. 124-126; Miller, *Sam Adams,* pp. 249-251.

[15] Hutchinson to Bernard, Jan. 29, 1772, Mass. Archives: Hutchinson Correspondence, XXVII, 285.

nances so low that he was "forced to strike any bold stroke that offered." Allegedly quoting him, Oliver declared that Warren had been faced with the alternative of conquer or die and had publicly announced that he would "mount the last round of the ladder or die in the attempt." Following Joseph Warren's death, John Adams, without quite charging him with ambition, wrote of his friend, "President of the Congress, Chairman of the Committee of Safety, Major General and Chief Surgeon of the Army was too much for Mortal. . . . For God's sake my friend let us be upon our guard, against too much admiration of our greatest friends."[16] If Warren did aspire to such dominance, he gave little evidence of his ambitions. He held no public office until 1774, nor in the eyes of the people of the colony did he seem to seek one. To all appearances he had come to oppose the Prerogative party because of a genuine American patriotism and his dislike of British rule and the growing aristocracy which dominated offices in the Bay Colony. Thus, he was able to talk with important Moderates and with the Boston artisans, whose political activities he directed, in a less self-interested pose than Adams.

Despite the political moderation of these years, Warren, Samuel Adams, and the others of the small core of popular leaders never flagged in their enthusiasm. They retained the Boston town meeting as a forum for attacks upon Hutchinson's administration and British policy, and in the annual orations commemorating the Boston Massacre they found a new way of using that body. In March, 1771, a committee of which Warren was a member suggested such an oration, and the town invited James Lovell to deliver the first speech on April 2. Lovell questioned parliamentary power in the colonies, but spoke quite temperately of the Massacre. His conclusion was a plea that the townspeople avoid violence and that even the commissioners of customs be granted protection of the laws—strange words from one who spoke at the behest of the Radicals.[17]

In 1772, Warren was to deliver the oration, a much more dangerous popular leader than James Lovell. The town committee appointed to solicit an orator reported to the selectmen that they

[16] Mayo, ed., "Additions to Hutchinson's 'History'," p. 45; Oliver, Origins and Progress of the American Rebellion, p. 186; Mass. Hist. Soc., *Warren-Adams Letters* (Boston, 1917), I, 74.

[17] *Boston Town Records, 1770 Through 1777*, pp. 47-48; *Orations Delivered at the Request of the Inhabitants*, pp. 9-11.

had obtained Warren's consent. But moderation had captured even the Boston selectmen, who well knew that a speaker like Warren, who had favored resistance in 1768, might arouse more passion than was wise. These officials, John Hancock and Samuel Pemberton among them, tried to block Warren's speech by refusing to call a meeting for March 5, until petitions of the inhabitants forced them to do so.[18]

March 5 brought bad weather to Boston. It had been a cold winter, and a driving snow storm moved in on that day, borne by an icy wind off the Atlantic. Still, some 4,000 people braved the blizzard to sit and stand in the Old South Meeting House, unheated except by a few footwarmers. The town meeting was called to order, and Dr. Chauncey preached a sermon.[19] Warren then mounted the black-draped pulpit and delivered a thirty-five-minute speech, which did much to shape the ideas of later generations of Americans on the Boston Massacre. A large part of it was devoted to a discussion of the colonial relationship with England. The final pages, however, plainly were designed to arouse the passions and to fix the events of March 5, 1770, in the minds of its hearers as a massacre of innocent inhabitants by the troops of a tyrannous king. This tone had pervaded the report of the tragedy printed in the *Boston Gazette* on March 12, 1770, and Samuel Adams played much the same theme in his articles following the acquittal of the troops. Warren resurrected and re-enforced this interpretation for patriot propagandists and chauvinistic historians of later years.

Warren's speech, like the preamble of his Suffolk Resolves, testifies eloquently to his ability. One is almost prone to agree with the judgments of Thomas Hutchinson and Peter Oliver, both of whom were political foes unlikely to indulge in rank flattery. The one credited Warren with both political and military courage and said that "if he had lived, he bid as fair as any man to advance himself to the summit of political as well as military affairs and to become the Cromwell of North America." Oliver charged that Warren was capable of any duplicity and dominated by avarice,

[18] Boston. *A Report of the Record Commissioners of the City of Boston, Containing the Selectmen's Minutes from 1769 Through April, 1775* (Boston, 1893), p. 110, hereafter cited as Boston, *Selectmen's Minutes.*

[19] Tudor, ed., *Deacon Tudor's Diary,* p. 38; Cunningham, ed., *Letters of John Rowe,* p. 225; Franklin B. Dexter, ed., *The Literary Diary of Ezra Stiles* (New York, 1901), I, 218; *Boston Gazette,* March 9, 1772.

but admitted that "had he conquered, Washington had remained in obscurity. . . ."[20] The choice of words, the balanced phrasing, the skillful combination of history and political theory make the oration of 1772 one of the finest in American revolutionary literature. The eighteenth-century theories of the origins of government in a social contract, of the rights of British subjects in the colonies, of the necessity of balancing the three Aristotelian elements of government—all of these Warren states as clearly and succinctly as any writer of the period. Comparisons of Joseph Warren's words with those of Thomas Jefferson are almost inevitable.

Warren opened his speech searching for the causes of those "mighty revolutions which have so often varied the face of the world," the rise and fall of great nations. Government, he said, originates in the quest of man for the greater *"strength and security* of all." A state remains happy only as long as its people fight for their rights and retain their initial devotion to a free constitution. Reflecting the classical education and the interest in ancient history which were marks of the eighteenth-century gentleman, Warren turned to Rome for his illustration. "It was *this* noble attachment to a free constitution, which raised ancient Rome from the smallest beginnings to that bright summit of happiness and glory to which she arrived; and it was the loss of *this* which plunged her from *that* summit into the black gulph of infamy and slavery." Her senators and soldiers, once inspired by the one to wisdom, justice, and heroism, later turned to corruption, plunder, and rapine. It was because the free constitution of England was being changed that the early settlers had come to the New World. The charter issued by William and Mary to the colonists had finally guaranteed their rights as British subjects. The most important of these rights, Warren said, was that a citizen should be governed only by laws to which he had given his consent.[21]

Next Warren discussed the constitutional problems arising out of British-American relations. He saw the House of Commons as embodying the democratic element of the British government; the

---

[20] Mayo, ed., "Additions to Hutchinson's 'History'," p. 45; Oliver, Origins and Progress of the American Rebellion, p. 186.

[21] Joseph Warren, *An Oration Delivered March 5th, 1772,* 2nd ed. (Boston, 1772), pp. 5-8. The oration is also printed in *Orations Delivered at the Request of the Inhabitants,* pp. 13-25, and in Jensen, *Colonial Documents,* pp. 753-759.

House of Lords was the aristocratic; and the king was the monarchical element. Balance among these three branches was essential to good government, and each of them must have a voice in the raising of taxes. Examining recent parliamentary statutes raising taxes in the colonies, he concluded that they were illegal, since they were enacted by the British legislative houses. The Massachusetts House of Representatives and Council, rather than the British Commons and Lords, formed the democratic and aristocratic branches of the Bay Colony's government, and the king, or his governor, was the only part of the British government which formed a part of Massachusetts' government as well. Only the king, then, could request taxes from the colony. When the people had protested against these unlawful acts, a further act of oppression had been committed—an army was sent in time of peace to enforce these unconstitutional acts.[22]

The rest of Warren's oration was a discussion of the evil of standing armies, as evidenced by ancient history and the British occupation of Boston. Rhetoric was substituted for fact, passion for reason, as he described the "mangled bodies of the dead" in King Street and exhorted the Bostonians to fight for the rights their forefathers had won. He questioned the acquittal of the troops and warned the men who had sought the stationing of an army in Boston to study their consciences before meeting their final judge. Finally, Warren asked the blessings of God upon the country, and concluded: "May our land be a land of liberty, the seat of virtue, the asylum of the oppressed, a name and a praise in the whole earth, until the last shock of time shall bury the empires of the world in one common undistinguished ruin!"[23]

Here were those concepts of an American destiny and of the essential superiority of the New World over the decadent kingdoms of Europe which were to reappear under guises as varied as the Monroe Doctrine and *Leaves of Grass*. And here, also, was a full-blown nationalistic sentiment which some historians have not marked in America until the early nineteenth century. In this oration, Warren served his party well by rising above party. A consistent opponent of the Bernard-Hutchinson faction, he was also an American nationalist who could appeal in all good faith to anti-British sentiment in Massachusetts. In doing so, he was

[22] Warren, *Oration Delivered March 5th, 1772*, pp. 8-11.
[23] *Ibid.*, pp. 12-18.

gathering strength for the Radical party in both the domestic political battles and the revolutionary crusade which lay ahead.

The annual orations on the Massacre were printed in pamphlet form, and were doubtless written with an intercolonial and English audience partly in mind. Within the Bay Colony, the annual instructions of Boston to its representatives in the General Court were an equally potent propaganda device. Most towns instructed their delegates, but the recommendations of the capital town of the Province received, of course, wide publicity and close attention. In 1772 the instructions were drawn by a nine-man committee, for which Warren again seems to have done the major work. The political calm of Massachusetts in this year must have made his words ring hollow in the ears of most men. "No people," he declared, "were ever in circumstances more truly alarming than those in which the people of the province now are." Illegal taxes by a foreign power had reduced them to "the despicable condition of slaves."[24]

Warren's instructions warned the representatives that "power without a check is tyranny" and asserted that the "only reasonable end of government is the happiness of mankind." If Governor Hutchinson refused the salary voted by the General Court and instead accepted payment from England, there would be serious danger of such tyranny. Certainly there was doubt, Warren said, that the governor was promoting the happiness of the people of his colony. This was clear from his obedience to instructions sent from 3,000 miles away. By instruction he moved the seat of the legislature; by instruction he turned over Castle William to British troops; by an instruction from home he vetoed the salaries voted him and the agents of the Massachusetts House in England. Finally, Warren recommended that Boston's representatives protest against the power of admiralty courts and the denial of jury trials.[25]

In these instructions Warren expressed virtually every possible issue except the payment of judicial salaries by the home country. When the committee presented its report, the town meeting voted to ask it to draft an article on this subject. Two members were

---

[24] *Boston Town Records, 1770 Through 1777,* pp. 80, 83. The extravagant alarm for colonial rights is characteristic of Warren, and the prose resembles his style closely. Certain articles are quite similar to those in his "List of Infringements and Violations of Rights" of 1772.

[25] *Ibid.,* pp. 83-85.

added to the committee, but the eleven men were unable to reach agreement. Warren and the other Radicals on the committee seem to have been outnumbered. It was then suggested that the town name a new committee, but the meeting voted to postpone further consideration of the question until October. At that time Joseph Warren and Samuel Adams avoided the mistake of allowing Moderates to ruin their plans. With Benjamin Church, they formed a three-man committee to draft an address to the governor concerning judicial salaries.[26]

The salary question, no new one at all, originated in Massachusetts' peculiar charter provisions, and was now aggravated by Britain's attempt to tighten imperial control over the colonies. Massachusetts was technically a royal colony, since the king appointed her governor; actually she was something of a hybrid, retaining features of the corporate colony she once had been. An elective Council in a royal province had been particularly distressing to Francis Bernard and some authorities at home. And, as in some other royal colonies, the governor was in the uncomfortable position of holding a royal appointment, while being dependent upon the colonial legislature for his salary. Judges were named by the governor and Council and drew their salaries from the colonial treasury. Freeing these officials from such dependence upon the General Court might both augment British power over the colony and further weaken the strength of the Radicals in party battles. Thus, Radical opposition to this move was intense, being based upon both party interest and their desire for home rule.[27]

Warren, Adams, and Church presented their report on judicial salaries at the town meeting of October 28, 1772. They mentioned a widespread rumor that the Superior Court judges were to be made independent of the General Court in order to "compleat the system of their slavery, which originated in the House of Commons," and asked Hutchinson whether or not he had any news of such a plan. The meeting approved the paper and appointed Warren to the committee that would present it to the governor. On October 30, he and his colleagues reported that Hutchinson

[26] *Ibid.*, pp. 86-89.

[27] Oliver M. Dickerson, "Use Made of the Revenue from the Tax on Tea," *New England Quarterly*, XXXI, No. 2 (June, 1958), 232-243, gives detailed information on salaries actually paid to colonial officials.

refused to lay any correspondence or advice on colonial affairs before a town meeting. The town named a new committee to prepare a petition asking the governor to call the General Court, and Warren's group carried this to Hutchinson. They met with a second refusal, Hutchinson arguing that he would be yielding his constitutional right to call the Court if he did it at the bidding of any town.[28]

Thus, the Boston political machine was stymied again, as they had been in 1768, in their attempt to rally provincial support through the General Court. Now, however, they made use of a new device to achieve their ends—a device which was to prove much more successful than the abortive convention of 1768. The development of committees of correspondence—called by a Conservative the foulest, most venomous serpent ever to issue from the eggs of sedition—grew directly from the Conservatives' refusal to call the General Court. Ironically, their growth forced Hutchinson to summon the legislature and did more than anything before to build among the opposition a political organization which extended throughout Massachusetts. Warren and Adams soon found that gaining support among politically like-minded men in other towns and counties by correspondence was much easier and infinitely more reliable than depending upon erratic meetings of the General Court or newspaper and oratorical propaganda of limited circulation.

Massachusetts Bay continued to present a peaceful political front during most of 1773. Establishment of the Boston Committee of Correspondence in November, 1772, however, marked the first step on the road to exciting political battles. At the town meeting of November 2, Samuel Adams moved that twenty-one persons be named to such a committee. John Hancock and other Moderates were noticeably absent from those who accepted appointments to it, and the Radical leaders—Adams, Warren, Church, Quincy, Young, Molineux—were assured of dominance on the committee. Adams' motion was that the group prepare a statement of colonial rights and violations of those rights and

[28] *Boston Town Records, 1770 Through 1777,* pp. 89-92. On the attempt of the Radicals to arouse other towns on the question of judicial salaries, see: Cushing, ed., *Writings of Samuel Adams,* II, 340-342, 344, 346-347, 350; Wells, *Samuel Adams,* II, 1-2; broadside, "Boston town meeting to the Selectmen of Medway," Boston, Nov. 20, 1772 (Boston Public Library).

that this paper be communicated to other towns and to the world at large.[29]

The statement of rights and grievances was one of the most important papers in the pre-revolutionary period of Massachusetts history. Thomas Hutchinson had felt little anxiety when he first heard of the new committee. After reading this paper and witnessing the formation of a network of committees, the governor wrote, "Thus all on a sudden, from a state of peace, order, and general contentment, as some expressed themselves, the province, more or less from one end to the other, was brought into a state of contention, disorder, and general dissatisfaction. . . ."[30] The committee met on November 3 and appointed three subcommittees to draft statements of colonial rights and violations of those rights and a letter to other towns. James Otis headed the group which was to draft the list of rights, though Samuel Adams actually wrote the paper adopted. Warren, as head of the second subcommittee, wrote the statement on the violations of those rights, and Benjamin Church was responsible for the letter to the towns. The committee reported to a town meeting on November 20. Adams' document was approved immediately, but Warren's statement was returned to the committee for the addition of articles on customhouse fees and the payment of the salaries of key administrative officials. In the afternoon session, the meeting approved the amended report and Church's letter to the towns, and issued instructions for distributing 600 copies of the entire report.[31]

Samuel Adams based colonial rights on three sources—those which were guaranteed by natural law, those which Christ guaranteed to Christians in the New Testament, and rights claimed under British law as subjects of George III. Natural rights included guarantees of life, liberty, and property, as well as freedom of conscience (except to papists), all of which were assured by the compact through which men created government. The rights granted by Christ included freedom of worship (except for Cath-

[29] *Boston Town Records, 1770 Through 1777,* p.93; Miller, *Sam Adams,* pp. 264-265.

[30] Hutchinson, *History,* III, 265, note.

[31] Boston, Committee of Correspondence, Minutes, Nov. 3, 1772 (photostats in Mass. Hist. Soc. Library); *Boston Town Records, 1770 Through 1777,* p. 94. Warren's paper is in the handwriting of William Eustis, one of his medical students.

olics), as guaranteed in the Toleration Act and the Massachusetts Charter. Finally, all of the colonists "are by the laws of God and nature, and by the common law of England, *exclusive of all charters from the Crown,*" entitled to all rights of persons born and residing in England. Among these rights were that the legislature shall not have arbitrary power; judges should be independent of prince and people; and property was not to be taken from a subject without his consent.[32]

Joseph Warren's "List of Infringements and Violations of Rights" went beyond Adams' statement to a virtually complete denial of parliamentary authority. It was meant to arouse Massachusetts from its political lethargy and to justify any extreme measures which the Radicals might take. It consisted of twelve articles which, he argued, were sufficient to justify any actions already taken or likely to be taken in order to redress grievances. This enumeration followed Adams' discussion of rights and the origins of government in much the same fashion used by Jefferson in the Declaration of Independence. Warren used the same form in the Suffolk Resolves, and it is found often enough in other writings of the period to suggest that part of Jefferson's clear, logical arrangement was due to adherence to an established literary form. The Suffolk Resolves were a masterly use of it, and this earlier effort by Warren forecasts the later achievement of that document as Jefferson's *Summary View* does his Declaration of Independence.

Several of the grievances stated concerned the right of Parliament to legislate for the colonists. Warren asserted that colonial consent was necessary not only for tax laws, but also for all legislation. In this period, as in later American history, the customhouses were prime resources of patronage dispensers. Royal control of these offices gave the Prerogative party a number of profitable places to distribute. Thus, Warren's third article complained that a number of customs officials had been appointed in violation of the charter, which vested such appointment in the General Court (which the Radicals controlled). These officers, he said, possessed illegal powers of search, so that houses and even bedrooms were "exposed to be ransacked." Also, Britain had sent armies in time of peace to aid these unconstitutional officers in

---

[32] *Ibid.*, pp. 95-98.

collecting these unconstitutional duties for unconstitutional purposes—the payment of the salaries of the governor and other officials who should be dependent upon the colonial legislature. Other articles concerned the changing of boundaries by the king and Council, the transporting of people accused of destroying boats or naval stores to Britain for trial, the prohibition of colonial manufacturing, and an alleged attempt to establish an episcopate in the colonies which would endanger "that liberty wherewith Christ has made us free." The list of infringements included others previously set out by Warren in instructions to the Boston representatives: the extension of vice-admiralty court jurisdiction, denial of trial by jury, and the extensive use of ministerial instructions. Specific as most of these grievances were, they were so encompassing that, as Massachusetts' leading Conservative pointed out, they led to the conclusion "that parliament had no authority in any case whatever."[33]

The Adams-Warren report startled Massachusetts like an electric shock. Thomas Hutchinson later wrote that it was calculated "to strike the colonists with a sense of their just claim to independence, and to stimulate them to assert it." Plymouth, Roxbury, Brookline, Charlestown—town after town—replied to the Boston committee with assurances that similar sentiments were widespread in their areas. Marblehead ordered the pamphlet on colonial rights lodged with the town clerk and read annually before the town meeting, and the names of Warren and the other committeemen were recorded in the town book as great patriots. As late as November, 1773, replies to the Boston letter were being received. Some of the votes of the towns were, according to Hutchinson, "highly inflammatory," and the governor foresaw total independence from Britain if the correspondence committees were allowed to develop.[34] The rapid growth of these committees threatened to bind into one political party the previously unorganized opposition factions, and in the future they might be used as a revolutionary organization. News of the town resolutions soon reached the new secretary of state in England, Lord Dartmouth, who some Americans thought was a friend of the colonies. He wrote Hutchinson that these papers were "of a very serious na-

[33] *Ibid.*, pp. 99-105; Hutchinson, *History*, III, 264.

[34] Boston, Committee of Correspondence, Minutes, Dec. 1, 1772, Jan. 12, Nov. 19, 1773; Hutchinson, *History*, III, 263, 265-266; Wells, *Samuel Adams*, II, 4.

ture," as the dangerous doctrine expressed had "a direct tendency to encourage violence and tumult."[35]

Hutchinson called the General Court into session on January 6, 1773, earlier than he had planned, hoping thereby to prevent further town meetings from giving their support to the Boston statement. His supporters in the country could argue that a town meeting was unnecessary now that the representatives were convened. The governor hoped that some members of the Assembly, in the absence of explicit instructions from their constituents, might have the courage to join with him in denouncing the Boston committee.[36] The governor did manage to prevent temporarily the further adoption of the Boston statement of rights, but he had opened a new hornets' nest which was to aid in driving him from the colony. As long as Samuel Adams, James Bowdoin, Joseph Hawley, and men like them sat in the General Court, he could never seriously hope for a peaceful legislative session.

Thomas Hutchinson opened the General Court with the greatest mistake of his political career—that famous speech in which he issued an outright challenge to the doctrine that Parliament was not supreme, which had been embodied in Warren's "List of Infringements and Violations of Rights." The central point was that sovereignty could not be divided, that either Parliament must be supreme or the colonies would be independent, that no line could be drawn between the two. Adams was doubtless correct in writing that the governor had shown an "imprudent zeal in bringing a matter into open controversy which the Ministry had hoped to have settled in a silent way."[37] The members who heard it delivered in the House expressed open surprise at the speech. Hutchinson, overconfident of his strength and misjudging the extent of Conservatism in the colony, had given the Radicals precisely the chance they had been awaiting. With the question of parliamentary supremacy or independence thus bluntly posed, they rose to answer with unfeigned delight. In their answer, they were willing to go as far as had Warren in his statement of griev-

[35] Dartmouth to Hutchinson, Whitehall, England, Feb. 3, 1773, Transcripts of Instructions to Provincial Governors, VIII, 2584.

[36] Cushing, ed., *Writings of Samuel Adams,* III, 19-20; Hutchinson, *History,* III, 275.

[37] Bradford, ed., *Massachusetts State Papers,* pp. 336-342, particularly p. 340; Hutchinson, *History,* III, 267; Cushing, ed., *Writings of Samuel Adams,* III, 52-53.

ances, willing to deny parliamentary supremacy and squarely face an independent future.

The Council answered the governor's speech on January 25, 1773, and the House did so on the following day. The boldness and openness with which both replies denied every shred of Parliament's power was unprecedented for a legislative body. If Parliament were supreme, the colonies would be slaves, and since it could not have been the intention of Britain to hold them as slaves, they must be free. If no line could be drawn between independence and parliamentary supremacy, they must be independent.[38] Hutchinson addressed the houses again on February 16, and they answered on February 25 and March 2. The basic points in the great debate had already been stated, however, and in the first reply of the Massachusetts House of Representatives men on both sides of the Atlantic had been given plenty to turn over in their minds for some months to come.

The only certain thing about the authorship of this outstanding state paper is that John Adams, persuaded to leave his political retirement now that constitutional issues were at stake, revised it at the request of Samuel Adams. Hutchinson believed that Samuel Adams and Joseph Hawley were responsible for the first draft, and there is a vague implication in Samuel Adams' words that bears this out. Many years later, however, John Adams declared that his cousin had solicited Joseph Warren to write it. On such points John Adams' memory was often unreliable, and the final paper bears no close resemblance to Warren's style. One is given pause only by John Adams' statement that he was handed an "eloquent" oration which was "full of those elementary principles of liberty, equality and fraternity, which have since made such a figure in the world." There were none of the legal and constitutional arguments which he wrote into the final version. Such a paper would be more characteristic of Warren than of a lawyer like Hawley.[39] Also, the most important point of the entire message—the denial of any parliamentary authority in the colonies—had been made by Warren just two months before in his

[38] Bradford, ed., *Massachusetts State Papers,* pp. 342-364, particularly p. 363.

[39] Hutchinson, *History,* III, 268; Charles F. Adams, ed., *Works of John Adams,* II, 311-313; John Adams to Mercy Warren, Quincy, Mass., July 30, 1807, Mass. Hist. Soc., *Collections,* 5th ser., IV, 347; Cushing, ed., *Writings of Samuel Adams,* III, 52-53, 430.

list of grievances. In fact Hutchinson had taken up the question precisely because of Warren's statement of the colonial case in the 1772 pamphlet, and it is reasonable to suppose that Warren played a part in replying to Hutchinson's denunciation of his ideas. But, authorship aside, the significance of the paper lay in its effect in reopening the imperial issue and reviving the strength of the Radical party. Thomas Hutchinson's speech on January 6 opened a year of renewed political activity, which Warren and his friends were to close with that eloquent repudiation of parliamentary power, the Boston Tea Party.

# Tea and Treason

CHAPTER VII

The great event of 1773 was, of course, the Boston Tea Party. Whether the Revolution began with the end of the French and Indian War in 1763, as some would have it, or with the very first settlement in America, as others contend, the Tea Party was the incident that began the train of events that led to war. Nevertheless, for most Americans the year was many things. Once a week the Concord farmer pored over the political news in the *Boston Gazette,* and every few months the Boston artisan sat in town meeting listening to speeches against Lord North and Governor Hutchinson. For the rest, they followed their plows along the rocky, New England furrows, hammered their metal into pewter tankards and plates, and built their sturdy frame houses. They haggled over the price of fish and vegetables at the market stalls, drank beer and punch in their neighborhood taverns, and, on Sunday, sat piously in their meeting houses. And so it was, this year 1773, for Joseph Warren, concerned though he was about political affairs.

Warren was, after all, a husband, a father, and a doctor before being a politician. Keeping office hours, visiting patients, mixing drugs, instructing apprentices—the work never ended. Masonic lodge nights and other social gatherings provided a welcome break in his professional routine. There was the happiness found with his wife Elizabeth and the four children she had borne him. But there was also worry about steadily mounting debts, and in April there was tragedy—Elizabeth died at the age of twenty-six.

The vital statistics of Boston, less full for the eighteenth than for the seventeenth century, do not record the births of Joseph Warren's children. By 1773 there were four youngsters in the family, the eldest of whom could not have been more than eight. Warren at this time lived, rather ironically, on Hanover Street, named for the British royal house whose rule he helped overthrow. From his home it was only a short walk to any part of Boston—a few blocks to the Green Dragon Tavern or to the coffeehouses and Province House in King Street. William Cooper, the town clerk and Warren's constant political associate, lived in Hanover Street and the commissioners of the customs had an office there in Concert Hall. In 1770, Warren rented a large house from Joshua Green and purchased a Negro boy to help with the chores. Green's aged mother lived on in two front rooms and kept a maid and Negro manservant, while some of Warren's medical students probably occupied other rooms. Thus, the old place was filled with activity, serving as home, boardinghouse, office, and dispensary.[1]

Warren spent considerable time handling the affairs of Nathaniel Wheelwright's estate, and was involved in court cases as executor from 1769 to 1772. John Adams served as one of his attorneys in the business, and while both men doubtless made some money from it, it was surely time consuming and bothersome. Wheelwright had turned over many of his holdings to Charles Apthorp, his former partner to whom he was heavily indebted, and Warren had to sue Apthorp, Benjamin Faneuil, and others for recovery of the estate.[2] By 1773 this business was finished, but

[1] George Green to Joseph Green, Boston, Dec. 5, 1770, and promissory note of Warren to Joshua Green, Boston, June 28, 1770, both in Samuel A. Green MSS, I (Mass. Hist. Soc. Library). Baptismal records of Joseph and Mary Warren are in Motte, ed., *Church in Brattle Square,* pp. 184-185, 188. The eldest son, Joseph, never married and died in his twenties, as did the second boy, Richard. The two girls, Elizabeth and Mary, married General Arnold Wells and Judge Richard Newcomb respectively.

[2] Material on the Wheelwright estate is in: Suffolk Court Files, particularly vols. 132, 592, 595, 599, and 786, which are well indexed (Suffolk County Courthouse, Boston); *Massachusetts Gazette,* May 25, Aug. 17, 1769; *Boston Chronicle,* Dec. 11-14, 1769; Chamberlain MSS: Samuel Adams and Joseph

he had plenty of worries of his own, as his finances had worked themselves into a tangled skein.

The estate of Warren's father was appraised at over £1,000, and in 1765 Probate Judge Thomas Hutchinson assigned it to Joseph and Samuel Warren. Joseph Warren was an active physician by then, and though he did see that the house was repaired, his younger brothers farmed the Roxbury land. Warren and his wife Elizabeth received some income from her family property, and Joseph became increasingly interested in buying real estate himself. Between 1765 and 1770, he purchased several small lots and took over a number of mortgages, one from his friend Josiah Quincy. One £800 property in west Boston he bought with money loaned by James Bowdoin, and, as with many of his debts, this large sum remained unpaid at Warren's death. Before his death in 1775, Warren had acquired two Boston houses and 300 acres of land in New Hampshire. Some of the property had deteriorated badly and in some cases he spent more for repairs than he had for the original purchase. Floors, cellar doors, shingles, laths and plaster, posts and fences—all these and more had to be repaired. The workmen were forced to wait for payment until the settlement of Warren's estate. He went to court to collect fifty pounds in rent for his house, but did not pay his own rent on the property he leased from Joshua Green.[3]

Part of the difficulty, of course, was his own inability to collect debts owed to him. Patients then as always felt that the bills of the fishmonger and greengrocer were more pressing than the doctor's. Warren reluctantly wrote his brother about the money owed for his medical tuition, but John, just beginning practice in Salem, was in even worse shape. In these circumstances, many of the daily

---

Warren, pp. 169-171. There is no evidence as to why a young doctor like Warren was named to administer Wheelwright's large, complex estate. Mr. Bernhard Knollenberg has suggested to me that it might have been a political plum. If it were, it may have been an attempt to win Warren to the Conservatives, since the appointment was made by Thomas Hutchinson.

[3] As in notes 2 and 4, the documents are too extensive to cite separately. See Suffolk County Probate Records, LXIV, 473-474; Suffolk Deeds, CX, 203, CXVI, 39, 175-176, CXVII, 127, 128, CXXV, 178, CXXXIII, 209-210; Suffolk Court Files, DCIII, 111-113, DCXIX, 10; mortgages and bonds signed with James Bowdoin, all dated July 9 and 10, 1770, Warren MSS, II; Chamberlain MSS: Miscellaneous Papers, V, 817, 855, 859, 925, 929, 943; Samuel A. Green, *An Account of Percival and Ellen Green and Some of Their Descendants* (Groton, Mass., 1876), p. 62.

household expenses went unpaid, and there were larger debts for sums he borrowed: £27 5*s*. 1*d*. to Samuel Grant and Son for sundries, thirty pounds to William Read, £142 12*s*. 13*d*. to Lee and Jones, and some four pounds to Gideon Frost for the delivery of eighty-three gallons of milk during a six-month period. When a ship came in with a cargo of new dry goods from England, it could mean a bill of thirteen pounds for purchases of four days—linen, calico, satin, buttons, and the like. Such purchases were made only occasionally; yet year by year the obligations mounted and by 1775 Warren was heavily in debt. After his death, his estate brought £475 3*s*. 3½*d*., while creditors filed claims of more than £2,200 against it, and this was after mortgages, including Bowdoin's £800, had been foreclosed.[4]

Warren's medical practice nevertheless continued to grow as he became the best-known physician in Boston. He was called out to treat stab wounds resulting from street fights by sailors, was asked to testify in a court case involving an epileptic, and had to be constantly alert to the danger of epidemics. In 1769 he had notified the selectmen of two smallpox cases, and speedy removal of the patients to the pox hospital prevented the disease's spread.[5] The bulk of his practice, of course, was the routine treatment of his regular patients and his rounds at the poorhouse. When a case had political significance, however, as in the caning of Otis or the killing of young Snider before the Massacre, Warren was always called in as the chief physician.

Some of Warren's time was devoted to training young Harvard graduates who came to him to study medicine. His younger brother, whom Joseph called Jack, received his degree at Cambridge in 1771. If Joseph attended the commencement exercises, as did many of the people of eastern Massachusetts, he may well have approved of the oration on patriotism and enjoyed the humorous speech on quackery in the professions.[6] John Warren studied med-

[4] Joseph Warren to John Warren, Boston, Jan. 23, 1774 [1775], Autograph Collection (Houghton Library); Chamberlain MSS: Miscellaneous Papers, IV, 771, 825, 829, 853, and V, 863; Suffolk County Probate Records, LXXVI, 645-649, LXXXIV, 34-35; notice of foreclosure on Warren's house, Sept. 11, 1776, Warren MSS, II.

[5] Medical certificate of Joseph Warren, March 21, 1765, Suffolk Court Files, DLXXII, 147; Boston, *Selectmen's Minutes, 1769-1775*, pp. 20, 23; *Boston Post-Boy*, Feb. 24, 1771.

[6] *Boston Gazette*, July 22, 1771.

icine with his brother, as did many another young Harvardman. As had his own teacher, James Lloyd, Joseph Warren was forced to accept promissory notes for their medical tuition. There were so many doctors practicing in Boston that he urged the younger men to establish practices in other towns. He wrote Edward Holyoke, the principal physician at Salem, recommending his brother for a vacancy created by the death of a doctor there. John Warren did establish a small practice at Salem, but it was minor indeed compared to the cases he handled in later years after he had become a distinguished Harvard professor and one of the best surgeons in the United States.[7]

Busy as Joseph Warren was, he became increasingly active in social, town, and colony affairs. The Boston town records noted his faithful attendance at the annual school visitation, an honorary duty of civic leaders. As grand master, he continued to lead the ancient masons of Boston actively, attending most lodge nights and the annual festivals of John the Baptist and John the Apostle. At the former feast, on June 24, 1772, the members gathered at the Concert Hall, near Warren's home in Hanover Street. They marched "all cloath'd in their respective jewells," with Warren at the rear of the procession, to Christ Church to hear a sermon and then to the mason's hall. After a short meeting, they dined under a tent in the garden and devoted themselves to "mirth and social festivity."[8] In 1771 one of Warren's chiefs aides, Paul Revere, was chosen master of Saint Andrew's lodge, and William Molineux and Thomas Crafts were becoming increasingly active masons.

Warren and Revere became close friends as the public-spirited silversmith assumed leadership among the town's artisans, whose political support Warren valued. Revere named one of his sons Joseph Warren and, in 1773, the two men were drawn closer together by the deaths of their wives. Elizabeth Warren died on Tuesday, April 26; Sarah Revere on the following Monday, May 3. A Latin epitaph and a poem of eulogy, both probably by Warren, were printed in the newspapers.[9]

---

[7] Joseph Warren to Edward A. Holyoke, Boston, Oct. 13, 1773, Warren MSS, II; John Warren to Joseph Warren, Salem, Mass., Jan. 29, 1775, *ibid.*

[8] Mass. Grand Lodge, *Proceedings, 1733-1792*, pp. 241-242; Cunningham, ed., *Letters of John Rowe*, pp. 230, 247.

[9] *Boston Gazette,* May 3, 17, 1773.

In 1772, Warren, with Revere's aid, gave a degree of organization to the political activities of Boston's artisan and laboring classes. Being younger, a better public speaker, and having a more winning personality, Warren provided a dramatic leadership which Samuel Adams could not. A "mechanics caucus," formed under Warren's direction, met first at a house in the North End and later at the Green Dragon Tavern. The latter, which had become the property of the masons, was in Union Street, a short distance from Warren's home. A two-story brick structure, its door was marked by a menacing dragon. Many of the men who were to be active in the Boston Tea Party passed under this sign to masonic and political meetings. By 1773 the Green Dragon was the most important political headquarters in Boston, and within its walls Warren's leadership was pre-eminent.

The revival of political activity in 1773 swept Joseph Warren into the center of the political vortex to an extent which makes it difficult to understand how he maintained his medical practice and looked after his domestic responsibilities. Warren participated in most commemorative exercises such as those on August 14, 1773, the seventh anniversary of the repeal of the Stamp Act. Some 400 persons met under a tent because of threatened rain in Roxbury, Warren's birthplace. Unfortunately, a table collapsed and some 200 of the guests were assailed by upset sauces, meats, rum, punch, dishes, and silverware. Undaunted, they set the table up again and sang "The Liberty Song." Here, perhaps, Warren received the inspiration for his "A Song on Liberty," which he penned to the tune of "British Grenadiers." A less able effort than the song by Dickinson, it was nonetheless a bit more grist for the propaganda mill. Samuel Adams nominated his cousin, John, and Joseph Warren to membership in the English Society of the Bill of Rights in April, and Warren likely was associated with Samuel Adams in publishing the letters of Thomas Hutchinson in June. These letters, sent from Engand by Benjamin Franklin, were printed against his expressed directions, and served as a basis for demanding the removal of both Hutchinson and Secretary Andrew Oliver from office.[10]

[10] Mass. Hist. Soc., *Proceedings* (1869-70), XI, 142; "Boyle's Journal of Occurrences in Boston, 1759-1778," New Eng. Hist. and Geneal. Soc., *Register*, LXXXIV (1930), 365; Arthur M. Schlesinger, "A Note on Songs as Patriot Propaganda, 1765-1776," *William and Mary Quarterly*, 3rd ser., XI, No. 1 (Jan., 1954), 80-81; Cushing, ed., *Writings of Samuel Adams*, III, 24-25; Bradford, ed., *Massachusetts State Papers*, pp. 405-409.

Warren, however, devoted most of his political energies to the Committee of Correspondence, the battle over judicial salaries, and the tea incident which ended the year. The correspondence committee perfected the details of its organization by early 1773. A five-man subcommittee was appointed to handle most of the correspondence, and many of the letters are in Warren's hand. The committee met from six to half-past nine in the evening, holding seven such meetings in the short month of February, and understandably voted to contribute one dollar each to buy some good Rhode Island beer for these long sessions. Besides answering letters of individual towns in Massachusetts, Warren served on a subcommittee to vindicate Boston from Hutchinson's charges, and drafted a letter to other towns and colonies warning them to remain watchful of their rights.[11] The correspondence of the Boston committee with other towns within the Province provided the unified political organization which the Radical party had been trying to build since 1765. There was now a focal point to which people in Salem and Braintree and Worcester might look for advice and leadership. Committees all over Massachusetts adopted the policies and plans outlined by Warren and Adams in the Boston committee, and, through instructions to the towns' representatives in the General Court, made them colonial policy.

The success of this system in Massachusetts led to the implementing of an intercolonial system of correspondence such as Warren, Adams, and Richard Henry Lee in Virginia had been envisioning for some years. The Bostonians commissioned Josiah Quincy to travel through the colonies to investigate sentiment on the plan. Warren had recently found his lawyer friend's health somewhat mended, and probably approved the journey for both medical and political reasons with as much alacrity as he did Quincy's later trip to London. Quincy sailed for Charleston in February and found many people in both Carolinas who were zealous for the scheme. Before he reached Williamsburg, Virginia had established a committee, and other colonies followed her ex-

[11] Boston, Committee of Correspondence, Minutes, Dec. 25, 1772, Feb. 2, March 8, 30, Sept. 10, 1773; broadside letter of Boston Committee to Danvers Committee of Correspondence, Boston, Sept. 21, 1773 (Boston Public Library); Harry A. Cushing, *History of the Transition from Provincial to Commonwealth Government in Massachusetts*, VII, No. 1, in Columbia University, *Studies in History, Economics, and Public Law* (New York, 1896), pp. 95, 96-97.

ample quickly.[12] Yet it was the committees of the larger towns which were to be most important in uniting the colonies, rather than those of the colonial legislatures, most of the members of which returned home as soon as their sessions ended.

Boston's Committee of Correspondence steadily usurped power from the town government, very likely with the latter's consent. Yet it could be less important than some of the other political groups which Warren directed. The writing of the instructions for Boston's representatives in 1773 provides an excellent clue to the real springs of political action in revolutionary Boston. On April 9, the Committee of Correspondence appointed Joseph Warren, Benjamin Church, Nathaniel Appleton, William Molineux, and Thomas Young to draft the instructions, a function which properly belonged to the town meeting. Both William Molineux and Thomas Young tended toward the demagogic. Warren had little respect for Young's medical skill, and their connection in politics seems to have been of the nature of an uneasy truce. Thus, Warren's North End caucus met on May 4, and this body nominated a committee to draft the instructions, from which Molineux and Young were excluded. The caucus named Joseph Greenleaf and William Cooper to serve with Warren, Church, and Appleton, and voted, "that if any person or persons are set up in opposition to the five above mentioned, we will oppose him or them with all our force." Further, the group voted to "attend the meeting, till the aforesaid persons are chosen." When the town met the following day, it elected the candidates of the caucus, rather than those of the committee of correspondence, and chose Thomas Cushing, the nominee of the caucus, as moderator. Such success was the result of careful planning by Warren and the leading artisans. The caucus appointed a group of its own to write party ballots for distribution, and sought the concurrence of the Middle and South End caucuses in its plans.[13]

Thus Joseph Warren, who held no government post until 1774, played a major role in controlling Boston politics, which

[12] Quincy, *Memoir of Josiah Quincy,* pp. 54, 83, 90, 92; Boston, Committee of Correspondence, Minutes, April 9, 1773; Bradford, ed., *Massachusetts State Papers,* pp. 400-401; Cushing, ed., *Writings of Samuel Adams,* III, 63-65.

[13] Boston Committee of Correspondence, Minutes, April 9, 1773; *Boston Town Records, 1770 Through 1777,* pp. 131-132; minutes of the North End caucus are printed in Elbridge H. Goss, *The Life of Colonel Paul Revere* (Boston, 1891), II, 640-641.

did so much to shape the policy of the Bay Colony. He was the only person who served on every committee for drafting instructions between 1769 and 1774, and in many cases wrote the instructions with little or no aid. The importance of the Boston instructions was indicated by the close relationship between them and the business transacted in the following sessions of the General Court. This power in shaping colonial policy Warren owed to his position as leader of Boston's Masons and the North End caucus and to his public reputation, as an honest, sincere defender of colonial rights and the most popular and best known of Boston's medical men. Warren served on the most important committees of the period, including that which drafted the influential statement of colonial rights and grievances in 1772. He was the only man to be appointed (or to appoint himself) twice as orator on the March 5 anniversaries. And the role of the North End caucus in electing all Boston officers from selectmen to scavengers gave Warren a hand in the largest patronage system outside of the Massachusetts government, which Thomas Hutchinson's Conservative party controlled.

It was important that the Boston instructions of May, 1773, be vigorous and be given wide circulation. There were rumors that Hutchinson, after the debacle of the January session, would attempt a coalition of parties in the new legislature. When the legislature did convene, the governor accepted all but three of the members elected to the Council, including Hancock, who again decided to remain in the House. His hope of gaining Moderate support had been quickened in April, when James Otis appeared in court to defend a commander of an English revenue cutter.[14] Thus, Warren seems to have written the instructions himself, assuming as high a tone as he had used in his list of violations of colonial rights in October, 1772.

Warren described the instructions from the English Ministry to the governor, which had made the colonial legislature impotent, as a destructive, clandestine, and capricious system of government. He warned Boston's representatives against surrendering the powers of legislation "to any usurper under heaven," since the General Court's authority within the colony was as complete as that of Parliament within Great Britain. Warren declared that

[14] Cushing, ed., *Writings of Samuel Adams,* III, 37, 39-40.

such powers were granted by solemn compact, and the people were "determined never to recede" from the full enjoyment of the rights of English subjects. Throughout the instructions, he spoke of the General Court as "the Commons in America," putting it on an equal footing with the House of Commons in England. Warren warned that an army was still in the Province, prepared to massacre the helpless colonists at the word of any master, and, to complete their "infernal plan of enslaving America," the enemies of colonial freedom were bribing judges and governors with crown salaries.[15]

On this issue of royal salaries for colonial officials, Warren and Samuel Adams steadily gained support. Once again constitutionalists like Warren's friend John Adams—no Radical he—were persuaded to enter the political lists. Newspapers of late 1772 and 1773 were full of letters on the subject, including a series in which John Adams discussed the views of English legal theorists on judges' salaries. In the early months of the struggle, Thomas Cushing and some of the other Moderates wanted nothing to do with the issue. Cushing declared to Hutchinson that he dreaded mobs being raised, and retracted the few words he had spoken on the salary question. But Warren and others of the Committee of Correspondence kept the issue alive, drawing a petition which Warren presented to the Assembly that led the representatives in March, 1773, to resolve against royal salaries for judges. The House also increased the pay of the Superior Court justices so that no excuse could be found for accepting the crown grants, and eventually took the unusual step of impeaching Chief Justice Peter Oliver, the only judge who dared take his royal pay.[16] Throughout this fight, Warren was active on town committees and probably worked closely with John and Samuel Adams in planning the moves in the General Court. The passage of the Tea Act in May, 1773, led to a new crisis which was to arouse every colony along

[15] *Boston Town Records, 1770 Through 1777*, pp. 131-133.

[16] *Boston Gazette*, Jan. 11–Feb. 22, 1773, including replies to Adams by William Brattle; Mass. Archives: Hutchinson Correspondence, XXVII, 457-458; Boston, Committee of Correspondence, Minutes, Feb. 25, 1773; Bradford, ed., *Massachusetts State Papers*, p. 397; Hutchinson, *History*, III, 279, 317-320; Articles of Impeachment of Peter Oliver, Feb. 24, 1774, and Statement of Grand Jurors of Suffolk County, Aug. 30, 1774, Miscellaneous MSS, XIV (Mass. Hist. Soc. Library); *Sibley's Harvard Graduates, 1726-1730*, VIII (Boston, 1951), 749-751.

the Atlantic seaboard as the question of judicial salaries in the Bay Colony had failed to do.

Boston was slow in reacting to the new legislation, and it was Philadelphia which took the first firm stand against the landing of tea that received wide notice. Boston later adopted almost verbatim the resolves passed in the Quaker City. Certainly, had the Boston merchants not been quite so drastically affected by the act, Warren's political party would still have fought it. But without the support of the merchant class its chances of success would have been much slimmer. The East India Company appointed two sons and a nephew of Thomas Hutchinson, all of whom had refused to sign the nonimportation agreement in 1768, as three of its Boston agents. If it had deliberately courted trouble, it could hardly have done more to provoke it. Such men were likely to attempt to take advantage of the preference offered them, and to resist intimidation as long as personal safety allowed.

The violence stemmed from the nature of the Tea Act, rather different from that of previous legislation. Nonimportation agreements had been possible in fighting the revenue measures of the previous decade, since many of the merchants had reasons of their own for opposing the acts. The importation of tea would be a monopoly of a handful of merchants whose obedience to British law was unquestioned. These men could not be pressured into nomimportation, nor was there a single reason why they should voluntarily refuse to import—they stood to gain much by doing so. Nonconsumption agreements were likely to be as ineffective as nonimportation. Just how many Americans were willing to drown their constitutional scruples in better tea at cheaper prices Warren and Adams could not know, but in 1773 there was reason to suspect that the number was large. A "Tradesmen's Protest" criticized the merchants' attempt to prevent importation of British tea, and asserted their right "to eat, drink and wear whatever we can honestly procure by our own labour; and to buy and sell when and where we please." Some months after the Tea Party, women at Kennebec denounced the act as a "scandalous invasion of our tea-table privileges," and claimed to detect a dread plot to force upon them "that detestable, pernicious and accursed liquor, New-England rum."[17] The love of a New Englander for tea was

[17] Broadside, "Tradesmen's Protest against the Proceedings of the Merchants," Boston, Nov. 3, 1773 (Mass. Hist. Soc. Library); *Boston Post-Boy*, June 6, 1774.

most happily illustrated by the attempt of one member of the Boston Tea Party to fill his pockets while pretending to dump it. Thus, the aim of Warren and Adams had to be the prevention of the landing of the tea; once it was landed, it would find buyers aplenty.

The North End caucus, under Joseph Warren's leadership, met at the Green Dragon Tavern and took the initial steps in opposition to the new law. On November 2, 1773, this body appointed Warren, Benjamin Church, and Thomas Young as a committee to draft a resolution which would be read to the tea agents. The doctors roused Richard Clarke and his family from bed that evening, and demanded his appearance at Liberty Tree the following day. At eleven in the morning on November 3, church bells rang throughout the town for an hour, but the consignees had gathered in Clarke's warehouse at the foot of King Street and agreed not to attend the meeting. At one o'clock, Warren, Church, and Molineux led a menacing crowd down King Street. Molineux, a good man for this type of work, served as spokesman, informing the consignees that they had insulted the people and asking them to pledge not to land or pay duties on the tea. Upon their refusal to give their word, he told the merchants to expect the resentment of the people. The committee left the warehouse and the crowd moved off a bit, but, under instructions from Warren and Molineux, turned and rushed the building. The merchants were not quick enough to bolt the outer door, but retreated to the counting room. The mob took the doors off their hinges and swarmed in, but the twenty defenders had the better of it, as they stood on a narrow staircase which could not be taken. Warren's forces turned away and blocked the tea agents in the warehouse for an hour and a half. This attack, as threatening as any made upon the customs commissioners, indicated that private merchants might be made of sterner stuff than royal officials. The threats failed to shake them, and the attorney and solicitor general in England viewed Warren's actions as high treason.[18]

The failure of November 3 led to calls for a town meeting to

[18] Goss, *Paul Revere,* II, 641-642; Cunningham, ed., *Letters of John Rowe,* p. 253; Francis S. Drake, *Tea Leaves* (Boston, 1884), pp. 282-286; Thurlow and Wedderburne to Dartmouth, London, Feb. 11, 1774, Gage MSS: English Series, XXIV (William L. Clements Library); anecdote in William Knox MSS, X, folder 25 (William L. Clements Library).

consider the question. At a meeting on November 5, a full-scale debate of the Tea Act was held. The town passed resolutions that the tax had been illegally imposed without the consent of the American people, and that the people would take "all means in their power to prevent the sales of the tea imported by the East India Company." A committee, most of whom were selectmen, failed to get the resignation of the tea consignees, and two new committees, consisting of Radical chiefs, were appointed to visit them. Warren served on both committees, the first of which talked with Richard Clarke, Benjamin Faneuil, and Joshua Winslow. The other committee chased back and forth between Boston and the family's country home at Milton in a comic-opera search for the Hutchinsons. Finally, all of the East India Company retailers sent letters to the town meeting denying that they had received confirmation of their appointments as company agents and refusing to act until they did. The town voted these letters "daringly affrontive," and Warren headed a subcommittee of the Committee of Correspondence to send the minutes of the meeting to every town in Massachustts.[19]

From this time, Warren and Adams increased their efforts to gain the support of the Province of Massachusetts, or at least of the towns nearest Boston, before taking action in the crisis. Inhabitants of other towns were admitted to the Boston town meeting, which called itself "the Body" during these discussions, and the Boston Committee of Correspondence invited the committees of other towns to its meetings. Warren, Adams, and their followers petitioned that a town meeting be held on November 19, claiming that the tea agents now had definite knowledge of their commissions, since Richard Clarke's son had just arrived from London. Once again a committee visited the tea merchants and again they unanimously refused to resign. Threatening letters had already been thrown into the agents' houses at night, and on November 17 a crowd of more than 100 people attacked Clarke's house for nearly two hours. On November 19, the agents petitioned the Council for protection of themselves and their property, so that the tea might be safely landed. The Council sug-

[19] *Boston Town Records, 1770 Through 1777*, pp. 141-146; broadside petition for a town meeting and letters of the consignees, both in Chamberlain MSS: Samuel Adams and Joseph Warren, pp. 69, 74, 82, 91.

gested that they approach the justices of the peace, nearly all of whom supported Warren's policies.[20]

On November 22, the correspondence committees of Roxbury, Brookline, Dorchester, and Cambridge met with the Boston committee, and named Warren to a subcommittee to write to the other towns of Massachusetts. The letter was in the excited tone characteristic of Warren, though Adams or Church may have written it. The writer argued that if the landing of the tea were opposed, the East India Company would force the Ministry to repeal all taxes on tea to America. If, however, the company succeeded in selling taxed tea in the colonies, England would soon impose other taxes. Tea taxes would take some £30,000 sterling, and since the company wanted cash rather than American products in payment, hundreds of thousands of dollars would be drained from the country to pay for the tea. Also, once having its monopoly, the company might raise prices as high as it pleased.[21] This letter, printed as a broadside, made a powerful appeal with both constitutional and antimonopolistic arguments, and, by the time the tea ships reached Boston, Joseph Warren and Samuel Adams had achieved a large degree of the unity they had sought.

The *Dartmouth,* sailed by Captain Hall, with 114 chests of tea aboard, arrived on November 28. Though a Sunday, the Committee of Correspondence met, and the selectmen held two meetings. The committee, of course, did the important work. A meeting of the Body was called for the following day, and Warren penned a letter inviting the attendance of committees of other towns. The meeting, adjourned from Faneuil Hall to the Old South Meeting House because of the crowd, adopted resolutions that no taxes should be paid on the tea and that it should be re-

[20] Hutchinson, *History,* III, 311; petitions for a town meeting, Nov. 17, 1773, and broadside, "Notification, the Town being greatly alarmed," Boston, Nov. 17, 1773, Chamberlain MSS: Samuel Adams and Joseph Warren, pp. 78, 83, 86; *Boston Town Records, 1770 Through 1777,* pp. 147-148; Mass. Archives, Council Records, XVI, 741, 744-748; petition of Richard Clarke and Sons, Benjamin Faneuil, and Thomas and Elisha Hutchinson to the Governor and Council, [Nov. 19, 1773], Gage MSS: American Series, CXIII (William L. Clements Library), also printed in Drake, *Tea Leaves,* pp. 309-310; Narrative Referred to the Attorney and Solicitor General, Feb. 5, 1774, Gage MSS: English Series, XXIV; *Sibley's Harvard Graduates, 1726-1730,* VIII, 557.

[21] Boston, Committee of Correspondence, Minutes, Nov. 22, 23, 1773; broadside, "Gentlemen, The present posture of affairs," [Boston, Nov. 23 (?), 1773], (Boston Public Library).

turned to England in the vessels which brought it out. A watch, of Paul Revere and others of Warren's dependable supporters, was appointed to guard the ships.[22]

The next morning, Tuesday, November 30, the meeting of the Body reconvened at nine o'clock, and hissed a letter from Governor Hutchinson ordering the meeting to dissolve. This meeting took actions which were as extreme as the forcible resistance which Adams and Warren had unsuccessfully urged in 1768, and which were to be viewed as near treason in England. The principal leaders in the debates were Joseph Warren, Thomas Young, Samuel Adams, and William Molineux. It was agreed that the tea importers had "justly incurred the displeasure of our brethren in other colonies," and anyone who aided such importation was to be considered an "enemy to his country." The people again resolved to prevent the landing and sale of the tea, and to enforce this resolve "at the risk of their lives and property." The meeting ordered the appointed watch guarding the ships to meet at the *Gazette* office, made arrangements for ringing the church bells to alarm the town, and alerted six riders to carry the alarm to the country. This system, which Warren used to good effect in 1775, was being developed as early as November, 1773. During this crisis, people again turned to Joseph Warren as the one man who could determine whether or not the Sons of Liberty would resort to violence. In the town meeting, John Singleton Copley, Richard Clarke's son-in-law, argued that the tea agents could not send the tea back and begged that they be allowed to store it subject to inspection. The town meeting rejected this proposal, and the painter then held private conversations to this end with Warren, but was unable to dissuade him from inflexible opposition. John Rowe, owner of one of the tea ships and Warren's fraternal rival as grand master of modern freemasons, promised to use his influence to send the tea back to England. When nothing seemed to come from this, it was Warren who visited him and pressed him about his vessel and its cargo.[23]

---

[22] Boston, *Selectmen's Minutes, 1769-1775,* p. 203; Boston, Committee of Correspondence, Minutes, Nov. 28, 1773; Mass. Hist. Soc., *Proceedings,* XIII (1873-75), 167-168; Samuel A. Green, ed., "Minutes of the Tea Meetings, 1773," *ibid.,* XX (1882-83), 10-11.

[23] *Ibid.,* pp. 12-15; Mass. Hist. Soc., *Letters and Papers of John Singleton Copley and Henry Pelham, 1739-1776* ([Boston], 1914), pp. 211-213; Great Britain. *Acts of the Privy Council of England: Colonial Series,* VI (London, 1912), 550-555; Cunningham, ed., *Letters of John Rowe,* p. 257; Channing and Coolidge, eds., *Barrington-Bernard Correspondence,* p. 301.

December 16 was the date by which the issue had to be resolved, since owners had to enter cargoes and pay duties twenty days after a ship's arrival or the goods could be seized. Warren worked to get the tea returned to England, accompanying Francis Rotch on December 15 in a visit to the customhouse to apply for a clearance to return to sea. The owner of the *Dartmouth,* which had been in port nearly twenty days, made it clear that he was forced at his peril to apply for the pass, but the customs officials refused to issue it. Next, the Body ordered him to apply to the governor. Hutchinson, of course, also refused. The following evening, December 16, the final meeting of the Body was held and the tea was dumped into Boston Harbor.[24]

Warren's role in the dumping of the tea is as shrouded in secrecy as is the whole affair of December 16, 1773. A persuasive case might be made that he was a leader aboard the ships, but it would be based on circumstantial evidence only. Of the high command of the Radical party, Samuel Adams, Thomas Young, and Josiah Quincy were at the Old South Church, which would leave Church, Warren, and Molineux as the most likely figures to head the boarding parties. They had directed the earlier attack upon the tea agents, and, if the tradition that many of the members of the Tea Party were masons has a factual basis, Warren would be a logical leader of the group. St. Andrew's lodge canceled meetings on the night the first tea ship arrived and on the night of the Tea Party. Whether aboard the *Dartmouth* or not, Warren's role as the leader in bringing on the Tea Party was clear to everyone. He had initiated the first opposition in the North End caucus, and witnesses named him as one of the four most important men in the resolutions and debates which led to the destruction of the tea. Of the four, Warren and Samuel Adams

[24] Green, ed., "Minutes of the Tea Meetings, 1773," pp. 15-17. Typical contemporary accounts and reminiscences may be found in: Great Britain, Privy Council, *Acts: Colonial Series,* VI, 550-555; Tudor, ed., *Deacon Tudor's Diary,* pp. 44-45; *Boston Post-Boy,* Dec. 20, 1773; Jared Sparks, ed., "Extracts from an Original Diary by Thomas Newell, Boston, 1773, 1774," Mass. Hist. Soc., *Proceedings,* IV (1858-60), 218-219; Winthrop Sargent, ed., "Letters of John Andrews, Esq. of Boston," *ibid.,* VIII (1864-65), 326; Benjamin Bassett to John Davis, Cincinnati, Ohio, Feb. 3, 1825, Lemuel Shaw MSS (Mass. Hist. Soc. Library); Wells, *Samuel Adams,* II, 121; Samuel Lane Boardman, *Peter Edes: Pioneer Printer in Maine* (Bangor, Me., 1901), pp. 62-63; Edward R. Snow, *Amazing Sea Stories Never Told Before* (New York, 1954), pp. 102-104, lists 119 supposed participants in the Tea Party.

were the chief policymakers, and Warren was the foremost of the five men against whom the English authorities found the strongest evidence for possible treason charges.

The attorney and solicitor general studied the facts referred to them, and informed Lord Dartmouth that the evidence against Warren and four others was sufficient to justify seeking indictments for treason. They, however, fearing that the Ministry would not support them, refused to issue the warrants of arrest. Dartmouth merely instructed Thomas Gage to collect evidence for a possible trial in colonial courts. Gage had an escape from this attempt to shift the responsibility to him, since his orders said that it would be better not to prosecute if it appeared that conviction were unlikely.[25] In all good conscience, Gage could refuse to act, knowing sentiment in Boston as he did. So, with adequate evidence to arrest Warren, the Ministry avoided this step and instead passed legislation to punish not only Boston but also the whole of Massachusetts.

It was nearly six months after the Tea Party that Boston had news of the new acts. During these months, the Boston politicians continued to fight British policy and the royal representatives in Massachusetts charged with its execution. In January, 1774, four barrels of tea were burned on Boston Common, and in early March "Indians" dumped twenty-eight chests in the harbor. When Elisha Hutchinson, one of the tea agents, returned to town in January, the Sons of Liberty tolled bells and forced him to leave in a severe snowstorm. The same month a street fight occurred between George R. T. Hewes, one of the Tea Party participants, and John Malcom, a supporter of British policy. Malcom hit Hewes with his cane, and the latter was rushed to Warren's office. The doctor dressed the wound, remarked jokingly that the

[25] Thurlow and Wedderburne to Dartmouth, Feb. 11, 1774, Gage MSS: English Series, XXIV; anecdote in William Knox MSS, X, folder 25; Carter, ed., *Correspondence of Gage,* II, 160-161. Much confusion has existed on the subject of indictments. None were actually issued, and the legal officials in England felt that the evidence in their hands justified indictments only of Warren, Molineux, Church, and two others. If more evidence were available, further indictments might be issued against Samuel Adams, Hancock, Young, Williams, the selectmen, members of the House of Representatives, and members of the Committee of Correspondence who had proposed resolutions in the town meetings and established the guard at the tea ships. Warren and Molineux might also be indicted on other charges, and the lawyers believed that the Massachusetts Council was guilty of a high misdemeanor.

patient was lucky to have such a thick skull, and urged him to seek a warrant of arrest against Malcom.[26]

The efforts of Warren and Adams to have Thomas Hutchinson removed from his governorship were now bearing fruit. The Ministry called Hutchinson to England, supposedly for consultation, but as Thomas Cushing foresaw, a new governor was shortly appointed to replace him. Before his departure from Boston, lawyers, merchants, and others sent addresses of respect to Hutchinson. Warren and other members of the Committee of Correspondence drew a counteraddress denouncing the governor, and some of the loyalist addressers had to retract their sentiments.[27] When Lieutenant Governor Andrew Oliver died in early March, Samuel Adams urged Hancock to refuse to lead his cadet company to the funeral. Hancock, questioning whether or not politics should follow a man to the grave, participated in the services, though the Sons of Liberty stood off a bit and cheered as the coffin was lowered into the earth. Yet Warren, as head of the committee to plan the Massacre celebration, found Hancock willing to deliver the commemorative oration that year. Authored by Samuel Cooper and Adams, it called for a congress of the colonies to discuss the questions of the Tea Act and crown salaries for judges and governors. The speech reflected Radical policy also in pointing out the value of a well-ordered militia, and urged the people of Massachusetts to be ready to fight and die if need be.[28]

The Boston Committee of Correspondence steadily assumed more leadership of the Massachusetts opposition in 1774, and extended its correspondence to other colonies as well. When William Goddard proposed a colonial postal system to replace the royal one, he found enthusiastic support in the Boston committee. Warren headed the subcommittee to study the plan, and

---

[26] Sparks, ed., "Diary by Thomas Newell," p. 219; *Boston Gazette,* March 7, 14, 1774; *Boston Post-Boy,* Jan. 17, 24, 1774; *Massachusetts Spy,* Jan. 27, 1774; [James Hawkes], *A Retrospect of the Boston Tea-Party, with a Memoir of George R. T. Hewes* (New York, 1834), p. 34; [Benjamin B. Thatcher], *Traits of the Tea Party: Being a Memoir of George R. T. Hewes* (New York, 1835), pp. 129, 132.

[27] Thomas Cushing to Arthur Lee, Boston, Jan. 23, 1774, Barton MSS (Boston Public Library); *Boston Post-Boy,* May 30, Oct. 31, 1774; Boston, Committee of Correspondence, Minutes, May 27, 1774.

[28] *Boston Gazette,* March 7, 1774; Anderson, "Note on Ebenezer Mackintosh," pp. 349-350; Allan, *John Hancock,* pp. 146-147; Wells, *Samuel Adams,* II, 139; *Orations Delivered at the Request of the Inhabitants,* pp. 50-51.

letters were sent to other towns urging that all assistance be given Goddard.[29] When news of the passage of the Boston Port Act arrived in mid-May, 1774, it was largely through the Committee of Correspondence that Warren and Adams planned those policies which were to affect not only Massachusetts, but all of the American colonies as well.

The Committee of Correspondence met several days consecutively from May 12 to decide upon the course to be taken in view of the news of the punitive legislation. Warren drafted a letter inviting the committees of neighboring towns to attend the May 12 meeting, where his report condemning the Port Act was approved. Besides declaring that the act violated the colonists' natural rights, Warren contributed an interesting argument to the debate in his contention that it was against international law. He also aided in preparing a letter communicating news of the measure to other colonies. When a means of sending the messages was studied, it was likely Warren who suggested that his masonic and political protégé Paul Revere be charged with the job of riding express. Warren was also active in the deliberations of the May 13 town meeting, serving on a committee to consider what the town's conduct should be in the new crisis. This meeting voted that an intercolonial agreement not to import or export goods from Britain and the West Indies might be the salvation of North America, a sentiment and a phrase which Warren had expressed several times in letters. Some weeks later, he embodied this policy in his famous Solemn League and Covenant.[30]

The committee on the conduct of the town, which came to be called the Committee on Ways and Means or the Committee of Donations, considered a number of proposals. On July 19, the group suggested building a wharf and some houses on town land to provide work for the unemployed. By September the unemployment crisis was acute. Like the leaders of the New Deal in 1933, Warren and his colleagues found that immediate relief was more important than large-scale construction or manufacturing projects. The only thing which could be executed "with the speed necessary to give bread and employ to the most indigent laborers" was street repair and paving. After the poorest were thus "kept

[29] Boston, Committee of Correspondence, Minutes, March 22, 24, 1774.

[30] *Ibid.*, May 12, 13, 1774; *Boston Town Records, 1770 Through 1777*, p. 174; Wells, *Samuel Adams*, II, 155-157.

from the dangers of idleness" and provided with bread, the committee considered plans for reviving the economic life of the town. A brickyard, employing more than 100 men, was established, and plans were laid for reviving shipbuilding and building textile looms. The committee was enlarged to include representatives of the artisan class from the north, south, and middle districts of the town and thus prevent complaints of favoritism. Still, there were rumors of corruption—that the committee members were receiving pay and that they were employing poor workers for themselves or rich men with whom they were associated.[31] Yet any comparison of events in Boston after the Port Act closed off her trade with New England reaction to the Embargo of 1807 must end in tribute to the political skill of Joseph Warren and Samuel Adams in keeping the loyalty of the lower economic classes in the face of poverty. After troops arrived in June, Boston carpenters, badly in need of work, followed the injunctions of their leaders against working for the British army.

Most of Warren's work on the Committee of Donations came to be that of receiving and distributing contributions sent to relieve the suffering population of Boston, rather than devising make-work projects. On July 7 Windham, Connecticut, made the first donation, 258 sheep for the people of Boston. Others soon followed this example, in an abundance which Warren found heart-warming. Forty pounds from the Union Fire Club of Salem, two barrels of flour from Charlemont, 400 bushels of rye from Farmington, 224 quintals of fish and £39 5*s*. 3*d*. from Marblehead, 3,000 bushels of corn from two Maryland counties, and five guineas from one Samuel Moody of Newbury Falls were only representative of the money and food which poured in. Warren wrote letter after letter thanking the senders for their generosity and, incidentally, taking the opportunity to make political propaganda. His letter to Montreal was designed as an appeal to any discontent with the Quebec Act that might exist there.[32]

[31] *Boston Town Records, 1770 Through 1777*, pp. 173, 175-176, 181-183; broadside, Boston, Committee of Donations, "The Committee . . . would gratefully acknowledge," Boston, Sept. 22, 1774 (Boston Public Library); Cushing, ed., *Writings of Samuel Adams*, III, 167-169.

[32] Boston, Committee of Correspondence, Minutes, July 7, 1774; [Richard Frothingham, ed.], "Correspondence in 1774 and 1775," Mass. Hist. Soc., *Collections*, 4th ser., IV, 12-14, 29, 44, 46-47, 54-55, 58-59, 61, 117-120, 123, 167, 235-236; Henry J. Cadbury, "Quaker Relief During the Seige of Boston," Col. Soc. of Mass., *Publications*, XXXIV (*Trans.*, 1937-42), 39-61.

Other colonies also provided political support, no less encouraging to Warren than the economic aid they sent. Newspapers urged the people of Massachusetts to remain firm, as they were fighting the battle of all America, and towns and colonies officially expressed similar sentiments. The Virginia governor dissolved the House of Burgesses for its expression of support. The New Jersey Assembly assured Boston that all colonies were equally concerned with the unconstitutional Port Act, and proposed a congress of the colonies, a scheme close to Warren's own heart. Warren aided in drafting letters to New York, Baltimore, Philadelphia, and several of the colonies, and recruited his brother John into the ranks of propagandists. One of his college friends in Connecticut wrote, as a correspondence committee member, to the younger Warren, asserting that, if American grievances were not soon redressed, the king's head would not be safe, much less his crown.[33] Thus, many an American outside of Massachusetts was coming, by the summer of 1774, to champion the nationalistic policy which Joseph Warren and Samuel Adams had urged upon Boston for some years.

While Warren and his friends were looking to means of relieving the poor of the town from the effects of the Port Act, they also took steps toward fighting the punitive legislation. The most important of these steps was Warren's Solemn League and Covenant. In May, Warren was a subcommittee of one, appointed by the Committee of Correspondence to prepare a preamble for an agreement of the Boston merchants to countermand orders for goods from England.[34] Nonimportation by Boston, however, was little short of absurd, since Britain had already ordered the port closed. What was needed now was agreement by the rest of Massachusetts, and by other colonies if possible, not to buy British manufactures. Warren proposed a plan which was much wider than the pledges signed after the Stamp Act and Townshend Acts were passed. Those had been nonimportation agreements signed only by merchants in the largest port cities. Warren boldly

[33] Broadside, Virginia House of Burgesses, "This House being deeply impressed," [Williamsburg], May 24, 1774 (Mass. Hist. Soc. Library); Committee of Correspondence of Assembly of New Jersey to Boston Committee of Correspondence, May 31, 1774, Boston, Committee of Correspondence, Minutes, pp. 709-710; Schlesinger, *Prelude to Independence,* pp. 195-196; Daniel Tyler to John Warren, Brookline, Conn., July 21 (?), 1774, Warren MSS, II.

[34] Boston, Committee of Correspondence, Minutes, May 20, 1774.

proposed nonimportation and nonexportation by all merchants in every port city, and nonconsumption oaths to be taken by all people of the colony. Retailers in all areas would pledge not to handle British goods, and the plan would be enforced by boycotting everyone who refused to sign an agreement.

All of the more important principles of the Continental Association, adopted by the Continental Congress some months later, were to be found in Warren's Solemn League and Covenant. Most important perhaps was that a means of enforcement was provided outside of normal governmental channels. Both the publication of the names of violators and the boycotting of businessmen, which were parts of the Association, were proposed by Warren in June, 1774. The attempt to get other towns of Massachusetts to deny themselves trade with Britain was a real test of the political ability, and of the support outside of their own town, of the Boston politicians. The suspicion was bound to arise that Boston was trying to prevent Salem and Marblehead, and perhaps the port cities of other colonies, from taking over Boston's defunct trade. One might argue that the Bostonians had perversely destroyed private property, Britain had closed their port, and now they were cagily using talk of liberty and rights to prevent other towns from profiting by what was only their own fault. The way in which Joseph Warren tried to get the plan adopted only added to suspicions that trickery was afoot. What might have been a masterpiece of political manipulation led to the most serious challenge to the existence of the Committee of Correspondence, and lessened the chance of unanimous adoption of the Covenant.

Warren was chairman of the subcommittee appointed on June 2 by the Committee of Correspondence to draft the plan and a circular letter to be sent with it to other towns. On June 3, his grand lodge of masons had to postpone its meeting, because Warren was "engaged in consequential public business." Warren brought his Solemn League and Covenant in on June 5, and the full committee adopted it as presented.[35] The preamble expressed concern over "the present distressed condition of this insulted province" due to the late acts of Parliament which tended to

[35] Mass. Grand Lodge, *Proceedings, 1733-1792,* p. 254; Boston, Committee of Correspondence, Minutes, June 2, 5, 1774; Miller, *Sam Adams,* p. 301, cites no evidence for his claim of Adams' authorship.

subvert both natural and charter rights. In Warren's emotional language, a suspension of commercial intercourse with Britain was the only alternative to "the horrors of slavery or the carnage and desolation of a civil war." The signers solemnly covenanted to end all commerce with Britain until the Port Act was repealed and charter rights restored. Further, they would agree not to "buy, purchase or consume" any goods entering America from Britain after August 31, and they would "break off all trade, commerce and dealings whatever" with anyone who continued to import or purchase such goods. Warren urged a boycott of anyone who refused to sign the Covenant or was unable to present a sworn statement that his goods had not been imported from Britain after the deadline. The circular letter which accompanied the Covenant argued that other towns and colonies would soon suffer the same fate as Boston, unless the nonintercourse agreement were signed.[36]

The Covenant, as drafted by Joseph Warren, had obvious flaws and was so strong that it led to protests from some parts of the colony. The provisions on nonexportation, which were implied in the Covenant, were ill defined and no methods to enforce them were specified. The time limit, August 31, set for nonimportation was too short, as it would not have allowed admittance of all goods already ordered from England. The demand that social ostracism, as well as economic boycott, be applied to nonsigners would split families, churches, and other social groups. Some committees of correspondence asked the Boston body whether or not they were expected to adopt the document literally. The Bostonians hastily reassured them that they did not intend to dictate to others in this or other matters, but felt that a compliance with the spirit of the Covenant would aid America. Worcester drew up a variation of Warren's agreement, the main differences being the lack of an oath for merchants to sign and no mention of social

[36] Broadside, "We the subscribers, inhabitants of the town of Grafton," July 4, 1774 (Boston Public Library). A blank copy of the Worcester version of the Covenant and two copies signed in Medway, the latter a part of the Chamberlain MSS, are also in the Boston Public Library, and three copies, each varying slightly in phraseology from the Boston version, are in the Mass. Hist. Soc. Library. A copy of the circular letter, dated Boston, June 8, 1774, and beginning "Gentlemen, The evils which we have long foreseen," is in the Boston Public Library.

ostracism. This, rather than the Boston agreement, was adopted in some towns.[37]

Only about fifteen towns in Massachusetts signed the Solemn League and Covenant before the Continental Congress met in September, 1774. Salem opposed it because it would be ineffective without other colonies signing such an agreement, and the approaching congress would likely take up the subject. Jeremy Belknap urged Dover to reject Warren's proposal, since it was unfair to merchants who had already ordered goods from Britain. Also, it had been drawn up by a Committee of Correspondence appointed for other purposes and without an expression of the popular will. Warren demanded that everyone sign or be branded a traitor, and Belknap found tyranny to be as odious in this guise as any other. Writers in the Boston newspapers emphasized the unfairness of Warren's scheme, and attacked the Boston committee for exceeding its authority and resorting to acts as unconstitutional as those of Parliament. Even as firm a leader of the opposition in the Massachusetts House as Joseph Hawley opposed Warren's proposed Covenant.[38]

The Boston Committee of Correspondence distributed the Solemn League and Covenant throughout Massachusetts, without submitting it to the town meeting for approval. In fact, Warren seems to have kept news of its adoption by the committee deliberately secret within Boston. From his circular letter, other towns derived the impression that the Covenant had already been circulated and widely approved in Boston. Such actions by the Committee of Correspondence constituted an extraordinary assumption of power, since it was set up to correspond with other towns, rather than to form major policy. The efforts of Warren to secure adoption quickly may have been aimed at widespread nonintercourse agreements in New England before open debate in the Continental Congress might result in a more moderate course. Delegates from New York, Philadelphia, or the southern colonies might be less enthusiastic about nonimportation to gain repeal

---

[37] Broadside, "Gentlemen, Whereas several of our brethern [sic]," Boston, June 10, 1774 (Mass. Hist. Soc. Library); broadside, "We the subscribers, inhabitants of the town," undated blank form of the Worcester Covenant (Boston Public Library); Albert Matthews, "The Solemn League and Covenant," Col. Soc. of Mass., *Publications,* XVIII *(Trans.,* 1915-16), 107-120.

[38] Matthews, "Solemn League," pp. 120-122; Mass. Hist. Soc., *Proceedings,* XXII (1885-86), 484-486; *Boston Post-Boy,* June 27, July 4, 1774; Taylor, *Western Massachusetts,* pp. 69-70.

of these punitive laws than they had been years before in fighting the Townshend legislation. Nonexportation was likely to be even more cooly received.

The way in which the Committee of Correspondence secretly adopted and circulated the document provided an excellent opportunity for the Prerogative party to challenge the Radicals. At the town meeting of June 17, the first remarks were uttered on this highhandedness, but Warren expertly handled the crisis, managing to push through a vote of confidence in the committee. His resolve that the group should be continued gave the committee a permanent existence which had been questionable, since the primary reason for its creation had been to distribute the pamphlet on American rights which Warren and Adams had penned in 1772. The town also recommended that the committee write to the other colonies, urging the meeting of a continental congress and pledging to abide by its decisions.[39]

Warren, of course, had long favored such a policy, and since he was the chief Radical leader at this town meeting, it is likely that he wrote the town resolve setting forth this major commitment. Less than two weeks before, he had penned one of his strongest appeals for colonial union, pledging that he would rather die than betray American rights. Unless, he said, the people acted like men and appointed a continental congress, they could expect the derision of schoolboys and the condemnation of posterity.[40] On June 15, unaware of the success which would be his in the town meeting just two days later, he wrote a discouraging letter to Samuel Adams at Salem. A tradesmen's meeting, which Warren had hoped would support his policies, had dissolved without taking action, and he felt that the party which favored paying for the tea was growing stronger. He prayed that Adams would do everything possible to hasten the calling of a colonial congress, and privately renewed the vow he had made in the newspapers. "Vigilance activity and patience are necessary at this time," he wrote to Adams, "but the mistress we court is *Liberty* and it is better to die than not to obtain her. If the *timidity* of some and the treachery of others in this town does not ruin us I think we shall be saved."[41]

[39] *Boston Town Records, 1770 Through 1777*, p. 177.

[40] *Boston Evening-Post*, June 6, 1774.

[41] Warren to Adams, Boston, June 15, 1774, Samuel Adams MSS (New York Public Library), also printed in Frothingham, *Warren*, p. 317.

On the evening of June 17, following the town meeting at which Warren had battled in defense of the Committee of Correspondence and gained the town resolve to support a congress, Samuel Adams returned from the session of the House at Salem with equally good news. The two friends met at Warren's home with Quincy, Cushing, and other Radical leaders, "a very important and agreeable company," as Thomas Young put it. Warren told them of his success, and Samuel Adams related how the House had appointed delegates to a congress. One of them read an encouraging letter from New York, and they rejoiced together over "an interchange of interesting advices from all quarters."[42]

The rejoicing was almost premature. The Boston town meeting of June 27 witnessed the most serious challenge to the leadership of Warren and Adams since the convention of 1768. The meeting ordered that all letters sent by the Committee of Correspondence and the answers received be laid before the town. The letters sent from Boston were read, and a motion was made that the committee be censured and "said Committee be annihilated." This was a mistake in strategy on the part of the opposition. Had they proposed that circulation of the Solemn League and Covenant be suspended, they might have stood a chance of victory, but some of their own supporters were amazed at the motion to abolish the committee. Samuel Adams vacated the moderator's chair and joined Warren, Molineux, Quincy, Young, and Benjamin Kent on the floor and spoke in defense of their conduct. Those who spoke or voted against them were not solely pensioners of Thomas Hutchinson and the British government; they included respected citizens like Ezekiel Goldthwait, who was popular enough to have been elected to office by the people of Boston over Samuel Adams, and moderate merchants like John Rowe. The question was debated until dark and the debates continued "very warm on both sides" the following day. But the vote went four to one in support of the Committee of Correspondence and against the resolution of censure.[43]

Having failed in this attack, the opposition turned to the news-

---

[42] Quoted in Frothingham, *Warren,* pp. 325-326.

[43] *Boston Town Records, 1770 Through 1777,* pp. 177-178; Cunningham, ed., *Letters of John Rowe,* pp. 276-277; Sargent, ed., "Letters of John Andrews," pp. 329-332; Matthews, "Solemn League," pp. 116-117.

papers and printed addresses of protest which had been circulated. The signers criticized both the Committee of Correspondence, as an unconstitutional body, and the Covenant. One such protest called Warren's scheme "a base, wicked, and illegal measure, calculated to distress and ruin many merchants, shopkeepers, and others . . . to put a check at once to our industry, by stopping the exportation of all the staple articles of our trade."[44] On June 29, Thomas Gage, the new governor of the Bay Colony, issued a proclamation denouncing the Covenant and ordering the arrest of anyone who circulated or signed it. Further, he called the attention of the Massachusetts attorney general to orders issued by the Ministry to collect evidence for prosecution of the Tea Party leaders, one of whom was Joseph Warren, author of the Covenant.[45]

Thus Warren's name was becoming well known in England, though he was still exercising his influence through secret party caucuses, the Committee of Correspondence, and the Boston town meeting, rather than from a high government post. His activities during the tea crisis made him the Ministry's best candidate for hanging at the end of a traitor's rope. In Massachusetts, as a leader of American nationalism, he was being granted, at the age of thirty-two, recognition as one of the colony's outstanding statesmen. As an orator and writer, he was the most eloquent defender in the entire colony of the right of Americans to govern themselves. As a political leader, he was second to none in vigor and courage, and shared with Samuel Adams the shaping of opposition policy in Massachusetts. Initially rejected by much of the Bay Colony, the principles embodied in his Solemn League and Covenant were later adopted by all America. This nonintercourse agreement is strikingly similar in its provisions to the Association, though with ten years of thought on the subject behind them, the men of the Continental Congress scarcely needed this example in planning their agreement. With his Suffolk Resolves, however, Joseph Warren, continuing his round of visiting patients in

[44] [Peter Force, ed.], *American Archives*, 4th ser. (Washington, 1837-46), I, 490; *Boston Post-Boy*, July 4, 1774; *Massachusetts Gazette*, July 7, 1774.

[45] Gage to Dartmouth, Salem, Mass., July 5, 1774, Carter, ed., *Correspondence of Gage*, I, 358-359; Alden, *General Gage*, pp. 208; Schlesinger, *Colonial Merchants*, p. 324, argues that there was no serious opposition to the Covenant.

Boston, determined the first important policies of the American Congress which was to meet 300 miles away in Philadelphia. And not long after this, he was to be one of the key figures in making the decision that plunged America into war.

# Resolves and Congresses

CHAPTER VIII

Increasingly, the question of peace or war depended upon events in Massachusetts, and there two men, Thomas Gage and Joseph Warren, might well have much to say as to which it would be. Either man might give orders, Gage to his troops and Warren to a mob, which would mean fighting, though the broader question of a prolonged war between America and Britain was beyond their control. Gage in particular had a difficult time in influencing policy. From the time of his arrival in Boston in May, he was shackled by the policy which his predecessors had established. He could do little but seek advice from members of the Conservative party who had done much to establish those political enmities that were to make his position so unhappy. Personally acceptable to the people of Massachusetts Bay, he was a prisoner of British policy, which demanded strict enforcement of the parliamentary acts to punish Boston, and of the Conservative party, which controlled the executive and judicial departments. He had attempted to alter British policy by suggesting that the punitive laws be suspended until the people had a chance to pay for the tea; he made an honest effort to understand conditions in the Bay Colony by seeking the advice of Joseph Warren and others outside of the circle of Conservative officials which surrounded him. In both cases he failed. George III thought his scheme of suspending the acts "the most absurd" that could be suggested, and Warren rejected Gage's overtures.[1]

Nobody can say at just what point reconciliation became impossible and the irrevocable step was taken which meant war would come. But if reconciliation had been possible through the efforts of any two men, Gage and Warren were two of the best hopes on this side of the Atlantic. They had a mutual respect, perhaps even a warmth, for each other, and were able to work closely to prevent street brawls which might touch off the fighting. This, however, was as much as they could do. What was needed now was a major change in policy. Either Britain would have to back down and repeal the Tea Act or the colony would have to pay for the tea and admit parliamentary supremacy. Warren had a stronger voice in shaping Massachusetts policy than did Gage in the councils of Britain, but he too was something of a prisoner of larger forces. Warren had preached unfettered opposition long enough to find it difficult even to consider compromise. He and Adams had set in motion the minds and hearts of the people to a degree that they would find hard to control should they want to. Certainly his conscience was touched occasionally when he wondered whether or not he should sacrifice some of his uncompromising demands to avert the war he foresaw, but it was only after the fighting began that Warren frankly regretted not accepting Gage's invitation to speak openly to him.

The truth, of course, was that even if Gage and Warren had had the power of averting war, they may not have recognized the opportunity. It was not until April, 1775, that they were confronted with the single, clearly stated question of war or peace, and could have realized that a single decision of theirs might shift the balance. Until then, they faced a host of problems to solve on the basis of immediate needs, each of which appeared to be too inconsequential to result in the outbreak of fighting. A petition,

[1] W. Bodham Donne, ed., *The Correspondence of King George the Third with Lord North from 1768 to 1783* (London, 1867), I, 216; Massachusetts Provincial Congress, *The Journals of Each Provincial Congress of Massachusetts in 1774 and 1775* (Boston, 1838), p. 519, note.

a resolve, an appointment to office, a veto—none of these surely would cause the fighting to begin. Yet each of these steps, every decision, made reconciliation more difficult and brought war so much closer.

In May the new governor took one such step, negativing the election to the Council of James Bowdoin, John Adams, and eleven others. Nothing could make clearer the fact that the old political wars were to continue on Conservative advice, for Gage had been in the Province only two weeks before he took this action. When he found it necessary to enforce the act which provided that town meetings were not to be held without the consent of the governor and that the Council was to be an appointed body, his initial popularity was at an end. Every attempt to muster support for the act and to suppress opposition to its enforcement failed. The political strength of Warren and Adams was too great, their devices for circumventing the act too many, for anyone to succeed in enforcing it in Massachusetts.

On July 19, 1774, the Boston town meeting appointed Warren and the other leaders of the Boston opposition to a committee to draft a declaration of its sentiments about the new acts. This declaration was to be addressed "to Great Britain and all the world." On July 26, the town created a committee of safety, including Warren, Quincy, Hancock, and the two Adamses. This group was to plan measures for the public safety during the crisis. When Gage issued orders against the convening of such town meetings, Warren developed an evasion of the prohibition by encouraging county conferences, which were not regulated by the Massachusetts Government Act.[2] Warren and Samuel Adams had talked of such a possibility before the latter had left for the Continental Congress. Now Warren mustered the selectmen and the Committee of Correspondence to choose delegates to a Suffolk County convention. Warren, Benjamin Church, Oliver Wendell, and John Pitts were the Boston delegates to the Suffolk meeting at Doty's Tavern in Stoughton on August 16. As it developed, this meeting was no more than preparatory. Some of the towns had

[2] *Boston Town Records, 1770 Through 1777,* pp. 183, 185; Boston, *Selectmen's Minutes, 1769-1775,* pp. 224-225; Warren to Samuel Adams, Boston, Aug. 15, 1774, Samuel Adams MSS, also printed in Frothingham, *Warren,* pp. 339-340.

not given their delegates power to act, so the convention arranged for a new meeting at Dedham on September 6.[3]

On August 10, Samuel Adams, Thomas Cushing, John Adams, and Robert Treat Paine, delegates to the Continental Congress, had left Boston for Philadelphia. Before their departure they met at a tavern in Watertown to say farewell to their friends. Doubtless Warren, left to direct affairs alone at home, was among the well-wishers who saw them off. In the future, as he served on town committees, directed the Committee of Correspondence, and arranged the county conference, he was to be so busy that occasionally he would be unable to write to his friends in Philadelphia. When he did find time, however, he wrote at length, explaining new developments in Boston, encouraging the delegates at Philadelphia to look after the interests of Massachusetts, and seeking their advice. Without the aid of Samuel and John Adams, Warren now had to shape policy for Massachusetts almost single-handedly. Other towns were used to looking to Boston for direction, and, in the remaining months before war broke out, Joseph Warren was the key figure in corresponding with them and seeing that they supported the policies which he was formulating.

Before the Suffolk convention reconvened, Worcester made just such a call upon Boston for leadership in developing a common policy for the Province. Both Bristol and Worcester counties had held meetings, but their conventions had lacked direction and resulted in no important actions. Warren, now heading the Boston Committee of Correspondence, planned a convention of the counties similar to that of 1768, to meet at Faneuil Hall on August 26, 1774. Delegates from Suffolk, Worcester, Essex, and Middlesex elected Warren chairman of the convention, and, under his leadership, wrote a general policy statement for the guidance of later county congresses. Most of the principles embodied in the resolves of Middlesex and other counties were stated here. The convention called for a provincial congress to combat despotism and to establish referees to replace the courts, which were now under parliamentary regulation. All legal officers acting in conformity with the Administration of Justice Act, from the attorney general to

[3] Boston, Committee of Correspondence, Minutes, Aug. 12-13, 1774; Frothingham, *Warren,* p. 342; Nathaniel Patten to Jonathan Adams, Roxbury, Mass., Aug. 18, 1774, Chamberlain MSS; M. P. Webster, "The Suffolk Resolves," *New England Magazine,* n.s., XXVII, No. 3 (Nov., 1902), 359-360.

justices of the peace, were declared to be acting unconstitutionally and to be traitors to colonial rights. The people should oppose the courts and boycott such officials, while supporting every defender of the colony's rights. The latter point was particularly important to Warren, for since the Tea Party, Gage had discretionary orders for his arrest and trial for treason. Finally, the Faneuil Hall convention encouraged the people of the colony to accelerate their military training in order to protect their rights by arms if need be, a policy which Warren had long urged. The preamble to this declaration rested the colonial case directly upon natural rights, which the people held from God and which were secure not only against Parliament but the king as well.[4]

On August 15, Warren wrote to Samuel Adams suggesting some resolves which he felt would more likely succeed if members from some other colony could be persuaded to introduce them. These were probably along the lines of the Faneuil Hall and Suffolk Resolves. Warren wrote at length of the necessity of opposing the councilors who had been appointed and of denouncing the Quebec Act. He urged the Massachusetts delegates to make clear to other members the dangerous implications for their charters of an arbitrary change in the Massachusetts government. If Britain could take away Massachusetts' right of electing councilors, she could deny the right of other colonies to elect even their representatives. Then, recalling the political sagacity that he had seen in Samuel Adams for years, he added that he was "perhaps too much like the declaimer who delivered a lecture upon the art of war to the illustrious General Hannibal."[5] A week later Warren urged Adams to promote the principles embodied in his Covenant as an intercolonial plan. He saw the stoppage of trade with Britain as the bare minimum to avert war within two months. Withholding flax seed from Ireland would be particularly helpful, as it might throw "a million of people in Ireland out of bread." He planned to investigate the amount of Britain's economic interest in Ireland and the number of members of Parliament whose chief wealth was there or in the West Indies.[6]

[4] Boston, Committee of Correspondence, Minutes, Aug. 26-27, 1774; Votes of Delegates to Faneuil Hall Meeting, Aug. 26, 1774, Miscellaneous MSS, XIV (Mass. Hist. Soc. Library).

[5] Warren to Samuel Adams, Boston, Aug. 15, 1774, Samuel Adams MSS.

[6] *Id.* to *id.*, Boston, Aug. 21, 1774, in *ibid.*, also printed in Frothingham, *Warren*, pp. 343-344.

Warren sent the same advice to the towns of Massachusetts. To a committee of Norwich: "We consider a suspension of trade through the continent with Great Britain, Ireland, and the West Indies, as the grand machine that will deliver us." He assured the people of Preston that nonintercourse would produce such changes in Britain as would force her to yield on every point to American demands. By this time, however, Warren was no longer placing sole reliance upon economic boycott. In these letters in late August, 1774, he considered seriously the possibility of peaceable coercion failing. In that case, appeal would have to be made to "the last resort" and, he said, "we flatter ourselves that we shall act like *men,* and merit the approbation of all America." By September, Warren was suggesting to Samuel Adams that it might be wise to test whether or not America would support Massachusetts in a more extreme policy than economic coercion, if that should become necessary.[7]

This is not, of course, to say that Warren wanted war; if war did come, however, he wanted the colony to be prepared. He saw the necessity, if violence were to be averted, of working toward that end in England, since Gage's power was severely limited. He desired to go abroad himself, but the sacrifice of his medical practice for such a trip was more than he could afford. He encouraged his ailing friend Josiah Quincy, for whom an ocean voyage might be good, to go to England. Warren wrote letters of introduction to his acquaintances in England, urged Samuel Adams to get letters from gentlemen at Philadelphia, and served as a witness to a codicil to Quincy's will. Death had hovered about the tubercular young lawyer for years, and he died on the return voyage, before having an opportunity of reporting to Warren the information he had gathered in England. Through letters to his wife, however, Quincy managed to send some reports on English conditions to Warren.[8]

Within Massachusetts, Warren's policies were becoming more radical and a few of his plans were more extreme than some peo-

[7] Warren to Committee of Norwich, Boston, Aug. 27, 1774, and *id.* to Committee of Preston, Boston, Aug. 24, 1774, Frothingham, ed., "Correspondence in 1774 and 1775," pp. 47, 55; Warren to Adams, Sept. [4], 1774, Samuel Adams MSS, also printed in Frothingham, *Warren,* pp. 355-357.

[8] *Id.* to *id.,* Boston, Aug. 29, 1774, *ibid.,* also printed in Frothingham, *Warren,* pp. 351-352; Quincy, *Memoir of Josiah Quincy,* pp. 209, 289, note; Frothingham, *Warren,* p. 358.

ple favored. Most immediate was the opposition which he believed had to be made to the courts and the mandamus council, as it was called under the new act. Working on the realistic assumption that the punitive laws would not be repealed, Warren encouraged the Province to prepare itself for eventual war and develop plans for a new government outside of the royal system. All of these policies for Massachusetts he expressed in the resolves that he wrote for Suffolk County. Even more important, these resolutions provided a policy statement that gave direction to the Continental Congress in Philadelphia. With the question of its adoption of these resolves, Congress was faced with the first of those issues that were to divide the members into two factions until the one attained the majority necessary to resolve upon independence.

Nineteen towns of Suffolk County appointed more than seventy delegates to the meeting which reconvened from its August adjournment at the house of Richard Woodward in Dedham on September 6, 1774. A document in the hand of William Cooper indicates how carefully Warren and his Boston colleagues had planned the course of the county congress. Written before the convention met, this document is the minutes of the meeting as the Bostonians proposed they should have been. Also, it is, in a sense, a first draft of the Suffolk Resolves. The finished document, however, is so much more polished and exciting that the draft in no way detracts from the credit accorded Warren for the final state paper. In any case, on most points the document in Cooper's hand so closely parallels Warren's stated views, and in some cases his very wording, that it seems likely he was its principal author.[9]

According to the Cooper "minutes," the Boston delegates intended to read the recent acts of Parliament and other papers at the opening of the convention, and to propose unit-voting by towns, so that an appearance of unanimity might be had. Next a series of resolves would be proposed and the convention would adjourn until the following Tuesday. The proceedings would be sent to the Boston Committee of Correspondence, likely their place of origin, for publication. However, instead of pushing these resolves through, Warren placed himself at the head of a commit-

[9] MS, At a Convention of the Representative Committees of the Several Towns and Districts of the County of Suffolk . . . (Mass. Hist. Soc. Library). So far as I am aware, the existence of this manuscript is unknown to historians of the period. Webster's "Suffolk Resolves," the only article on the subject, takes no notice of it.

tee to consider a county policy, thus giving the appearance that delegates from other towns had a part in the proceedings. After appointing the committee, the congress adjourned to meet at Daniel Vose's home in Milton on September 9, rather than September 13 as the Cooper "minutes" had suggested. The September 6 meeting had been so brief that Warren was able to return to Boston and make a number of professional calls that day.[10]

The Cooper draft of the resolves to be introduced at the Suffolk convention asserted that the rights of the people of Massachusetts had been invaded by the recent parliamentary acts. This was sufficient justification for the colony to resume its first charter, which had been unjustly abrogated, or to take any other prudent measures. However, the people wished that the old harmony with Britain might be restored, and to effect this they pledged to halt all commercial intercourse with Britain. Another step toward this end, the resolves said, was the holding of town meetings which should plan county conventions. The counties, in turn, should provide for a provincial convention, which might correspond with similar bodies in other colonies. The people of Suffolk County pledged submission to the acts of the Continental Congress, and proposed as a permanent settlement with Britain that the colonies pay an annual sum into the British treasury, rather than submit to having illegal revenue officers in America. Other resolves provided: that home manufacturing and agriculture be encouraged; that the Quebec Act, designed to establish popish despotism, be opposed by a firm union of the British colonies; that the unconstitutional councilors and other officials appointed by the recent acts were traitors and should be brought to trial when the times permitted; that anyone fined or punished for opposing the punitive laws be compensated by the county; and that a county committee of correspondence be appointed.[11]

Here, surely, was an extreme enough policy for most people in the colonies. In its provision for establishing a government on the basis of the first charter, which would allow for an elected governor and the barring of royal revenue officials from the colonies it envisioned a virtually independent state within a British commonwealth of nations. Parliament would have no right to

[10] Webster, "Suffolk Resolves," pp. 361-362, 371-372; Warren, Ledger, Sept. 6, 1774.

[11] MS, At a Convention of the Representative Committees . . . of Suffolk.

regulate the colonies in any way, and the people declared their willingness to fight for home rule, or protection of rights, as it was usually put. Yet the proposal of annual grants to support the Empire indicates a sincerity about restoring harmony with Britain, and suggests that Warren and his friends had a well-developed conception of a sovereign America tied to Britain only by affection and economic interests. Adoption of Warren's Solemn League and Covenant, which had not been widely popular, was suggested as the best way of forcing Britain to accept Suffolk's policy.

The resolves which Joseph Warren presented to the convention when it reconvened in Milton on September 9 were different in certain respects from these Cooper "minutes." The entire document compares favorably with the Declaration of Independence, and the preamble is as exciting as Jefferson's great state paper. It recited, in general terms, the past oppressions by Britain "which of old persecuted, scourged and exiled" the ancestors of the American colonists. These early settlers had acquired this savage desert by their toil, treasure, courage, and blood, and had willed it to later generations. It was a sacred duty of the men of 1774 to transmit this heritage and land, free of shackles, to the future. On their fortitude and wisdom hangs "the fate of this New World, and of unborn millions." If they consented to live in slavery, their names would live in infamy forever; if they resisted the unconstitutional invasions of their rights, their names would be praised until "the streams of time shall be absorbed in the abyss of eternity."[12]

The resolves which followed this preamble frankly faced the imminence of war, with no proposals for restoring harmony, such as annual grants to Britain. After a routine acknowledgment of allegiance to the king, Warren declared that the recent acts of Parliament violated rights granted by Nature, by the British Constitution, and by the Massachusetts charter, and that no obedience should be paid to them. Warren had already decided that the courts could not be allowed to sit under the new act,[13] and resolves six and seven urged that the royally appointed judges be opposed. The county would support sheriffs and other officials who refused to execute orders of these courts, and, in order to maintain peace in the absence of courts, Warren asked the people to avoid disputes over paying debts which fell due and to submit

[12] Force, *American Archives*, 4th ser., I, 776.
[13] Warren to Adams, Sept. [4], 1774, Samuel Adams MSS.

disputes which might arise to arbitration. Mandamus councilors were ordered to resign their seats or be branded enemies of their colony, but Warren shrewdly dropped the suggestion of the Cooper draft that the royal officials be brought to trial as traitors, which might have alienated public opinion. Other resolves protested against fortifications which Gage was constructing at Boston Neck and the Quebec Act to establish Roman Catholicism in Canada, considered to be "dangerous in an extreme degree to the Protestant religion, and to the civil rights and liberties of all America." Warren's protest against the Quebec Act, while more temperately phrased than the charge of "popish despotism" in the Cooper "minutes," played a part in spreading that anti-Catholic agitation which was a part of much revolutionary propaganda thereafter. Realizing the powerful appeal that could be made to some people on this issue, newspapers and conventions took up the charge in the Suffolk Resolves and elaborated it.[14]

Warren proposed several means by which opposition to British policy might be made, and in them one has an accurate road map of the actual course which the colonies were to follow in succeeding months. Once again Warren suggested his pet scheme—nonintercourse with Britain and the encouragement of home manufacturing. The resolves again called for a provincial congress, and asked the towns to elect delegates to meet at Concord on the second Tuesday of October. Warren wrote this resolve on the assumption, or the hope, that the meeting of the General Court scheduled for October 5 in Salem would fail. Lest other colonies fear that Massachusetts was creating a powerful, independent government, a pledge of submission to the acts of the Continental Congress was added, and Warren made no mention of taking up the original charter. Though Warren favored the erection of a full government for Massachusetts Bay, he admitted to Samuel Adams that even resumption of the old charter was a subject which had to be "handled very gently and cautiously whenever brought upon the tapis."[15]

The rest of the nineteen Suffolk Resolves looked toward war.

---

[14] Force, *American Archives,* 4th ser., I, 777-778; Sister Mary A. Ray, *American Opinion of Roman Catholicism in the Eighteenth Century,* No. 416, in Columbia University, *Studies in History, Economics and Public Law* (New York, 1936), pp. 279, 286-288, 294-295, 309. See further, Margaret W. Willard, ed., *Letters on the American Revolution, 1774-1776* (Boston, 1925), p. 67.

[15] Frothingham, *Warren,* p. 358.

Warren prayed that militia-training be encouraged and all militia commissions be resigned so that new officers might be chosen, presumably to eliminate all of doubtful loyalty to the American cause. Should Britain try to arrest the defenders of American rights, the people would seize every royal administrative official in the colony. Warren promised that Suffolk County would establish a courier system to warn the country in case of troop maneuvers, but he warned the people against riots and unwarranted attacks upon private property. Most important of all, resolve twelve said that the people would "act merely upon the defensive, so long as such conduct may be vindicated by reason and the principles of self-preservation, but no longer."[16] Here was a full acceptance of the possibility of war, and a public notice that the people of Suffolk County would fight. When the Continental Congress approved the Suffolk Resolves, it pledged to support Massachusetts in a defensive war, without further defining the conditions which would justify it than Warren had done in resolve twelve. Thus, the question of war or peace for all of America was placed in the hands of the leaders of the Massachusetts opposition party.

The only other action of the Suffolk convention was the adoption of an address to Gage protesting his erection of fortifications at Boston Neck. The Boston selectmen had already remonstrated about this in an address drawn by a subcommittee, headed by Warren, of the Committee of Correspondence. He likely wrote the county address also, as he was named chairman of the committee to wait upon Gage with it. The address said that such fortifications aggravated the miseries of the town by preventing necessary intercourse with the country and were intended as an unjust reflection upon the loyalty of the people of Massachusetts, who had no intention of injuring the troops. Gage replied that he planned to report to the king the general disobedience to the Port Act, a reply which the committee voted unsatisfactory. Warren, in conversations with Secretary Thomas Flucker, tried unsuccessfully to get Gage to accept a second address on the subject.[17]

The adoption of the Suffolk Resolves by the Continental Congress was one of the most important acts in America in 1774.

[16] Force, *American Archives,* 4th ser., I, 778-779.

[17] Boston, Committee of Correspondence, Minutes, Sept. 8, 1774; Boston, *Selectmen's Minutes, 1769-1775,* pp. 227-228; *Boston Post-Boy,* Sept. 19, 1774.

There were, of course, similar resolutions by other county congresses. Most of them called for a provincial congress and recommended opposition to the parliamentary legislation and the officers who acted under it. But most of these resolves were patterned upon those adopted by the Faneuil Hall meeting in August or upon the Suffolk Resolves. Bristol County felt it unnecessary to express its sentiments, this having been done so well by Suffolk County. And none of the resolves went so far toward preparing for war as did those which Warren wrote for the Suffolk convention. Thus, although the Middlesex Resolves were laid before the Continental Congress on September 14, no action upon them was taken. Samuel Adams and his colleagues were awaiting Warren's resolutions, which Paul Revere was carrying to Philadelphia.[18] Revere arrived on September 16, and the Suffolk Resolves were brought into Congress the following morning. They provided the issue needed to evoke a frank exchange of opinions from the members as to the course which America should pursue. Thus far lacking in direction, the Congress was now asked to decide between humble petitions and quiet submission or disobedience and a defensive war.

The debates were "long and warm," according to Joseph Galloway, though adoption was voted the day the Resolves were introduced. Congress approved all of Warren's proposals and encouraged the people of Massachusetts to pursue "the same firm and temperate conduct" expressed in his Resolves. In short, they were to oppose royal officials and parliamentary acts, and to prepare for a defensive war. As Galloway put it, thus "the foundation of military resistance throughout America was effectually laid."[19] And thus, also, the principles of nonintercourse which were to be embodied in the Continental Association were adopted. The Congress also voted that the colonies should continue to contribute to the relief of Boston. The members of Congress applauded as the Resolves were read, and the people of Philadelphia received them enthusiastically.[20] No other action in the

---

[18] *Ibid.*, Oct. 10, 1774; Force, *American Archives*, 4th ser., I, 750-752, 795-801, for the county resolves; U.S. Continental Congress, *Journals of the Continental Congress, 1774-1789* (Washington, 1904), I, 31.

[19] *Ibid.*, I, 37-39; [Joseph Galloway], *Historical and Political Reflections on the Rise and Progress of the American Rebellion* (London, 1780), pp. 68-69.

[20] Cushing, ed., *Writings of Samuel Adams*, III, 156; Edmund C. Burnett, ed., *Letters of Members of the Continental Congress* (Washington, 1921), I, 34, 35.

fall of 1774 was so important in crystallizing opinion on both sides of the Atlantic.

When Thomas Gage heard of the adoption of the Suffolk Resolves by the delegates at Philadelphia, he wrote Lord Dartmouth that he did not "expect much good from their deliberations." A loyalist source suggested that the only excuse for this vote of the delegates was that they had just drunk thirty-two bumpers of madeira. The Resolves convinced a Conservative writer in New York that independence was the Radical goal, and he dropped his newspaper activities. In England, Thomas Hutchinson felt that the Resolves were "more alarming than any thing which had yet been done." Warren's policy was "undoubtedly treasonable," and both he and William Knox, a former royal official in Georgia, thought that any chance of concession was now hopeless. Dartmouth was thunderstruck, and viewed Massachusetts as "plainly in a state of revolt or rebellion" as did the king. In November, George III wrote Lord North, "Blows must decide whether they are to be subject to this country or independent." On February 9, 1775, he addressed Parliament, formally declaring Massachusetts to be in a state of rebellion.[21] The resolves of Joseph Warren and the other delegates who met in the little town of Milton on September 9 had hit their mark.

The formation of this bold policy was only half the job, however; Warren had also to execute the plans which he had set out for Massachusetts. In September, 1774, his most immediate problems were effective opposition to the new, royally appointed officials and the creation of a government for the Bay Colony. The latter question Warren had deliberately avoided in his Suffolk Resolves. Though privately he seems to have favored a new, fully elective government for the colony, he realized that such plans had to be delicately broached. His friends in Philadelphia recommended an extremely cautious policy, not entirely congenial to Warren's spirited temperament and not well designed to provide effective government should war break out. Many people in the western counties favored reviving the first charter as a basis of government, while others, particularly in the eastern part of

[21] Carter, ed., *Correspondence of Gage,* I, 377; Donne, ed., *Correspondence of George the Third,* I, 214-215; *A Few Remarks upon Some of the Votes and Resolutions of the Continental Congress . . .* (1775); Hutchinson, *Diary and Letters,* pp. 272-273, 284, 285, 302; Davidson, *Propaganda,* pp. 253-254.

the colony, felt that the king had broken the compact with the people and that they might create an entirely different form of government.

Either of these courses would have been more radical than simply abiding by the charter of 1691, which the delegates at the Congress recommended. John Adams wrote that even resuming the first charter was a startling proposal to the people at the Congress, and that the general opinion was that Massachusetts should "live wholly without a legislature." Samuel Adams, dreading disunity between the eastern and western sections of the colony, proposed that the second charter be used, the last elected Council serving with the House of Representatives. The delegates to the Continental Congress, he said, feared that the Bay Colony was aiming at total independence, and would overpower the other colonies if this were achieved. They would support Massachusetts in a defensive war, but not if she set up a new form of government. Warren, however, was faced with the problem of creating an effective government in Massachusetts or abdicating control of the colony to the royal governor and the royal council. He argued that nothing in Philadelphia could be more important than this subject, and begged Samuel Adams to send intelligence and advice immediately.[22]

Congress gave more support to Warren's policy of opposing royally appointed officials, embodying in a special resolution his Suffolk Resolve that anyone who took office under the Massachusetts Government Act was an enemy of the country. The people of Massachusetts, through force and intimidation, made his policy the "law" of the colony, compelling mandamus councilors to resign and preventing the courts from sitting. The demand that councilors resign and the attempt of Gage to confiscate the colony's supply of ammunition nearly precipitated hostilities. Early in the morning of September 1, some 250 troops were ferried across Boston Harbor, and moved the powder and cannon from the Charlestown powder house to a barn near the shore. Despite the attempt at secrecy, the news was soon out and a story circulated that a skirmish had resulted in the killing of six people. Dispatches

[22] [Joseph Warren] to [Samuel Adams], Boston, Sept. 12, 1774, [Samuel Adams] to [Joseph Warren], Philadelphia, Pa., Sept. 24, 1774, *id.* to *id.*, Sept. 25, 1774, all in Samuel Adams MSS, also printed in Frothingham, *Warren*, pp. 375-376, 377, 378-379; Burnett, ed., *Letters of Members of the Continental Congress*, I, 48.

were sent west toward Springfield, northwest to New Hampshire, and southwest to Connecticut. Israel Putnam forwarded a letter to Philadelphia which threw the Congress into a state of alarm. Bodies of armed men began to collect throughout Massachusetts, and there was a real danger of several thousand attempting to take Boston and drive out the troops. The selectmen and the committees of correspondence of Boston and Charlestown hastened to the scene of action. Warren received word that there were angry crowds about the homes of two mandamus councilors in Cambridge and a plea that someone from Boston go there to avert trouble. A second messenger told him that the roads from Sudbury to Cambridge were lined with people in arms, and urged him to take steps to prevent violence. Warren gathered as many of his Boston committee as he could on short notice, and they crossed to Charlestown. There they were asked to go on to Cambridge. They met Lieutenant Governor Thomas Oliver, who was hastening to Boston to plead that Gage keep his troops in the town. The large assembly at Cambridge was peaceful, and Warren, Young, and other leaders spent three hours with it and secured verbal satisfaction from local royalists. That evening Warren missed one of only three masonic lodge meetings he failed to attend as grand master. Well ordered as the crowd had been, Warren sensed that not a man would have been saved had the troops marched more than five miles out of Boston. The day after this mass demonstration, Gage wrote home that his army was too small and that he needed a body of irregular troops for special missions.[23]

This crisis of early September occurred just before the meeting of the Suffolk County convention, and Warren's resolves on an alarm system, electing new militia officers, and preparing for a defensive war, were a warning to Gage about such expeditions in the future. The news had spread almost too rapidly on September 1, and men from Worcester and Concord asked the Boston Committee of Correspondence to work out an effective system which would prevent needless alarms. Warren's skill in developing an organization of spies, couriers, and alarm signals became clear

[23] Sparks, ed., "Diary by Thomas Newell," p. 221; Sargent, ed., "Letters of John Andrews," p. 350; Dexter, ed., *Literary Diary of Ezra Stiles,* I, 477, 481-485; Warren to Adams, Sept. [4], 1774, Samuel Adams MSS; Carter, ed., *Correspondence of Gage,* I, 371-372; Wells, *Samuel Adams,* II, 238.

in April, 1775. On September 17, some Bostonians stole a page from the British manual of cold-war tactics and took four brass cannon during the night from a gunhouse near the Common. In the course of the escapade, William Dawes suffered a slight injury, and, according to a family tale, Warren treated him and expressed sympathy with the action.[24] A more official action in September was the boycotting of the British army. The Boston Committee of Correspondence warned laborers against working on the barracks which were being built, and John Warren wrote to New York asking that no carpenters be sent to the army from that city. The laborers quit work and Gage went so far as to propose that, if work were resumed, he would allow goods to enter Boston from Charlestown under the guise of king's stores. The nights were becoming cold already, and the troops could not sleep in tents much longer. However, the correspondence committees of Boston and neighboring towns established committees of observation to prevent lumber and other supplies from entering the town, and the Roxbury Sons of Liberty burned a load of straw intended for the army.[25]

The seizure of colonial powder on September 1 also led Joseph Warren to think increasingly of the possibility of war. He wrote Samuel Adams early in September that the time had come either to yield all rights and speak no more of freedom, or to oppose the enemy and no longer "rest upon our arms." By November he was suggesting that the wisest step was for Britain and America "fairly to separate," if the punitive laws were not to be repealed. If Britain should remain adamant, it would mean that the two countries would "spend their blood and treasure in destroying each other." And there were other, more moderate men agreeing with Warren by late 1774. In October, Joseph Reed wrote Josiah Quincy, Jr., "Should this bloodless war fail of its effect, an infinite majority

---

[24] Boston, Committee of Correspondence, Minutes, Sept. 19, 1774; Sparks, ed., "Diary by Thomas Newell," p. 222; Henry W. Holland, *William Dawes and His Ride with Paul Revere* (Boston, 1878), p. 34.

[25] Boston, Committee of Correspondence, Minutes, Sept. 24, 1774; John C. Warren, *Genealogy of Warren with Some Historical Sketches* (Boston, 1854), p. 82; Warren to Samuel Adams, Sept. 29, 1774, Samuel Adams MSS, also printed in Frothingham, *Warren*, pp. 381-382; Sargent, ed., "Letters of John Andrews," pp. 368-369; facsimile broadside, Boston, Committee of Correspondence, "Gentlemen, The committees of correspondence of this and several of the neighbouring towns," Sept. 27, 1774 (Boston Public Library); Force, *American Archives*, 4th ser., I, 807.

of all the colonies will make the last appeal, before they resign their liberties into the hands of any ministerial tyrant." John Dickinson told Quincy that all of the colonies were aroused, and, unless Britain changed her policy quickly, civil war was unavoidable. Two months later, Quincy wrote a letter from England to his wife, probably intended for Warren, in which he vowed that the Americans would have to *"seal their cause with their blood."*[26]

As the possibility of war loomed larger, Massachusetts became hungry for news of the Continental Congress' proceedings, which the Congress had ordered to be kept secret. The one breach of this order was the confidential report which Samuel Adams sent to Warren about the prayer offered by an Episcopalian clergyman. Adams, sometimes called the last Puritan, had declared on the floor that he was not a bigot and could hear a prayer by anyone who was a friend to his country. In concert with the other Massachusetts delegates, he suggested the Reverend Jacob Duché, in order to gain support of Episcopalians. One delegate privately said that there was never a cleverer political tactic, and John Adams felt that he had never heard a better prayer. Warren published part of Samuel Adams' letter on the subject with a note of his own, in which he offered this as proof that the Episcopalians were generally supporting Boston and the American cause. To his friends in Philadelphia, he sent apologies for printing portions of Adams' and Cushing's letters, which had done much to aid morale in the Bay Colony.[27]

The Radicals developed plans for a provincial congress to govern Massachusetts before Governor Gage decided not to summon the General Court. Warren was the organizer of this movement, and the Faneuil Hall resolves of August set a pattern for the county convention resolves calling for such a meeting. In Boston he controlled the election of its delegates, seeing to the choice of the right Liberty party members to represent the town. He wrote Samuel Adams that he hoped they could count on his

[26] Warren to Adams, Sept. [4], 1774, Samuel Adams MSS; Warren to Josiah Quincy, Jr., Boston, Nov. 21, 1774, Quincy MSS, p. 76 (Mass. Hist. Soc. Library), also printed in Frothingham, *Warren*, pp. 394-396; Quincy, *Memoir of Josiah Quincy*, pp. 167, 168, 224.

[27] Burnett, ed., *Letters of Members of the Continental Congress*, I, 26-28; Charles F. Adams, ed., *Familiar Letters of John Adams and His Wife Abigail Adams During the Revolution* (Boston, 1875), p. 37; *Boston Post-Boy*, Sept. 26, 1774.

services, and asked whether it would be all right to have John Adams and Thomas Cushing elected. On September 22 the town meeting chose Warren, Church, and Nathanial Appleton to serve with the town's four representatives in the proposed Congress. The day before, the town had voted against a motion to instruct the representatives, but Warren gained enough votes for reconsideration of the question, and the meeting named him chairman of a committee to draft instructions. These instructions, reported at the same meeting on September 22, were short and concerned only with refusing to recognize the Massachusetts Government Act and forming a provincial congress. Warren ordered the representatives to recognize the Council elected in May as the only constitutional council for Massachusetts. Since an honest discharge of their duties would likely lead to dissolution of the General Court, he instructed them to meet with such other delegates as might be appointed to a congress.[28]

On September 1, Gage had issued his call for the General Court to meet at Salem on October 5. His proclamation canceling these writs was dated six days after Boston adopted Warren's instructions, and cited those instructions and the county resolves as reasons for his action. Had the General Court met, there clearly would have been a struggle over the question of which was the legal council, the one elected in May or the one appointed by the king.[29] Warren had made certain of that by carefully organizing most of Massachusetts to support his policy on the question. Thus, Gage annulled the writs summoning the representatives, but was unable to prevent their meeting without him and the mandamus council. They met at Salem, passed a resolve declaring Gage's revocation of the writs to be unconstitutional, and formed themselves into a congress. Warren now took his seat in the new body, the first colonial office he had held. The members chose John Hancock chairman and Benjamin Lincoln clerk, and then adjourned to October 11 at Concord.[30]

The first session of the Provincial Congress took a number of steps toward providing a government for the colony and preparing for war. It invited members of the Council elected in May and those who had been appointed mandamus councilors, but

[28] [Joseph Warren] to [Samuel Adams], Boston, Sept. 12, 1774, Samuel Adams MSS; *Boston Town Records, 1770 Through 1777*, pp. 190-192.

[29] Mass. Prov. Cong., *Journals*, pp. 3-4; Cushing, *Transition*, pp. 71-73, 81.

[30] Mass. Prov. Cong., *Journals*, pp. 5-6, 16; *Boston Post-Boy*, Oct. 10, 1774.

had refused to act under their commissions, to join with the Provincial Congress in governing the colony. This system of government, based on the second charter, was not all that Warren desired, but it was the best that could be had. He and his friends had to govern Massachusetts with an inadequate governmental machinery, which depended largely upon persuasion to get popular support. The Congress ordered that all Province money be paid to Henry Gardner, who was appointed receiver general, rather than to the royal treasurer. In a move to gain financial support for the new government, the Congress instructed towns to carry out the assessments voted by the last General Court and to pay all taxes. One of the most important actions of the Congress was the establishment of a commitee of safety, which was to become the executive of the revolutionary government.[31]

Joseph Warren was active on the Committee on the State of the Province, which recommended the most important policies that the first session of Congress adopted, and on several minor committees. The Committee on the State of the Province drafted an address to Gage similar to those which Warren had already written for Boston and Suffolk County, expressing concern with troops being quartered in the Province and with the fortifications being built on Boston Neck. The governor replied that those fortifications were there only because of the colonists' warlike preparations, and warned the Provincial Congress to halt its "illegal and unconstitutional proceedings." Other resolves of the session provided that the body's proceedings be kept secret, that a committee report a nonconsumption agreement, and that a committee investigate the state of the army. The latter group suggested that arms, field pieces, mortars, powder, and shot costing £20,800 were necessary to defend the Province. The provision on nonconsumption was a new attempt to gain wider acceptance for Warren's Solemn League and Covenant.[32]

The origin of the Committee of Safety is to be found in an important report of October 26. Declaring that "nothing but slavery ought more to be deprecated than hostilities with Great Britain," this report cited the presence of troops and invasion of the colonists' liberties as justifying preparation for war. A committee of safety was to be established with the power to alarm and muster the colony's military forces whenever necessary for the

[31] Mass. Prov. Cong., *Journals,* pp. 19, 38-39, 40.
[32] *Ibid.,* pp. 16-18, 20-21, 22, 25, 28, 30.

defense of the lives, liberty, and property of the people. All officers and soldiers were to obey the orders of this committee. A committee of supply should also be named to purchase and distribute arms, ammunition, and artillery to the troops upon their muster. The people were encouraged to provide themselves with arms and ammunition, and the militia units were to proceed with the election of officers. All officers and soldiers mustered were assured of pay by the Province. On October 27, the Congress elected Joseph Warren one of nine members of the Committee of Safety, and appointed five commissaries and three general officers for the militia on the same day. On October 29 the Congress adjourned to November 23, but before doing so ordered the Committee of Safety to communicate its proceedings and votes to the Continental Congress. Also, William Heath, Joseph Warren, and Benjamin Church were named to hide the colony's military stores "with the greatest secrecy" someplace in the country.[33]

The creation of the Committee of Safety, with power to alarm and muster the military forces, placed the decision of war or peace for the American side in the hands of nine men in Massachusetts Bay. John Hancock was chairman of the committee at first, but often did not attend its meetings, and Joseph Warren was its actual leader. Concerned about the rashness of Warren and other Bostonians, the Provincial Congress had insisted that there never be more than three members on it from that town. The direction of the military, for which the committee was established, was the function for which it seemed least suited. The membership of the committee in the Provincial Congress might have promoted close liaison between it and the legislature, but under Warren's leadership the Committee of Safety steadily assumed more independence from its parent body. Its powers were specifically delegated, but in vague terms which created fears of its assuming too much power in some minds and occasionally resulted in a too cautious exercise of its powers. Most serious were the conflicts between the military officers and the committee, which arose in part because of this imprecise definition of powers.[34]

[33] *Ibid.*, pp. 31-34, 35, 38, 41, 42, 48; broadside, Provincial Congress, "Whereas in consequence of the present unhappy dispute," Cambridge, Mass., Oct. 26, 1774 (Boston Public Library).

[34] Agnes Hunt, *The Provincial Committees of Safety of the American Revolution* ([Cleveland, Ohio], 1904), is a useful study of these bodies, though her description of their characteristics does not seem applicable to the Massachusetts committee in some respects. See particularly pp. 151-158.

During the adjournment of the Provincial Congress, the Committee of Safety began serious organization for war. The Committee of Supplies was instructed to collect arms, ammunition, food, and other supplies at Concord and Worcester. Gage had only poor intelligence of the Congress' actions and committees. He did have knowledge of the plan to organize several thousand men to be ready on a minute's warning, but was uncertain as to the purpose of this army. His reports said that some in the Congress favored an attack upon the army in Boston, others demanded that the town be set afire, while the more moderate members suggested inviting the Bostonians to evacuate the town.[35]

From Philadelphia, John Adams sent a warning that the Continental Congress would not support Massachusetts if she embarked upon an offensive war. There was little possibility of that body voting men or money for defense at that session. Warren did, however, continue to press for strong support from the Continental Congress. He headed the Boston Committee of Correspondence now, which met almost daily and repeatedly sought the advice of Congress in order to get national approval of Warren's policies. The report of Gage's fortifying Boston resulted in a resolution of Congress approving Massachusetts' opposition to the punitive laws. If force were used to execute these laws, the Congress declared, "all America ought to support them in their opposition." The Continental Congress sent a letter to Gage, asking that he desist from fortifying Boston and confiscating property, and pledging continental support of Massachusetts.[36]

The people's faith in the Congress was the only thing that enabled Warren "to keep people from action at some particular times." Disputes between the troops and the townspeople did break out occasionally, and he feared that there would have been bloodshed already except for the actions of the Congress. Though favoring all-out preparation for a defensive war, Warren tried to avert senseless quarrels in Massachusetts. He held several private conversations with Gage and found him to be "a man of honest, upright principles." The general seemed to desire the restoration of harmony, rather than continuing the tension in order to have a place for himself as some public officials might have done. On

[35] Mass. Prov. Cong., *Journals*, p. 506; Carter, ed., *Correspondence of Gage,* I, 382; Force, *American Archives,* 4th ser., I, 880.

[36] Burnett, ed., *Letters of Members of the Continental Congress,* I, 65; U.S. Continental Congress, *Journals,* I, 56-58, 60-62.

November 7, a committee of which Warren was a member reported recommendations for maintaining peace and order to the Boston town meeting. The number of the watch should be increased and should patrol the streets all night, while all peace officers were to call upon the inhabitants in dispersing unruly gatherings. It was further suggested that servants and children be subject to a curfew, and that there be stricter enforcement of the laws relating to taverns serving disorderly patrons. One British officer noted that the troops' drunkenness was at "a very great pitch," because of the cheapness of liquor. Warren's committee carried the town recommendations to Gage, and the governor promised on his side to arrest any soldiers engaged in any disturbance and to prohibit the carrying of side arms in the streets.[37]

Though Warren worked with Gage on this problem, he spent much more effort in promoting Boston's revolutionary activities and organizing town meetings in direct violation of the Massachusetts Government Act and under the nose of the general, who was charged with the law's enforcement. Warren and other political leaders, as well as craftsmen like Revere, were constituted a town committee to execute the resolves of the Continental Congress. Warren also served on a committee to thank other colonies for their donations, and on another with Church and Samuel Adams to consider Gage's misrepresentations of the conduct of the town. On December 13, Warren ordered word sent to Newport, Rhode Island, that some 300 soldiers were headed that way. The same day Paul Revere was dispatched to Portsmouth, New Hampshire, with a letter suggesting that the powder be captured from Castle William and Mary. Some 400 men were mustered, and the powder was taken after token resistance by the captain and four or five gunners garrisoned there. Later another body carried off some 1,500 small arms and everything resembling artillery.[38] Such activities originated in the Boston Com-

[37] Warren to Adams, Boston, Sept. 29, 1774, Samuel Adams MSS; Warren to Josiah Quincy, Jr., Boston, Nov. 21, 1774, Quincy MSS; *Boston Town Records, 1770 Through 1777*, pp. 194-195; John Barker, *The British in Boston* (Cambridge, Mass., 1924), pp. 3-4, 18, 21-22.

[38] *Boston Town Records, 1770 Through 1777*, pp. 205-207, 209-211; Dexter, ed., *Literary Diary of Ezra Stiles*, p. 501; Charles K. Bolton, ed., *Letters of Hugh Earl Percy from Boston and New York, 1774-1776* (Boston, 1902), pp. 46-47; Fortescue, ed., *Correspondence of King George the Third*, III, 160-161; Force, *American Archives*, 4th ser., I, 1041-42.

mittee of Correspondence, and, tending as they did toward an offensive war, were not supported by many men who sat in the Provincial Congress.

In December, Charles Lee, one of the more experienced military men in the colonies, visited Boston, spending all of his time in the company of Warren and other Liberty party leaders. Lee doubtless referred to Warren when he said that a physician at Boston had vowed that the last act of nearly every dying father he visited was to gather his sons about his deathbed and charge them never to desert their country's cause. Lee spoke of the man who told him this as being "of exceeding good sense and the greatest candour." And Warren was just that—so patently honest, sincere, and sensible that one was almost persuaded to believe such obvious propaganda.[39] William Gordon, who wrote the history of the revolutionary struggle, entered the cause of the Massachusetts opposition largely through the persuasion of Warren's personality. He had come to the colonies in 1770, and was pastor of the Third Church in Roxbury, Warren's birthplace, by 1772. The story of his initial struggles is told in the Massachusetts Council's authorization of the payment of £12 6*s*. 6*d*. to Joseph Warren's mother for "dieting nursing and cloathing one William Gordon, a poor stranger." By December, 1774, Gordon was preaching in defense of the American cause, and it was Warren who appointed him to edit the letters of Thomas Hutchinson which were found at the former governor's estate.[40]

The Provincial Congress, which had reconvened on November 23, soon chose delegates to the Second Continental Congress and a committee to consider the actions of the First Congress. This committee, of which Warren was a leading member, naturally approved the Continental Association and other acts of that body, and urged the towns of the colony to establish inspection committees to enforce the Association. Manufacturing, including arms, powder, and saltpeter, was encouraged to offset the economic repercussions of nonintercourse. Warren served on the committee on the state of manufactures which recommended this policy, and also on one to correspond with the inhabitants of Canada and to

[39] Willard, ed., *Letters on the American Revolution,* p. 35; Frank A. Mumby, *George III and the American Revolution: The Beginnings* (Boston and New York, 1923), pp. 360, 362-363.

[40] Davidson, *Propaganda,* p. 205; Mass. Archives, Council Records, XVI, 757.

gather intelligence of that area. On December 10, this short session adjourned, noting that frequent elections were necessary to prevent endangering liberty. The Congress recommended that new elections be held for a Provincial Congress to meet at Cambridge on February 1, or earlier if members from Boston and surrounding towns felt that a crisis demanded it.[41]

The Boston delegates to the Second Provincial Congress were Thomas Cushing, Samuel Adams, John Hancock, Joseph Warren, Benjamin Church, Oliver Wendell, and John Pitts. While in attendance Warren served on the most important congressional committees and when absent was directing military preparations through the Committee of Safety, which was often ahead of the Congress in aggressive sentiment. The collecting of stores and encouragement of militia-training had been going on for some months. The Provincial Congress had even appointed general officers to command the army, and the Committee of Safety had been empowered to muster this army in certain circumstances. Yet the Province was scarcely prepared for war, militarily or mentally. Many people still shuddered at the thought of full-scale war, and important members of Congress refused to adopt vigorous measures which might provoke it. The brief meeting of the first session of the second Provincial Congress, February 1-16, 1775, marked another step on the road to Lexington. During this period, the majority in Congress gave up their faint hope of redress of grievances and concurred in Warren's policy of preparing the mind of the colony for war.

Much of the Congress' work was, of course, routine. Warren helped in devising a means of paying the delegates to the Continental Congress, including the forty-six pounds which Robert Treat Paine had "accidentally lost out of his pocket while on his journey to Philadelphia." Warren and others studied means of obtaining the vital saltpeter, and recommended that directions for its manufacture be printed and that the Congress buy all of the product made during the next year. He helped create a Committee of Correspondence for the Provincial Congress, served on a committee to consider a report from Scituate that royal troops were stationed in Marshfield, and on another to prepare an address to the people on taxes. Such work had to be done, and it was the Congress which had to do it, for the Committee of Safety

[41] Mass. Prov. Cong., *Journals*, pp. 55, 56-58, 59, 61, 62, 63-65, 73-74.

had neither the authorization nor the public recognition necessary to perform such functions.[42]

The most important action of this session of the Congress was the adoption of a firmer statement of the people's determination to fight if necessary. Such a statement was by no means unique. The colonists had declared such sentiments for months; in fact, they had done so for years, and that was the point. Declarations of their willingness to fight in defense of their rights made in June, 1774, were made with quite as little expectation of soon having to do so as were similar pledges in 1765 or 1770. Always such resolves had been accompanied by assurances of loyalty to George III and expressions of their hope that harmony would be restored. Now, in February, 1775, the horizon of war seemed much closer, the probability of conflict much greater, and the chance of Britain yielding to colonial demands much, much smaller. When the Provincial Congress admitted that there was little hope of redress, that conflict was imminent, nothing remained but to prepare to fight or admit that ten years of brave words had been gasconade.

Warren's party had an argument for adoption of this firmer policy in the troop movements conducted by Gage. In mid-December the people about Boston had been alarmed by a march of the King's Own Regiment into the country. Gage had to keep his men busy and healthy, and short marches became common in succeeding months. On February 10, alarming reports reached the Provincial Congress about a body of troops on the way to Cambridge to disperse the Congress. The Congress quickly appointed a committee to observe these troop movements, and, on the Boston side of the river, Warren and Church rushed to the ferry in a chaise "determined to share with our brethren in any dangers." The alarm proved to be false, but on the following day the Congress appointed Warren one of a seven-man committee to report a resolution setting forth the people's determination "coolly and resolutely, to support their rights and privileges, at all hazards." Warren favored such a resolution, and wanted a schooner sent to England to make it clear to the British people that the colonists were not cowards and were in earnest about defending their rights.[43]

[42] *Ibid.*, pp. 87, 88, 93, 95, 96, 98, 100.

[43] Warren to Adams, Boston, Feb. 10, 1775, Samuel Adams MSS, also printed in Frothingham, *Warren*, p. 414; Mass. Prov. Cong., *Journals*, pp. 94, 97-98.

The resolve which Congress adopted on February 15 represented the death of the Moderate faith that harmony with Britain could be restored by pledges of allegiance to the king. Warren's months of work had led a majority of the Congress to consider seriously the prospect of a civil war with the mother country. The resolve warned the people of the Bay Colony that there was little reason to hope that their grievances would be corrected. Rather, it appeared that "the sudden destruction of this colony" was intended, and the people should prepare against surprise attacks. The militia and minute companies should be readied, and the Congress pledged to purchase all arms and bayonets made in the colony.[44] Warren's policy for Suffolk County had now become the policy of Massachusetts. If Warren and Adams had their way, the colony was going to be mentally and militarily on constant alert. In view of the policy declared in this session of Congress, the legend of the colonial minuteman, with his gun beside his plow, would appear to have much truth to it. There were still men who deplored this bold policy, and there were many who worried that defensive measures might easily become an offensive war. A street fight, a tavern brawl, a march into the country—any of these might touch off the explosive situation. And in March, 1775, there was real danger of the powder keg igniting as Warren delivered an oration commemorating the Boston Massacre of 1770 in a town meeting attended by British officers.

By this time, the demands for inspired leadership made upon this young Boston doctor had become rigorous indeed. In August, 1774, his closest friends and advisors had gone to Philadelphia, leaving him to plan policy for Boston and the Bay Colony. In the absence of the Adamses and with Josiah Quincy in England, there was no intimate among the party chiefs in whom he could confide his fears. Convinced as he was that America must rule itself, Joseph Warren was not yet certain of the wisdom of leaving the Empire and establishing an independent nation. A weak policy might lose everything, and too daring a course might lead to war. Warren was called upon to head the Boston Committee of Correspondence, organize the county conventions, plan the establishment of a new government for Massachusetts, and shape a policy for America. Working through the county conventions and the

[44] *Ibid.*, pp. 101, 103.

committees of correspondence, he developed support for the Provincial Congress to govern the colony. And in his Suffolk Resolves he called upon the colony and all America to be prepared to fight a war. It was the adoption of this policy by the Continental Congress which led the English authorities to declare that Massachusetts was in a state of rebellion. But the future was laden with even more serious decisions and harder work. In April, 1775, the true temper of Joseph Warren was to receive the acid test: would he be able to make the decision that would begin the fighting and put two countries at war? Once that decision was made, there was the question of his ability, as an inexperienced executive without power, to organize a badly disciplined, ill-equipped army to win a war. Warren responded to these new demands as he had to earlier ones—with valor, vigor, and intelligence. Between April 19 and June 17, he worked unceasingly, fought courageously, and finally gave his life for the cause in which he believed.

# Crucible of War

CHAPTER IX

March 5, 1775, was a Sunday, so Warren's address in commemoration of the Boston Massacre was planned for March 6. All of Boston marked the date. John Tileston dismissed school that morning for the rest of the day. People going to the town meeting carried bludgeons with them. The town was alive with rumors of a fight or, possibly, an assassination of Warren and other leaders by the British troops. Samuel Adams foresaw being attacked in their trenches, and agreed that it was wise to have Warren, "an experienced officer in the political field," deliver the address. John Adams was anxious because of Warren's spirit and fire. He felt that some phrase might bring upon Warren "more malice and influence some dirty tool to stir up to revenge and bloodshed." Everything pointed to the possibility of a new massacre, and Warren had displayed a cool courage in volunteering to give the oration. On that tense day he nonetheless went about his professional duties and visited five patients.[1]

[1] *Boston Town Records, 1770 Through 1777,* p. 215; "Extracts from the Diary of Mr. John Tileston," New Eng. Hist. and Geneal. Soc., *Register,* XX, No.1 (Jan., 1866), p. 11; Cushing, ed., *Writings of Samuel Adams,* III, 195-196; John Adams to Samuel Savage, Boston, March 4, 1775, Samuel F. Savage MSS, II (Mass. Hist. Soc. Library).

It took courage—there could be no doubt of that. Warren was going to deliver the oration in a Boston town meeting which was illegal under the Massachusetts Government Act. He knew that a number of British officers and seamen planned to attend, and that morning the Forty-third Regiment took another of its marches into the country, which always created some alarm. He knew of the plan for a disturbance, but was unable to discover its nature and had to be prepared for anything. One rumor was that if Warren spoke against the king an officer would throw an egg at him, the signal to draw swords and assassinate the Radical chiefs.[2] What was more, General Gage had discretionary instructions for the arrest of Warren because of his role in the tea incident. It took courage, and the town knew Warren possessed that quality. But discretion was called for also, and there were many who questioned whether or not Joseph Warren's judgment would control his hot temper.

The meeting convened at 11:30 in the morning in the Old South Meeting House. Samuel Adams was moderator, and seeing some forty British officers enter, invited them to take front pews "that they might have no pretence to behave ill." Warren arrived about 12:30, and ascended the pulpit, which was draped with the black cloth that John Hancock had furnished. He put his left hand in his pocket, held a handkerchief in his right, and began his address. The troops behaved well, though there were occasional hisses, drowned out by the applause of the townspeople.[3]

Warren's oration lacked the power and skillful wording of his first address, but it was moderate only insofar as he avoided a direct attack upon the king. He excoriated the British Ministry, condemned standing armies, and evoked memories of the tragedy in King Street in what was intended as unparalleled emotionalism. Warren began by asserting that every man has a natural right to personal freedom, from which arises a right to property. But arbitrary government always attempts to deprive men of their property without their consent. Thus, in the seventeenth century, men had left England because tyranny was being established there, and had fled to a wilderness among savages. They had

---

[2] Hutchinson, *Diary and Letters,* pp. 528-529.

[3] Cushing, ed., *Writings of Samuel Adams,* III, 206; Allen French, ed., *A British Fusilier in Revolutionary Boston* (Cambridge, Mass., 1926), pp. 37-38; Wells, *Samuel Adams,* II, 278-279.

realized that even anarchy, "that bugbear held up by the tools of power," was less dangerous than despotism. Their title to the lands which they took came from purchasing them from the Indians, and they had clearly believed that King James of England had no right to grant a charter to them. These ancestors received no aid from England, either in building an economy or in defending this new country. Only when they had enriched the colony did the British Ministry become interested in it, and then only in order to despoil the people of their property in violation of their rights. Finally, an army had invaded the colony in order to force submission to this ministerial plan.[4]

Following these general historical remarks, Warren re-created the events of the evening of March 5, 1770. He called upon the widows of the slain to bring their children and behold the murdered men dying in the street. "Take heed, ye orphan babes, lest whilst your streaming eyes are fixed upon the ghastly corpse, *your feet slide on the stones bespattered with your father's brains.*" After this tragedy, Warren said, one would not have expected to see again a British army in the town of Boston. Now, however, the people once more saw troops in the streets and ships-of-war in the harbor. Knowing that liberty "is far dearer than life," they would not be intimidated by this show of force. Warren denied that independence was the aim of the colonists; rather, they desired that the two countries, like the oak and the ivy, would grow in strength together. But, if the measures of the Continental Congress did not succeed and safety could be found only "thro' fields of blood," Warren urged the people never to turn from this trial, but to fight until tyranny was defeated.[5]

Just as the oration ended, the Forty-third Regiment returned from its march and halted opposite the Old South Meeting House. Samuel Adams left the pew where he had been sitting with the selectmen, and resumed his position as moderator. He moved that the thanks of the town be extended to Warren and that an oration be delivered the following year. The British officers held up their hands in the negative, nominated persons, and finally be-

---

[4] Joseph Warren, *An Oration Delivered March Sixth, 1775* (Boston, 1775), pp. 6-12, 14. The oration was printed in the *Massachusetts Gazette* and the *Boston Post-Boy,* March 20, 1775, and Warren's manuscript of it is in the museum of the Massachusetts Historical Society.

[5] Warren, *Oration Delivered March Sixth, 1775,* pp. 15, 17, 21-22.

gan shouting and banging canes against the floor. A number of people cried "Fie! fie!" which was mistaken for a cry of fire. Confusion ensued, and some, fearing a fire or an attack by the regiment in the street, jumped out of windows. Order was restored, but following the meeting Gage forbade the exhibition and procession planned for the evening and alerted his troops.[6]

Warren's speech sounds absurd in certain passages and as a whole was mere bombast, but the call to face the possibility of war and to fight when it did come indicated the road that Warren and his friends were taking. Though he believed that accommodation might still be possible, Joseph Warren was personally prepared to fight if necessary and even to declare for independence. For him the point of no return would be a march by Gage into the country to enforce the punitive laws. If that should happen, he felt that Great Britain could "take her leave at least of the new England colonies" and perhaps of all America. Warren used his March 6 oration on the Massacre to prepare the colony for war, if that should come.[7]

The militia and minute companies had been arming and drilling for months, and the Congress had called for a census of these companies and their arms in February. Many men shared the opinion of Peter Oliver, Jr., who wrote that the "great preparations on both sides for an engagement" made hostilities very likely indeed.[8] The question was what actions would justify armed resistance, and on this men differed. They differed also on the question of whether or not Massachusetts alone should decide upon war. Warren believed that it should, trusting that the commencement of hostilities would force the other colonies to support Massachusetts. On this issue his views were far from having unanimous support. Until the Provincial Congress adjourned on April 15, a large party in the legislature fought the war policy of the Boston politicians.

[6] Barker, *British in Boston,* 25-26; Jeremy Lister, *Concord Fight,* [ed. by Harold Murdock] (Cambridge, Mass., 1931), pp. 20-21; French, ed., *British Fusilier,* pp. 38-39; Mass. Hist. Soc., *Proceedings,* XIV (1875-76), pp. 101-102; John C. Warren, *Genealogy of Warren,* pp. 72-73.

[7] Warren to Arthur Lee, Boston, Feb. 20, 1775, Lee MSS, II (1773-76), 32, also printed in Frothingham, *Warren,* pp. 418-419.

[8] Cushing, ed., *Writings of Samuel Adams,* III, 170-171; broadside, "In Provincial Congress, Cambridge, Feb. 14, 1775. Whereas it appears necessary for the Defence" (Boston Public Library); Hutchinson, *Diary and Letters,* p. 371.

Opposition developed particularly to the power of the Committee of Safety to muster the provincial forces to the defensive. Joseph Hawley thought much of this "most critical, most important, most arduous trust" following the February session of the Congress. He saw that once the soldiers were mustered the decision for war would have been made. They would assume that America had vested the decision in Massachusetts, and that the colony had given discretion to the Committee of Safety. The Committee of Safety was to summon the militia when it decided that an attempt was being made to carry the acts of Parliament into execution by force. This, wrote Hawley, was too vague a definition of the actions which would justify war, and the pledge of support by other colonies was equally vague. The resolution of the Continental Congress, which there was no evidence of the entire continent supporting, said "all of America *ought* to support" Massachusetts. The colonies ought to do so, but would they and could they? Hawley asked, "Is this a treaty offensive and defensive of sufficient precision to make us secure of the effectual aid of the other colonies in a war with Great Britain?"[9] He hoped to postpone hostilities until the Continental Congress voted to declare war. Should Massachusetts' Committee of Safety make the decision, the other colonies might well desert, and the Bay Colony would be left to its fate.

Warren, too, was interested in seeing that the colony was justified "in the sight of *God* and man" before taking up arms.[10] But all good Americans knew whose side God was on, and clever propaganda, such as Warren used to make March 5, 1770, appear a massacre, might depict the events of an April 19 as "barbarous murders" and secure the support of the other colonies. In the days following the fighting at Lexington, Warren was to prove his ability in penning propaganda that made the inhabitants appear to have been innocent victims at the "butchering hands of an inhuman soldiery." His reports, containing hardly any concrete details of the action at Lexington and Concord, led colonists from Connecticut, Rhode Island, and New Hampshire to march to Boston, and aided in getting, ex post facto, the commitment

[9] Joseph Hawley to Thomas Cushing, Northampton, Mass., Feb. 22, 1775, Mass. Prov. Cong., *Journals,* pp. 748-750.

[10] Warren to Arthur Lee, Boston, April 3, 1775, Force, *American Archives,* 4th ser. (Washington, 1839), II, 255-256.

from the other colonies that Joseph Hawley had craved. Warren was gambling, to be sure, but it was a gamble on which he worked night and day during early April in order to reduce the odds. Within the Provincial Congress, he fought for the creation of a standing army, and without he led the congressional committees in preparing the militia for action on a minute's notice.

The new session of Congress met at Concord on March 22. Financial problems still loomed large, and again the Congress asked the towns to pay their taxes, warning that collectors could no longer be indulged in their "unreasonable neglect."[11] If the members of Congress were able to agree on such policies, there were other issues of equal importance which broke them into factions. The bare resolves in the records of the Provincial Congress tell nothing of the long struggles over the questions of mustering the militia, creating a regular army, and adopting articles of war. Many of these questions were posed to the Congress by the Committee on the State of the Province, which was dominated by Warren and others who favored a bold policy. The Boston politicians' attempt to make this committee a policy-making body was indicated by the plans it brought into Congress—plans it had not been instructed to formulate.

During the last week of March, the Committee on the State of the Province held long meetings on "business of the utmost importance." This business was the drafting of a resolve for adoption by the Provincial Congress on the question of precisely what would justify calling out the militia. Even within this committee, Warren found some opposition, as the moderate members vigorously debated this and the closely related questions of the place of rendezvous for the militia and the means of giving the alarm. Many delegates in Congress followed Hawley in insisting that the other colonies pledge aid by treaties before hostilities were begun. The Congress debated the appointment of agents to confer with the other New England governments on policies to be pursued. Finally, it approved a resolve that the country should be alarmed when any body of troops with baggage and artillery should march out of Boston. In such a case, the people would "oppose their march, to the last extremity."[12] The Committee

[11] Mass. Prov. Cong., *Journals,* p. 114.

[12] *Ibid.,* p. 112; John Hancock to Dolly Quincy, Concord, Mass., March 25, 1775, Chamberlain MSS: John Hancock, p. 54; Allen French, *General Gage's Informers* (Ann Arbor, Mich., 1932), pp. 16-18.

of Safety had possessed the wider power to call the militia when an attempt was made to execute the punitive laws by force. The new resolution narrowed the committee's authority by specifying that the expedition had to include baggage and artillery, and Gage, knowing of this resolve, sent none of either with the infantry on April 18. Warren, ignoring this fact and in direct violation of this congressional resolve, which had been the result of Hawley's long struggle to limit the committee's power, sent his couriers hurrying through the night to call out the militia to begin the war. To most minds, the size of this expedition and its obvious aim of destroying the colony supplies at Concord, while not an attempt to execute the parliamentary acts, seemed to justify Warren's action. If Warren personally acted culpably by using wide discretion in interpreting the congressional resolve, Congress nevertheless had made it clear to Massachusetts that the militia should fight when the Committee of Safety mustered it, and the action on Lexington Common must be viewed as a planned, official resistance, rather than the spontaneous efforts of unorganized farmers.

Though the Congress did approve the mustering of the militia in certain circumstances, there was dissent on the proposal to establish a standing army. Warren's party found that some members had been instructed to vote for such a measure, others lacked instructions on it, and Salem decidedly opposed it.[13] A long fight was also waged on the adoption of articles of war, and by the end of March there seemed to be every possibility that the moderate faction would destroy Warren's hope of getting a full-scale army ready for action.

On April 2, Warren received a letter from Arthur Lee telling him that both houses of Parliament were supporting the king, and that re-enforcements were on the way to Gage. Warren and Adams called all of the absent members of the Provincial Congress to attend the session immediately, and Warren used the letter to arouse the members and to try to get his policies adopted. He wrote Lee that the letter had enabled him to prevent the members from falling into "that state of security into which many have endeavoured to lull them." The reading of Lee's letter caused "great consternation" in Congress, and the legislative body

[13] *Ibid.*, pp. 20-21.

approved a report on raising an army and sending delegates to seek aid from Connecticut, New Hampshire, and Rhode Island. Still there was opposition to actually putting a Massachusetts army in the field with the extraordinary expense it would involve, and on April 15 the Moderates won the majority necessary to force an adjournment until pledges of aid from the other New England colonies could be obtained. Though many delegates opposed the raising of a regular army, Congress saw the danger of relying upon untrained volunteers for artillery units, and authorized the Committee of Safety to enlist six additional companies. These men would be trained immediately, kept on active service, and paid from the colony treasury.[14]

Even before the disappointments of this session of Congress, Warren had come to depend upon the Committee of Safety to get his policies through. This body acted more vigorously than its parent, and Warren was able to develop plans there which he might not have dared to bring into the legislature. During December and January, the committee had collected all the artillery and shells available, and thereafter ordered the Committee of Supplies to purchase all necessities—powder, brimstone, beans, molasses, tents, and the like. If Warren and his friends could not get the Congress to raise a standing army, Warren could persuade his committee to acquire stores "for an army of fifteen thousand men to take the field." Warren sought artillery officers and gunners from the Boston company which had existed for some years, and investigated to see what medical supplies would be necessary for a large army. Such supplies as were acquired were stored at Concord, Stow, and Worcester, and guards were posted at them. Night watchmen were employed at Charlestown, Roxbury, and Cambridge, the three routes out of Boston, and Warren developed his corps of couriers to be sent to the towns where the magazines were located, in case the British army came out at night. He kept a close personal check on these supplies, and on April 18 the Committee of Safety ordered a general redistribution of supplies and arms to provide a balanced defense of the colony and to prevent the loss of too many supplies by a surprise raid. Warren's group directed that musket balls at Concord be buried and

[14] Warren to Arthur Lee, April 3, 1775, Force, *American Archives,* 4th ser., II, 255-256; French, *General Gage's Informers,* pp. 21-22, 23, 24, 27; Mass. Prov. Cong., *Journals,* pp. 135, 137, 141-142.

ammunition and provisions be removed to other towns. Letters summoning the militia and minutemen, to be used when the British marched, had been printed as early as Februay 23.[15]

If the Radical party was ready for war by April 19, the British Ministry was no less so. On April 14, Gage received a letter from Lord Dartmouth informing him that the home government considered Massachusetts to be in a state of rebellion and authorizing him to impose martial law. He encouraged him to arrest the principal Radical leaders, but gave Gage discretion as to that. Dartmouth's main point was that a test should be made, on this issue or any other, of the people's willingness to fight. He instructed Gage to make such a show of force that the people of Massachusetts would have to fight or submit entirely. The Ministry had decided it would be better, if there were going to be a war, that it be brought on immediately, rather than after the Americans had had time to develop a large, well-supplied army.[16] The British Ministry had ordered just the type of action which Massachusetts had agreed would justify a defensive war.

Warren kept in touch with Samuel Adams at Concord during April through messages carried by Paul Revere, and likely knew that Gage had sent two spies to map the country between Boston and Concord. Within Boston, he depended upon some thirty members of the North End caucus to observe the troop movements and gather intelligence. On April 15, Gage relieved the grenadiers and light infantry of all duties, and about midnight Warren's men saw the boats of the men-of-war launched. Warren sent Paul Revere with word of these movements to Samuel Adams, who was staying at Lexington. On his return through Charlestown, Revere arranged a signal system to warn leaders there in case the British came out of town at night. By April 18, Warren was convinced from a number of reports that an important move was planned for that night, and he contacted a spy who obtained news of Gage's intention of marching to Concord. The British troops were formed about nine in the evening, and Warren had dispatched William Dawes to ride by way of Boston Neck and Cambridge before Revere arrived at Warren's home at

[15] *Ibid.*, pp. 506-514, 516-518; Warren to Adams, Boston, Feb. 10, 1775, Samuel Adams MSS.

[16] Dartmouth to Gage, Whitehall, England, Jan. 27, 1775, Transcripts of Instructions to Provincial Governors, VIII, 2699-2706.

ten o'clock. Warren believed that Gage aimed to capture Hancock and Adams, as well as the Concord supply depot, and urged Revere to cross by boat to Charlestown and ride to Lexington to warn his friends there. Warren had declared in his Suffolk Resolves that the people should defend all patriot leaders, and the Congress had ordered the Committee of Safety to muster the militia when Gage marched out of Boston. Talking with Revere late on the evening of April 18, Warren realized that the time had come to act. At that moment the decision of war or peace presented itself to him as clearly as it ever does to any man, and Warren instructed Revere to arouse the militia on his ride to Lexington, the step which he was virtually certain would mean war before sunrise. Knowing his own personal danger, Warren did nothing to escape until the following morning.[17]

The Provincial Congress, after long debate and careful consideration of the question, had resolved that the mustering of the colony's military forces would be done by a vote of the Committee of Safety. Warren, the only Radical leader left in Boston, was unable to contact his fellow committee members on April 18, and made this decision alone, in direct violation of the congressional resolution, which had been specifically designed to prevent Warren and the other Boston members from taking this final step rashly. The Committee of Safety met in Cambridge that evening, and did send word to Lexington of an advance party of British officers which had been seen on the road. However, it was Warren's much more alarming message that a large body of troops had left Boston which alerted the Massachusetts countryside.

[17] Barker, *British in Boston*, p. 29; Paul Revere to Jeremy Belknap, Boston, Jan. 1, 1798, Mass. Hist. Soc., *Proceedings*, XVI (1878), 371-374; Sparks, ed., "Diary by Thomas Newell," pp. 85-86; Holland, *William Dawes*, pp. 9, 35-36; Forbes, *Paul Revere*, p. 252; Richard Frothingham, *The Alarm on the Night of April 18, 1775* ([Boston, 1876]), pp. 3-4. Revere said Warren instructed him to warn Adams and Hancock, but adds that he aroused the countryside. It is, of course, possible that Revere notified the militiamen on his own initiative, but it seems a fair supposition that Warren instructed him to do so. Jonas Clarke, writing within a year of the battle at a date much nearer the events than Revere's letter, was struck by Warren's warning that the British army was coming to destroy the stores at Concord, rather than his warning to Hancock and Adams. The tone of Clarke's account gives the impression that Warren's message was a general alarm to the countryside, rather than only a personal message to Adams. Also, Revere did try to go on to Concord to warn the minutemen there. Jonas Clarke, *Opening of the War of the Revolution, 19th of April, 1775* (Lexington, Mass., 1901), p. 3.

From Charlestown to Concord, his colleagues, who had sat in the Provincial Congress and knew that word of such a march was the signal for war, worked throughout the night, mustering men in towns along the British route. The fact that resistance was not made until the British reached the town of Lexington probably was not fortuitous. Samuel Adams was in Lexington, and he and Joseph Warren were of one mind on the question of opposing Gage's march. That Samuel Adams did nothing, during that long night of waiting for the redcoats to appear, to arouse the militia and confer with the officers on the stand to be taken is too much for human credibility. Thus, the Massachusetts militia was rallied by Warren and Adams, without a full vote of the Committee of Safety, and the decision which Joseph Hawley had dreaded was made. There was to be no declaration of war by a Continental Congress or defensive treaty with other colonies before the fighting began.

The British troops had a hard day's work ahead when, after wading through swamps and slips of the sea, they finally began their march toward Lexington about two in the morning. Except for the capture of men sent from Lexington to check on the movement, the march was an uneventful tramping in wet boots along the dark road. Lieutenant Colonel Smith ordered Major Pitcairn forward with six companies to secure the bridge at Concord. As this advance party approached Lexington Common, dawn was just breaking, and Pitcairn saw the militia company assembled and a number of armed spectators scattered about. Unable to leave this body in the rear of his march to Concord, he ordered them to lay down their arms and disperse. Some of them began running off with their arms, and the British troops broke ranks and went shouting after them. A general exchange of fire began and a number of Americans were killed.

By the time the British reorganized and marched to Concord, militia and minutemen from several towns had gathered there, and the Americans had much the better of the fight at the North Bridge. Still, the British were able to execute a part of their aim, the destruction of stores and artillery, before beginning their return march. Sporadic fire was maintained against them, and their ammunition was becoming depleted by the time they met Lord Percy's re-enforcement at Lexington. Percy, taking command now, chased off the provincials by firing the two field pieces he had brought from Boston, and rested the troops who had been on the march for more than twelve hours and had fought two engagements. Percy used his fresh troops to bring up the rear when he moved out about three in the afternoon, but the American militia, now arriving from several miles away, made the march to Charlestown a five-hour nightmare of sniping from houses, trees, and fences.[18]

Joseph Warren left Boston at dawn on April 19, several hours before Percy came out with his re-enforcements. It was cool, windy weather as Warren crossed to Charlestown in a boat with Isaiah Thomas, printer of the *Massachusetts Spy*. By ten in the morning, he had news of the engagement at Lexington, and rode hastily out of Charlestown toward the scene of the action. For a short distance, a medical colleague rode with him. At Watson's Corner, they found two soldiers trying to steal a horse, the old man who owned it pulling one way and the soldiers the other. Warren drove them off and continued on toward Lexington, but ran directly into the rear of Lord Percy's columns. He tried to pass the British army, but was stopped by bayonets and narrowly escaped capture when two officers, who fortunately did not recognize him, rode up and asked where the troops were. Warren claimed not to know, and went off on a crossroad to get around Percy's force. On this road he fortunately met William Heath, a Roxbury friend with some military experience. Heath, "very corpulent and bald-headed" as he described himself, did good work that day. He had already sent men to take up the planks of the Cambridge bridge and barricade the far end of it in case Percy should return by the route he had taken out of Boston. Now the two men worked together to organize the unconnected militia and minute companies into a coherent resistance.[19]

Warren and Heath managed to get around the British and reached the militia at Lexington just after Percy made contact with Colonel Smith's retreating men. They found the American forces disorganized and temporarily terrorized by the British

[18] Lister, *Concord Fight,* p. 30; *General Gage's Instructions of 22nd February 1775* (Boston, 1779), pp. 18-19; French, ed., *British Fusilier,* pp. 50-55.

[19] Thomas, *History of Printing,* I, 169; Harold Murdock, *The Nineteenth of April, 1775* (Boston, 1923), p. 55 and note; petition of Jacob Rogers, Cambridge, Mass., Oct. 10, 1775, Richard Frothingham, *History of the Seige of Boston* (Boston, 1851), p. 371; Frothingham, *Warren,* pp. 457-458; William Heath, *Memoirs of Major-General Heath* (Boston, 1798), pp. 7, 12-13.

artillery fire. Warren and Heath tried, as best they could, to form a rough regiment from the scattered troops during the hour or two that Percy rested his men.[20] Warren appeared on the field as the leading member of the Committee of Safety, the body which had full authority to order and dispose of the militia, and may well have made the decision to harass the British army all the way back to Boston. Insofar as any order was brought out of the confused mass of men and any organized tactical direction given, Warren and Heath were responsible for both.

Warren pursued the British back along the road to Boston, and at Menotomy he and Heath managed to bring the hottest fire of the day to bear upon the enemy. The long street of the town was lined with houses from which the Americans maintained a crossfire. Percy's supply of artillery shells was exhausted, but a number of Americans were caught in houses between the main body and the flanking column and were bayoneted. The Americans had no bayonets for hand-to-hand fighting, and half the American casualties of the day occurred near Menotomy. Warren and Heath were in the thick of the fight, exposing themselves to heavy gunfire as they entered the town and on an open area near the meeting house. At one point, a British musket ball knocked a pin out of the lock of hair that Warren wore near the ear. After passing through Menotomy, Percy wisely decided to head for Charlestown rather than the Cambridge bridge, and altogether did fine work in bringing his men nearly fifteen miles from Lexington to the safety of Bunker Hill. There, after twenty-four hours without sleep, several hours without drink, and a forty-mile march, Colonel Smith's troops threw themselves down at eight in the evening. Warren and Heath stopped on Charlestown Common, and, seeing the strength of the British position, turned the militia back to rest in Cambridge.[21]

The initial alarm of the British expedition, sent by Warren, was followed by a hastily scribbled message after the action at

---

[20] *Ibid.*, p. 14; Arthur B. Tourtellot, *William Diamond's Drum: The Beginning of the War of the American Revolution* (Garden City, N.Y., 1959), p. 194.

[21] Heath, *Memoirs*, p. 14; [Harold Murdock, ed.], *Late News of the Excursions and Ravages of the King's Troops on the Nineteenth of April, 1775* (Cambridge, Mass., 1927), p. 24; *General Gage's Instructions*, pp. 19-20; Bolton, ed., *Letters of Hugh Earl Percy*, p. 50; Murdock, *Nineteenth of April, 1775*, pp. 95-96.

Lexington. Joseph Palmer, a member of the Committee of Safety, made no direct call for troops in the note he wrote at Watertown on the morning of April 19, but it served quite as well. The message was carried south by riders, and troops began their march from Connecticut and Rhode Island, and from New Hampshire to the north, toward Boston. This skirmish need not have been the beginning of an eight-year war; there was still a possibility of peace. At an important meeting of militia officers in Cambridge on April 20, however, the formation of plans for an army to fight a full-scale war was discussed. Warren was the leader in promoting this design, which appeared "new and unexpected" to the leader of the Salem militia, who argued that the engagement did not make a war inevitable. Warren's participation in the battle made him the hero of the hour and gave him an influence such as no other man in the colony could command. Since the Provincial Congress was not in session, Warren was able to use his personal popularity and his position of dominance on the Committee of Safety to organize the regular army which many in Congress had opposed. He set up a makeshift headquarters at Cambridge, and, as a semiofficial commander-in-chief, directed the generals in the work of organizing the army. On April 21, his Committee of Safety voted to raise an army of 8,000 men to serve for seven months, and asked the general officers to make returns of those in the militia who might be taken into the Massachusetts army. Thus was the decision made not to disperse the militia but to pen the British army in Boston by a seige operation that was to last nearly a year.[22]

The first days following the battle were filled with confusion and feverish activity for Warren and his generals at Cambridge. They sent out a company to bury the dead, and began makeshift arrangements to care for the wounded at the Vassal mansion. Warren personally was concerned with seeing that the prisoners received good medical care, and doubtless was responsible for ordering officers of the guard to treat them "in the kindest manner, and procure good surgeons to attend the wounded." On April 21, he wrote Gage a letter pledging that his men had been

[22] MS copy of Joseph Palmer's message (Mass. Hist. Soc. Library); John H. Scheide, "The Lexington Alarm," Amer. Antiq. Soc., *Proceedings,* n.s., L, Part 1 (April, 1940), 59-60, 62; photostat, statement of Timothy Pickering, Windham, Mass., June 26, 1807, Warren MSS, Ia; Mass. Prov. Cong., *Journals,* pp. 519-520, 521.

"treated in every respect with much humanity," and a British surgeon sent to treat them would receive a safe conduct. One lieutenant was near death, and Warren, anxious to do everything possible "to gratify the unhappy gentleman," assured Gage that the adjutant might be sent from Boston to see the prisoner. Troops were arriving hourly in the town, and Warren worked with his general officers in assigning them to positions along the defensive lines, which were quickly erected in Cambridge and Roxbury to block Gage in Boston. Many inhabitants had fled Cambridge, and Warren had to see that measures were taken to prevent looting of property. A summons had to be sent to the scattered members of the Provincial Congress and arrangements made for their sitting.[23] And, in the confusion of it all, Warren saw that fuller accounts of the battle and requests for aid were forwarded to the other colonies.

Warren recognized at once the propaganda value of the Lexington engagement in rallying public sentiment and achieving unity in Massachusetts and throughout America. Also, there was a permanent army to establish, and he perceived the use which might be made of the action on April 19 in stimulating enlistments and raising troops. In writing his propaganda, Warren had a good starting point in his personal belief that the British had fired the first shot. In the margin of a broadside account of the battle, he wrote, "The people say the troops fired first and I believe they did." Many people, in fact, charged that Gage had given Colonel Smith orders to shoot first. Warren expressed his personal opinion, privately, that Gage was deceived by officers and Tories into believing that the Americans had begun hostilities.[24] His own conviction that the British had fired first gave Warren's propaganda a sincerity and a tone of genuine outrage which gained wide credence for his version of the affair. Not only people in his own day, but also Americans for generations to

[23] "Orderly Book of Colonel William Henshaw," Mass. Hist. Soc., *Proceedings,* XV (1876-77), 88-89; Batchelder, "Harvard Hospital-Surgeons of 1775," pp. 501-502; Mass. Prov. Cong., *Journals,* p. 147, note 1; Warren to Gage, Cambridge, Mass., April 21, 30, 1775, Gage MSS: American Series, CXXVII.

[24] Broadside, "A Circumstantial Account of . . . 19th of April 1775," with marginal comment by Warren (Mass. Hist. Soc. Library); Warren to Arthur Lee, Cambridge, Mass., May 16, 1775, Lee MSS, II, also in Frothingham, *Warren,* pp. 488-490.

come saw the action on Lexington Common as a massacre of innocent yeomen by the troops of a tyrannous king, and the propaganda written by Joseph Warren in the two weeks following the battle was largely responsible for this conception. His broadside appeal to the towns of Massachusetts for troops, following the "barbarous murders of our innocent brethren," is an example of his propaganda at its best. He warned that it was imperative that an army be raised immediately "to defend our wives and children from the butchering hands of an inhuman soldiery," which would "ravage this devoted country with fire and sword." The note of immediacy and the emotional fervor of this message flowed from the sincere indignation of a young idealist:[25]

> We conjure you, therefore, by all that is dear, by all that is sacred, that you give all assistance possible in forming an army: our all is at stake. Death and devestation are the certain consequences of delay, every moment is infinitely precious, an hour lost may deluge your country in blood, and entail perpetual slavery upon the few of your posterity, who may survive the carnage. We beg and entreat, as you will answer it to your country, to your consciences, and above all as you will answer to God himself, that you will hasten and encourage by all possible means, the inlistment of men to form the army....

In the days immediately following the battle, Warren sent the first specific appeals for troops to the other New England colonies, writing in a tone of equal urgency and fire. His first letter of April 23 assured the Connecticut governor that the British troops had fired "without any provocation," and begged aid "to save our country from absolute slavery." Acutely aware as he was of the shortage of everything from food to arms at Cambridge, he pleaded that Connecticut send ample supplies with its troops. One day later, he reported to Connecticut and New Hampshire the "slaughter of the innocent inhabitants" and the British retreat, which had been marked by "depredations, ruins and butcheries, hardly to be match'd by the armies of any civiliz'd nation on the globe." Boston, Warren said, was shut up and "the miserable inhabitants pent up there with a licentious soldiery." He informed both colonies of a plan Gage had to destroy the other New England colonies as well as Massachusetts. Massachusetts' Provincial Congress had voted to raise 13,600 men, and Warren

[25] Broadside, "Gentlemen, The barbarous murders," Watertown, Mass., April 30, 1775 (Mass. Hist. Soc. Library).

urged the other New England colonies to bring the total force to 30,000.[26]

Actually, some people in the other colonies still questioned the decisions for war and creation of a large New England army. James Sullivan, sent to New Hampshire to secure aid, was politely received, but he found some opposition to sending troops to Massachusetts. Despite Warren's urgent appeals to Connecticut for aid, that colony sent delegates to confer with Gage about an armistice. Warren met with these agents, William Samuel Johnson and Oliver Wolcott, after their conference with the general, and wrote in alarm to Governor Trumbull. "We fear," he said, "that our brethren of Connecticut are not even yet convinced of the cruel designs of Administration against America. . . . No business but that of war is either done or thought of in this colony. . . . Our only relief now must arise from driving General Gage with his troops out of the country. . . ." Trumbull assured Warren that he need not fear Connecticut's firmness in the common cause, and expressed his hope that the embassy to Gage had not created difficulties.[27]

While engaged in these propaganda activities and convening the Provincial Congress as its new president, Warren was also planning his most masterly stroke of all. He saw the importance almost at once of the question of who had fired the first shot on Lexington Common, and wanted to get his account of the fight to England as quickly as possible. If his version beat Gage's accounts of the skirmish, he might do much to embarrass the North Ministry and rally public opinion to the American side. The Congress appointed a committee to take depositions from witnesses of the action, another to draw up an account of it, and a third, headed by Warren, to write a letter to Benjamin Franklin and an address to the people of Great Britain. In his address, Warren swore that the British troops had fired first upon the inhabitants at both Lexington and Concord, and represented the

[26] "Letters of John Hancock, Joseph Warren, Thomas Gage, James Warren and Governor Trumbull," Mass. Hist. Soc., *Collections,* 5th ser., X (Boston, 1888), 284, 286; Massachusetts Provincial Congress to the Colony of New Hampshire, Watertown, Mass., April 23, 1775, Sparks MSS: New England Papers, 355 (Houghton Library), also printed in Force, *American Archives,* 4th ser., II, 378.

[27] James Sullivan to Warren, Exeter, N.H., April 25, 1775, Force, *American Archives,* 4th ser., II, 393; "Letters of John Hancock, Joseph Warren . . . and Governor Trumbull," pp. 287, 296-297, 301-303.

affair as an inhuman butchery. On their retreat, the British troops had burned houses, shot old men, and driven women in childbed naked into the streets. Warren warned that his countrymen would not tamely submit to persecution and tyranny, and, appealing to Heaven for the justice of their cause, were determined to die or be free. He placed the blame for the mother-country's cruel program upon the Ministry, rather than the king, and prayed that the British people would repudiate this policy. His letter to Franklin asked that the accounts be printed and distributed throughout England and, particularly, be given to the lord mayor and council of London. Franklin was urged to assure the people that the colonists would sell their liberty "only at the price of their lives."[28]

The Congress chartered a special packet to carry the news to England, a plan which Warren had favored after the Boston Massacre, and he issued orders for the sailing of the *Quero* of Salem, with John Derby as captain. Warren instructed Derby to make for an Irish port and then cross to England to escape cruisers in the channel, keeping Warren's orders "a profound secret from every person on earth." The *Quero,* sailing in ballast, left four days after the *Sukey,* the dispatch ship which carried Gage's accounts, but arrived in England on May 28, nearly two weeks before her rival. The following day Derby delivered Warren's messages, the depositions, and copies of the *Salem Gazette* to the lord mayor. The publication of the news was so embarrassing to the Ministry that, it was said, one of the cabinet members actually went to church and offered prayers for the arrival of the *Sukey*. Thomas Hutchinson was wise enough to digest the American accounts with more than a grain of salt, but Dartmouth sent lamentations to Gage on the slowness of the dispatch service and the financial world watched the stocks nervously. When the *Sukey* did arrive, the Ministry could counter Warren's story of how the fight had begun, but was hard put to soften the impression he had made of a rout with significant casualties.[29]

---

[28] *Ibid.,* pp. 148, 154-156; Warren to Benjamin Franklin, Watertown, Mass., April 26, 1775, Seventy-Six Society MSS (Mass. Hist. Soc. Library), also printed in Force, *American Archives,* 4th ser., II, 488.

[29] Mass. Prov. Cong., *Journals,* p. 159 and note; Robert S. Rantoul, "The Cruise of the 'Quero': How We Carried the News to the King," Essex Institute, *Historical Collections,* XXXVI, No. 1 (Jan., 1900), 5, 6-7, 9-10, 13; Carter, ed., *Correspondence of Gage,* II, 199.

When Joseph Warren called the Provincial Congress to order on April 23, that body was faced with as serious a decision as any government had ever been confronted with in the British colonies. The Continental Congress was not to meet until May 10, and the Massachusetts Congress had no constitutional standing. The men of the Bay Colony could appeal to no higher authority on the issues of establishing an army or assuming full government, much less the profound question of war or peace. The first day of its meeting the legislature voted to raise an army of 13,600 men and to send delegates to the other New England colonies, thus ratifying Warren's decision, already approved by his Committee of Safety, to develop a standing army to fight Gage. During the remaining days of April, the Congress heard a report from the treasurer—money was needed badly now—and adopted resolutions on reorganizing regiments, appointing army engineers, impressing horses, and obtaining powder, artillery, and other essentials.[30]

Several towns petitioned the Provincial Congress for powder, and it ordered towns with adequate supplies to sell part of their powder to those which had none. The Congress instructed the Committee of Supplies to appeal to Connecticut and Rhode Island and to purchase all military stores necessary. The beginnings of an administrative system for the revolutionary government were made in the authorization given this committee to employ as many assistants as necessary. Warren, after convening the Provincial Congress, spent much of his time with the Committee of Safety. Looking to his duties as chairman of this important body, he occasionally failed to answer communications from the Congress. On April 30, Warren ignored two messages, while the legislature sat idle all morning awaiting his reply before sending a peremptory third note demanding an answer. John Murray acted as president of the Congress in Warren's place until May 2, when that body, having failed to get James Warren to accept the chair temporarily, wrote Joseph Warren, asking that he attend his duties as president.[31]

Actually the Committee of Safety appeared to be more important than the Congress in many ways, and Warren's leadership of

[30] Mass. Prov. Cong., *Journals,* pp. 148-149, 150, 151, 152, 153, 157, 165.
[31] *Ibid.,* pp. 157-158, 165, 172-173, 178.

the committee was as essential as his attendance in the Congress. It was as head of the committee that he had alarmed the countryside on April 18, and many of the congressional resolves, such as that creating a regular army, were only ratifications of actions already taken by Warren's committee. After Lexington, the committee maintained a general oversight of the organization of the army at Cambridge, directed the Committee of Supplies in many of its activities, and increasingly became a policy-making body. The troops, whose very numbers were unknown, had to be housed, fed, and supplied with arms and ammunition. Many men had come without rations, extra clothing, bedding, or so much as saying farewell to their families. These men wanted to return home and the Committee of Safety had to get the towns to send replacements. It saw that Dr. Isaac Foster had beds, bedding, and food for the hospital, and arranged for teams and wagons to transport to Cambridge those supplies at Concord that had escaped destruction. Warren took a census of the artillery in the colony—only twenty-three pieces, many of which were light and lacking shells. Many of these plans stemmed directly from Warren, and he conferred closely with the generals, planning troop disposition and general strategy. As early as April 23, he was contemplating an attack upon the British entrenchments at Boston Neck.[32]

In the eighteenth century, military intelligence work was usually directly under the commander of the army, and it was thus natural that Warren assumed direction of this activity in his position as head of the Committee of Safety. He heard of a rider carrying a mail pouch to Gage, and ordered John Thomas, commander at Roxbury, to search all travelers on the road to Boston. On the evening of April 22, at a meeting of the Committee of Safety, Benjamin Church startled those present by declaring that he intended to go into Boston to see what he could learn of enemy plans. Warren had often had doubts about this medical colleague of his. Now he stared, asked Church whether or not he was serious, and pointed out that he might well be hanged if he attempted it. Church was determined, however, and Warren decided to take advantage of this mission to smuggle out knives and medicines

[32] *Ibid.*, pp. 171, 522, 527, 529; Massachusetts Committee of Safety to the Towns of Massachusetts, Cambridge, Mass., April 29, 1775, Force, *American Archives*, 4th ser., II, 447; Jeremy Belknap to his wife, Cambridge, Mass., April 23, 1775, Belknap MSS (Mass. Hist. Soc. Library).

for his surgeons. Warren did not live long enough to learn that Church conferred privately with Gage the next day, beginning a more serious type of collaboration than his prewar scribbling for the Conservative party. His later activities were to lead to his trial and conviction as a traitor and to banishment from the country aboard a ship which disappeared at sea. Eventually a system was worked out for slipping men in and out of Boston disguised as fishermen—men more reliable than Benjamin Church. Gage had scarcely laid plans for fortifying Dorchester Heights and Bunker Hill before Warren had news of them.[33]

Such activities properly fell within the authority of the Committee of Safety, but Warren also assumed for it other functions for the execution of which no other department existed. Most important, he made of it a policy-forming body that shaped many of the plans adopted by the Provincial Congress. On April 28, it voted to recommend to the Congress that it prevent the towns from obeying Gage's precepts for a meeting of the General Court. Warren had opposed the recognition of Gage and other royal officials and had favored the assumption of full government by the Province for some months. On these issues and most others, he was the most influential member of the Committee of Safety in determining policy, and then used his position as president and leading member of the Congress to get the committee's recommendations adopted. How he was able to win majority support for his policies when Joseph Hawley was in opposition, a feat which Samuel Adams could seldom execute in the General Court, remains a mystery. A large part of the answer may have laid in his warm, friendly personality, for Warren's graciousness was known to have won some support where Samuel Adams' cold reserve had failed. Warren also expressed for the Committee of Safety its sentiments regarding a letter from Lord Dartmouth to the other colonies, and headed a subcommittee to consider the state of the town of Boston.[34] The latter subject was of particular concern to Warren, whose children were still in Boston, and he personally developed and persuaded the Congress to adopt the cautious policy on evacuation which was pursued.

---

[33] Massachusetts Committee of Safety to John Thomas, Cambridge, Mass., April 29, 1775, Thomas MSS (Mass. Hist. Soc. Library); Mass. Hist. Soc., *Proceedings,* XVI (1878), 374-375; French, *General Gage's Informers,* pp. 117, 169-170.

[34] Mass. Prov. Cong., *Journals,* pp. 525, 526.

The story of the agreement between Thomas Gage and the Boston selectmen to allow the townspeople to remove from the town, if the Provincial Congress would permit people to enter Boston from the country, speaks well of the high sense of honor and integrity of Joseph Warren. On his part, he observed the complete spirit of the agreement, while the accusation that Gage broke faith has some truth to it. On April 20, Warren wrote Gage, suggesting that much suffering might be avoided if the two sides could rely upon the good faith of each other in any agreements which might be made. He promised, "As far as my influence goes, every thing which can reasonably be required of us to do, shall be done, and every thing promised shall be religiously performed." He urged that as many wagons as were available be allowed into Boston to remove the personal effects of the people who wished to evacuate. Gage refused to answer this letter to avoid recognizing any authority in Warren, and negotiated with the selectmen of Boston instead. A town committee, headed by James Bowdoin, conferred with the general, who asked the committee to write Warren to use his influence in permitting royal supporters to enter Boston.[35]

Warren encouraged the selectmen to sign an agreement, though the men who came out would have to lodge their arms with the selectmen and promise not to engage in any attack which might be made upon Boston. There was talk of assaulting the British fortification at Boston Neck by pushing bundles of wet hay in advance of the troops, and Warren seems to have desired a speedy evacuation partly for this reason. Many, however, opposed the agreement—many who were not captives in Boston. Jeremy Belknap compared it to the offer of Rome to the Carthaginians—safety if they would deliver up their arms—but they "were not such fools as to comply." When the subject came before Congress, James Warren and others did not favor the proposal, but Joseph Warren's persuasive arguments and charming personality carried the day. James Warren "voted for it more to gratifie my friend Warren, than from any other motive." In any case, Warren had already committed the Province to this policy before he brought it up in Congress. Aside from his desire to clear the town before

[35] Warren to Gage, Cambridge, Mass., April 20, 1775, *ibid.*, p. 519, note; "Boyle's Journal of Occurrences," pp. 11-12.

attacking Gage's army, Warren was seriously concerned about the people in Boston; even the British would soon be reduced to salt provisions and there might be no food for the townspeople. Warren turned his own gun in to the selectmen, and saw that the Americans observed the agreement, even after Gage had reneged on his promise that the inhabitants might take their effects out of town.[36]

Warren received a copy of the agreement which had been made on April 23, and urged the town committee to aid the poor in evacuation by using the money which had been received by the Committee on Donations. He promised that Loyalists would be allowed to pass into Boston unmolested. Congress circulated a broadside announcing the agreement and specified locations in Charlestown and Roxbury where those wishing to enter Boston could obtain passes. Another proclamation urged the towns of the colony to receive and aid the poor who were evacuating the town. The Congress, early in May, resolved that those who chose to remain in Boston be allowed to send into the country for their effects, another reflection of Warren's humane policy on this question. Some of the army officers thought such compassion absurd, and harassed the Loyalists who passed through American lines. Warren refused to tolerate either this persecution or disobedience by the military of the colony's civil authorities, a danger which worried him deeply. The Congress ordered that the army execute its resolves "without any levity, or indecency of expression or behavior." Yet in May, Lady Frankland was insulted and obstructed in removing to Boston, and one man was brought before Congress to answer for his conduct. Warren "gently admonished" him and informed him "that the Congress were determined to preserve their dignity and power over the military." He named a congressional committee to search Lady Frankland's goods, and furnished a guard of six men to escort the poor soul to town. Warren personally visited the wife of his friend Francis Dana, who was in England, and offered her and Judge Edmund

[36] Warren to Boston Selectmen, Cambridge, Mass., April 22, 1775, Gage MSS: American Series, CXXVII, also printed in Force, *American Archives,* 4th ser., II, 374; Jeremy Belknap to his wife, Cambridge, Mass., April 23, 1775, Belknap MSS; *Warren-Adams Letters,* I, 48; Boston. *A Volume of Records Relating to the Early History of Boston, Containing Miscellaneous Papers* (Boston, 1900), p. 329.

Trowbridge, at whose house she was staying, a letter to protect them in moving.[37]

Warren did more than could be expected in living up to the agreement, and his good faith was doubly honorable during those tense days. Party enmities had not subsided; feeling, in fact, ran higher against the Conservatives who cast their lot with their king than it did against the British troops. James Abercrombie compared it to the time of Cromwell, and believed that were there "not a red coat in the country they would cut one anothers throat." One British officer, who had no love for the "rebels," wrote with great pity of the poor quitting the town, not knowing where to go and facing possible starvation.[38]

As more passes were denied by Gage, even Warren lost hope. He served on a committee to make a "spirited application" to Gage on his treatment of the inhabitants, and he sent a secret letter to Gage pleading that the general abide by the agreement. Gage had refused to correspond with the Provincial Congress or its president, but Warren asked that he not sacrifice the peace of Britain and the colonies for the sake of formalities. Warren wrote that the people would not suffer the agreement to be violated without taking revenge, and appealed to Gage's humanity and conscience to honor the treaty. In a postscript, Warren vowed that no other person knew or would ever know that he had written, an invitation for the British commander to write directly to him in complete confidence. Warren also asked Samuel Adams in Philadelphia to propose a remonstrance to Gage from the Continental Congress, and even suggested that all royal officials in the colonies be seized and held until Gage released the Bostonians. By May 20, the Provincial Congress had decided to retaliate. It prohibited Loyalists still in the country from taking anything but furniture and clothing into Boston, and warned the people against taking deeds or leases on the property of mandamus councilors. Further, the people were to prevent Loyalists from leaving the

[37] Force, *American Archives,* 4th ser., II, 424; copy, Warren to Boston Selectmen, Cambridge, Mass., April 24, 1775, Warren MSS, II; broadside, "Whereas an agreement has been made," Watertown, Mass., April 30, 1775 (Boston Public Library); Mass. Prov. Cong., *Journals,* pp. 142-143, 176-177, 183-184, 195, 238, 239; *Sibley's Harvard Graduates, 1726-1730,* VIII, 519.

[38] Abercrombie to Cadwallader Colden, Boston, May 2, 1775, Mass. Hist. Soc., *Proceedings,* XXXI (April, 1897), 306; Barker, *British in Boston,* pp. 42, 44.

country without permission of the local committee of correspondence.[39]

The use of committees of correspondence, committees of safety and inspection, and the selectmen of the towns was the only method by which the Congress could hope to enforce its resolves. Lacking constitutional standing and executive officers, the revolutionary government had to rely upon local government. As early as April 12, the Provincial Congress had recommended that all towns appoint committees of correspondence and committees of safety to see that its plans, and those of the Continental Congress, were executed. It urged the people to aid these local bodies in "suppressing the efforts of the enemies of America," and in May ordered local authorities to impose stricter controls on people who were unsympathetic to the American cause.[40]

Increasingly, the need for courts also became clear. The Congress, and the Committee of Safety on several occasions, sat as courts of inquiry, but were unable to impose sentences. Joseph Warren headed the three-man committee which heard witnesses against one of his former students, Nathaniel Bond of Marblehead, who was accused of being unfriendly to the colony. Warren's committee found the young doctor to be a friend of American liberties, though imprudent at times, and recommended him to the good will of his countrymen. When the decision went against a defendant, the Congress ordered him confined to the jail in Concord, until the further decision of this or a future Congress was known. Joseph Hawley, the best lawyer in Congress, headed a committee to investigate the problems posed by the lack of a court system. On May 27, 1775, he recommended the establishment of a permanent court of inquiry to hear charges of treason and breaches of the public peace and security. Judgments would be based on the laws of the colony and "those of reason and equity."[41]

---

[39] Mass. Prov. Cong., *Journals*, pp. 208, 212-213, 245, 249, 546, 551; Warren to Gage, Cambridge, Mass., May 10, 1775, Gage MSS: American Series, CXXVIII, also printed in Force, *American Archives*, 4th ser., II, 798; *id.* to Samuel Adams, Cambridge, Mass., May 14, 17, 1775, Samuel Adams MSS, also printed in Frothingham, *Warren*, pp. 483-485; broadside, "Whereas some of the inhabitants of this colony," Watertown, Mass., May 15, 1775 (Boston Public Library).

[40] Broadside, "WHEREAS the preservation of our country from slavery," Concord, Mass., April 12, 1775 (Boston Public Library); Mass. Prov. Cong., *Journals*, pp. 139, 205, 226-227; broadside, "Whereas there are divers persons," Watertown, Mass., May 8, 1775 (Boston Public Library).

[41] Mass. Prov. Cong., *Journals*, pp. 212, 262, 315-317, 555.

Joseph Warren had fought for the establishment of a full government in Massachusetts for some months. In November and December, 1774, he and his party friends raised the question in the First Provincial Congress but "the hot leaders," as Gage called the group, could not "bring the majority into their schemes." Again in February, they suggested that the Congress choose a governor, but this proposal was defeated.[42] The need for government became frighteningly apparent after April 19. Aside from the vexing question of organizing the army, the problems of finance, of preserving the public peace, and of maintaining civil control of the military were extremely trying. Warren foresaw the troops plundering the people unless something were done, and desired that all steps possible be taken to combat those things which were weakening the respect for right and wrong, "more especially with regard to property." Few laws were necessary, he felt, but there had to be vigorous punishments for violations of those which were enacted. He denied that he was "a little angry" with the people or had a lower opinion of them than formerly. As with all people, when they got arms they began to feel superior to the civil government. The plundering of property had begun against those enemies who had refused aid to the men who had come to Cambridge on April 19-20, with little but the clothes on their backs. It was now becoming infectious, and Warren hoped that swift action would be taken to create a full, constitutional government in Massachusetts.[43]

Warren's fears were not entirely the groundless anxieties of an eighteenth-century mind confronted with vague talk of distributing private property. Somebody in Cambridge, pretending to act under General Ward's orders to search for arms, was committing a string of robberies. Raids on the liquor cellars of deserted homes added further to the disorders of the town. Also, many among the military had a contempt for the Congress and its doings. Soldiers on guard duty stopped congressmen, and passes had to be issued to them. When the Congress heard charges against a militia colonel and refused to commission him in the army, a spectator remarked, "By God, if this province is to be governed in this

[42] Boston Public Library, *Bulletin*, X, No. 4, Whole No. 87 (Jan., 1892), 319-320; Carter, ed., *Correspondence of Gage*, I, 387, 393.

[43] Warren to Adams, Cambridge, Mass., May 26, 1775, Samuel Adams MSS, also printed in Frothingham, *Warren*, pp. 495-496.

manner, it is time for us to look out, and 'tis all owing to the committee of safety, a pack of sappy-head-fellows. I know three of them myself." General Ward complained so to the Congress about the Committee of Supplies that the members of the committee remonstrated about "such ungenerous treatment." Warren, caught in the middle of a fight between the same committee and the commissary, had to use every bit of diplomacy he possessed to extract an apology from the committee in order not to lose his commissary. On May 18, the Congress appointed a committee to bring in a resolve that no army officers be elected to the Congress, hoping thereby to check the growing power of the military.[44]

A further problem, which probably could be solved only by a constitutional government, was the need for money, which became crucial after April 19. The Massachusetts Congress resorted to everything short of that interesting device of renting out the navy which the Texas Republic used many years later. Warren accepted a gift of $420 from Philadelphia intended to relieve the poor of Boston, and Congress was delighted to receive a £500 loan from a gentleman at Salem. A congressional committee was sent to confer with the import master to see if he had any colony money, but found that he had diverted the duties to pay for oil for the lighthouses. On May 3, Congress directed the receiver general to issue bonds to the sum of £100,000, payable at 6 per cent interest on June 1, 1777. Warren was one of the committee that chose Paul Revere to engrave a plate and print off the securities. This plan, though the bonds sold for as low as four pounds, brought in so little cash that the Congress resorted to printing paper currency. By June 3, troops were threatening to return home if they were not paid, and the Congress sent an urgent message to Receiver General Henry Gardner, asking him to come at once and sign the bills with "utmost despatch." The Congress asked Revere to work all night at printing the bills, but by the next day the troops had become so menacing that congressmen visited the print shop to see how many notes had been struck off and whether or not the press was going. The Congress passed resolves preventing people from receiving these notes at below par value and making the

[44] Mass. Prov. Cong., *Journals*, pp. 175, 206, 236, 301, 305, 532; Committee of Supplies to Provincial Congress, Watertown, Mass., May 22, 1775, Force, *American Archives*, 4th ser., II, 676; Elbridge Gerry to Warren, Watertown, Mass., May 1, 1775, Washburn MSS; copy, Warren to Gerry, Cambridge, Mass., May 2, 1775, Warren MSS, II.

currency of Rhode Island and Connecticut, whose soldiers had only their own colony bills, legal tender in Massachusetts.[45] Such proclamations, even with the force of an established government behind them, have been known to fail, and in Massachusetts, without such a government, the currency soon depreciated sharply.

The need for executive departments other than a treasury was equally apparent, if not quite so urgent. In May, Congress adopted resolves for appointing postmasters, setting mail rates, and establishing routes for post riders. Also, John Pigeon, the commissary, was authorized to appoint deputies and to employ men for his department. The routine executive work upon which Congress wasted time is best illustrated by the case of Mr. Emerson's horse. A committee appointed on June 1 was to see that the resolve of Congress approving the delivery of one horse to the Reverend Emerson for his use was carried out. On June 5, Congress named a second committee to describe the horse as a sorrel, this having not been made clear by the first group.[46]

Warren, in his two roles as president of Congress and chairman of the Committee of Safety, was becoming the symbolic executive of the revolutionary government. Abigail Adams looked to him to get a major's commission for her Braintree brother-in-law, and several of Warren's former students, including his brother John, hoped that he could place them in the medical corps. Warren wisely insisted that these young doctors send recommendations from the generals in whose army they wished to serve and that they be "strictly examined" in their medical knowledge. According to a reminiscence of John Adams, Warren spoke a charge to every officer commissioned before Congress, and "never failed to make the officer, as well as all the Assembly, shudder upon those occasions." Also, Warren was called upon to preside at the clergy's annual dinner and other ceremonial functions. But of legal power there was little, and Warren had to handle most of his corre-

[45] Copy, Warren to Joseph Reed, May 15, 1775, Warren MSS, II, printed in Frothingham, *Warren*, pp. 486-487; Mass. Prov. Cong., *Journals*, pp. 185, 187, 236, 255-256, 296, 297, 299, 300, 530; Massachusetts Provincial Congress to Henry Gardner, Watertown, Mass., June 3, 1775, Force, *American Archives*, 4th ser., II, 900; Davis Rich Dewey, "Economic and Commercial Conditions," Albert B. Hart, ed., *Commonwealth History of Massachusetts* (New York, 1929), III, 342-343.

[46] Mass. Prov. Cong., *Journals*, pp. 208, 222-223, 242, 286-287, 299-300.

spondence and executive duties himself, having as an executive staff only one clerk, William Cooper, Jr. When young Cooper did not attend his duties promptly, Warren asked that he come to Watertown immediately, as he was burdened with correspondence and needed a number of papers copied for the use of Congress.[47]

Warren worked assiduously throughout May and early June to improve this situation. On May 4, as chairman of the Committee of Safety, he asked that the Provincial Congress consider a resolve that "the public good of this colony requires, that government in full form ought to be taken up immediately." The following day, as president of the Congress, he signed a resolve, which he had written, to be circulated throughout the colony in broadside form, absolving the people from obedience to Governor Gage and declaring him to be "an unnatural and inveterate enemy to this country." Congress postponed the debate on establishing government until May 12, so that all members could be present. The best that could be obtained at that meeting was the appointment of a committee, including Warren, to ask the advice of the Continental Congress. The address to that body urged the necessity of civil government in order to maintain control over the militia and, incidentally, asked the Continental Congress to take over the direction of the army at Cambridge. In putting these questions up to the Continental Congress, Massachusetts was asking that body to become a central government whose word would be law, and to end its pose as a consultative assembly of delegates from sovereign states. Always alert to the dangers of jealousy on the part of other colonies, Warren saw that a committee was appointed to confer with delegates from New Hampshire in order to get its consent to the Bay Colony's assuming full government.[48]

Warren worked privately toward this end, writing to Samuel Adams in Philadelphia and setting out his own ideas of the kind of government he wanted for Massachusetts. These letters are

---

[47] *Ibid.*, p. 542; Abigail Adams to Warren, Braintree, Mass., May 13, 1775, Hart, ed., *Commonwealth History*, III, photograph between pp. 220 and 221; Joseph Warren to John Warren, Boston, April 10, 1775, Warren MSS, II; J[oseph] Warren to Lemuel Hayward, Cambridge, Mass., June 3, 1775, *ibid.*, II; Charles F. Adams, ed., *Works of John Adams*, III, 277; Frederick Tuckerman, ed., "Diary of Samuel Cooper, 1775, 1776," *American Historical Review*, VI, No. 2 (Jan., 1901), 309; Frothingham, *Warren*, p. 482.

[48] Mass. Prov. Cong., *Journals*, pp. 192-193, 197, 219-220, 230-231, 536; broadside, "Whereas his Excellency General Gage," Watertown, Mass., May 5, 1775 (Boston Public Library).

particularly interesting, because they indicate that Warren's fight against aristocratic rule of the colony and his words in defense of liberty had not been insincere propaganda. Now that he had power and place himself, he was not going to turn his back upon the people for whom he had said he was fighting or desert the principles he had preached. He wanted a government that would "give every man the greatest liberty to do what he pleases consistent with restraining him from doing any injury to another." Rejecting the idea of government for the few and foreshadowing the general-welfare concept of American constitutional theory, Warren demanded a government that would "most contribute to the good of the whole, with the least inconvenience to individuals." Most interesting of all, he had a clear conception of modern democratic theory, believing that only a fully democratic government would be able to secure the general welfare of the people and rejecting the "rule for the many by the few" notion of many of his contemporaries. Massachusetts had been plagued too long by "unprincipled villains," who acted as if they had a right to plunder their countrymen, and the reason for this had been their independence of the people. Warren hoped never to enter political battles again once the present fight was won, and disliked the thought of resuming the last charter, which in its appointive executive contained the seeds of despotism. Thus, he hoped that an entirely new, thoroughly democratic government would be established. "I would therefore wish that the government here might be so happily moulded that the only road to promoters may be through the affection of the people, this being the case, the interest of the governor and the governed will be the same. . . ."[49]

While awaiting news from Philadelphia, Warren found the Provincial Congress willing to strengthen the powers of the Committee of Safety. Congress gave it full discretion in summoning and disposing the militia and ordered all army officers to obey its orders. As head of the Committee of Safety, Warren now became a more official commander-in-chief, since the Congress made it clear that the general officers of the army were to obey his committee's orders in stationing troops and planning strategy, as well as on other subjects.[50]

[49] Warren to Adams, Cambridge, Mass., May 14, 17, 1775, and *id.* to *id.*, May 26, 1775, Samuel Adams MSS.

[50] Mass. Prov. Cong., *Journals*, pp. 236, 238, 241.

On June 9, 1775, the Continental Congress considered the address of Massachusetts on the subject of creating a government. It resolved that no obedience was due to the Massachusetts Government Act or to the governor and lieutenant governor of the colony. However, it urged Massachusetts to abide by the spirit of the second charter. The governor's office should be considered vacant, the Assembly should elect a Council, and these two houses should govern until the king appointed a governor who would obey the charter. There was nothing in this program, except the election of a new Council, that Massachusetts had not already done, and the Provincial Congress, before receiving news of this resolution, sent a more urgent request to Philadelphia. In this appeal, Warren pleaded the difficulty of maintaining public peace, and warned of some "alarming symptoms of the abatement of the sense . . . of the sacredness of private property."[51] Many people in America, however, clung to the hope of restoring harmony with Great Britain, and feared that Massachusetts would become independent if she were allowed to create a new government. Warren had to try to govern the Bay Colony and bring order out of the confused mass of troops at Cambridge by persuasion. The weaknesses of the supply system and the lack of discipline and coordination in the army were fully apparent before the first major battle on June 17. That Warren was able to accomplish as much as he did with the instruments at hand speaks well of his executive ability.

[51] U.S. Continental Congress, *Journals,* II, 76-78, 83-84; Mass. Prov. Cong., *Journals,* p. 319.

# Laurel on His Brow

## CHAPTER X

By May, 1775, now that Samuel Adams and John Hancock were away at the Second Continental Congress, Joseph Warren's leadership in the Provincial Congress was virtually unchallenged. Once war came, Joseph Hawley, James Warren, and other strong leaders, who might have served as rallying points of an opposition party, gave Warren their firm support. In minor matters the Congress simply approved his personal wishes, as in its appointment of Samuel Cooper, Warren's minister in Boston, and William Gordon, his Roxbury friend, as chaplains for the members. Warren named Gordon to edit Thomas Hutchinson's letter books, and probably was the person who decided to suppress certain letters that reflected on John Hancock's patriotism. As to more serious issues, there were yet some divisions of opinion, but Congress did give more support to Warren's war policy than it had before April 19.

Warren himself retained faint hope of remaining within the British Empire, and pledged himself to work for the benefit of Britain and the colonies. However, the terms which had been acceptable before Lexington would no longer do. The hope of reconciliation, Warren knew, was faint indeed, and he thought increasingly about seeking foreign aid. He had been a prime mover in establishing correspondence with discontented elements in Canada, urging people in Montreal to fight "every imposition, whether civil or religious." His Montreal correspondents expressed their sympathies for New England, but professed themselves unable to do much else. Actually, Warren placed more hope for America's salvation in an attack upon England by some European country, France being the likely ally. His belief in the likelihood of a long, hard war proved to be infinitely more realistic than that of Thomas Cushing, who believed the time had come to begin discharging part of the army.[1]

On May 5, the Second Provincial Congress, declaring that frequent elections were necessary even in a time of crisis, called upon the people to choose a new legislature. The Third Provincial Congress met on May 31, the Reverend Samuel Langdon, Harvard's president, opening the session with an appropriate sermon on restoring full government, one of Warren's favorite subjects. Though the Congress chose Warren president of the new body, Joseph Hawley, as vice president, played an important role in its deliberations. Warren devoted more and more of his time to the work of the Committee of Safety and the planning of strategy. His friends in Philadelphia soon complained about the little news he sent from the Provincial Congress.[2]

One of the problems with which Warren was concerned was the creation of a revolutionary navy. The seaport towns were open to attacks, and sent Warren appeals that something be done to defend them. The danger of such attacks upon these ports was potential rather than immediate, and a navy would be more important in preventing supplies from reaching the British army in Boston. One British ship seized two sloops at New Bedford in order to carry sheep from Martha's Vineyard to Boston. A group of Americans recaptured both vessels and thirteen British sailors aboard them in a short battle. At Machias, Maine, a patriot expe-

---

[1] Warren to Arthur Lee, Cambridge, Mass., May 16, 1775, Arthur Lee MSS, II, 52; *Warren-Adams Letters,* I, 57; French, *General Gage's Informers,* pp. 140-141; Warren to James Price and Alexander Hay, Boston, March 15, 1775, Frothingham, ed., "Correspondence in 1774 and 1775," pp. 235-236.

[2] Broadside, "WHEREAS the term for which this present Congress," Watertown, Mass., May 5, 1775 (Boston Public Library); Mass. Prov. Cong., *Journals,* pp. 273, 280; "Letters of John Hancock, Joseph Warren . . . and Governor Trumbull," p. 293.

dition seized two sloops from an armed British schooner, and then fought and captured the king's ship as it fled the harbor. On June 7, Congress asked Joseph Warren to head a committee to consider the establishment of a small naval force to "cruise on our seacoasts, for the protection of our trade, and the annoyance of our enemies." It was not until after the Battle of Breed's Hill, however, that a program was approved.[3]

Much more important was Warren's work in trying to organize the confused, ill-equipped army about Boston, which had gathered from the four New England colonies. Nathanael Greene's 1,500 Rhode Islanders were the best-disciplined troops in Cambridge or Roxbury. Shortly after April 19, some Connecticut militia companies marched to Boston, and on April 26 that colony's assembly appointed general officers for a proposed army of 6,000 men. The Massachusetts Committee of Safety asked Connecticut to send 3,000 to 4,000 well-supplied troops, but received answer that only 2,000 men could be spared. A number of New Hampshire troops had gone to Cambridge when news of Lexington arrived, and the colony incorporated them in the 2,000-man army which it created in late May. This was far short of the 16,400 men that Warren hoped Massachusetts' neighbors would raise, and the number actually at Cambridge fell short of those voted by these colonies. On June 7, 1775, the Massachusetts Congress proposed a meeting of delegates from the four governments to settle the number of troops to be raised and their subsequent disposition.[4]

In Massachusetts neither the Provincial Congress nor the Committee of Safety did much better than the other colonies in raising men and creating a well-ordered army. Warren had only one clerk to help in executing his duties as head of both of these bodies, and he himself was frequently ill during these days. Partly for these reasons, important work in organizing the army occasionally went undone or was seriously delayed. On May 8, Warren named himself to head a committee of doctors to examine persons

[3] Mass. Prov. Cong., *Journals*, pp. 291, 294, 308-309; Octavius T. Howe, "Massachusetts on the Seas in the War of the Revolution (1775-1783)," Hart, ed., *Commonwealth History*, III, 31.

[4] Warren to New Hampshire Congress, Watertown, Mass., May 26, 1775, Force, *American Archives*, 4th ser., II, 717; Mass. Prov. Cong., *Journals*, pp. 307, 536; Allen French, *The First Year of the American Revolution* (Boston and New York, 1934), pp. 77-80, 83-86; Frothingham, *Seige of Boston*, p. 99.

recommended as army surgeons. By May 20, Congress was making arrangements for army chaplains, and the ministers wrote to Warren volunteering their services in line with his suggestion. However, there were more immediate demands which remained unsatisfied a month after the Battle of Lexington. John Thomas asked the Committee of Safety to appoint adjutant and quartermaster generals, and Artemas Ward wrote Warren of the need to settle the number of regiments, commission the officers, and pay the troops. It was not until May 19 that Warren signed the commissions of Ward as general and commander-in-chief, and of Thomas as lieutenant general. On the same day, Congress appointed a committee to settle the rank of the regiments, a touchy problem, and on May 23 it decided to appoint a lieutenant general, two major generals, four brigadiers, two adjutants, and two quartermaster generals.[5]

Of the size of the army, only a good guess could be made—a guess that might be far from the truth one day later. On April 22, some 500 New Hampshire men, saying Ward had told them they were no longer needed, started for home. Massachusetts troops were even more likely to take furloughs on their own authority. The Provincial Congress had to investigate reports that the numbers of the army were dangerously reduced, order the general officers not to allow the men to leave camp, and urge the selectmen of the towns to send deserters back to Cambridge. On June 7, the Provincial Congress named a committee to confer with Ward on obtaining accurate returns from the regiments, and warned that officers who made false returns would be cashiered. James Warren saw the troops "continually going and coming," and was most tentative in estimating their number at 6,000 on May 7. One week later, Joseph Warren guessed that there were about 7,000 men, far from the 30,000 he hoped to muster. The Provincial Congress flatly rejected the suggestion that the military forces be augmented by recruiting slaves. The war was being fought for the liberties of free colonists, and the use of slaves would be inconsistent "and reflect dishonor on this colony." Warren, however,

[5] Mass. Prov. Cong., *Journals,* pp. 203, 236, 243, 247, 253, 283-284, 290; John Thomas to Committee of Safety, Roxbury, Mass., May 12, 1775, Force, *American Archives,* 4th ser., II, 581; Artemas Ward to Warren, May 19, 1775, *ibid.,* II, 647; MSS Commissions to Artemas Ward and John Thomas, signed by Warren, May 19, 1775 (Mass. Hist. Soc. Library).

conferred with Indian leaders, hoping for defensive alliances or at least a declaration of Indian neutrality. He wrote to Samuel Adams, suggesting that the Continental Congress send presents to the Six Nations, and asked the New Hampshire Congress to help.[6]

Actually the colony was fortunate in having no more troops at Cambridge than there were. The army was large enough to keep Gage in Boston, and nothing could be done offensively without artillery. More men would only have made more serious the already difficult problems Warren and his generals faced of feeding, housing, and paying the troops and of maintaining order and cleanliness in the camps. While there was some confusion, such as troops at Chelsea having to send to Watertown for their meat rations, the real problem in the supply system was simply a shortage of everything needed. The Provincial Congress urged the towns to supply their troops with blankets, and the scanty food stored at Concord was brought to Cambridge. The commissary, headed by John Pigeon, had to see that each man got his ration of bread, meat, peas or beans, butter, vinegar, beer, milk, and soap. Ward urged Pigeon to do as best he could "without spending time for exactness," but this broad grant of power helped little enough. At one point, Pigeon threatened to resign unless the Committee of Supplies approved a purchase he had made. Warren and Ward persuaded him to remain on the job, while Warren sent a hastily written message to the committee, asking it to apologize to Pigeon. His friend Elbridge Gerry, who headed this group, in turn became irritated with Warren and almost quit. Besides the problem of feeding the army, the Provincial Congress had to meet the request of at least one town for food to avert famine. The Committee of Safety worked with Quartermaster General Joseph Palmer in solving the housing problem. Since sufficient tents were unavailable and the supply of sailcloth was shortly exhausted, they had to lease houses near the camp for quartering troops. On May 4, Congress approved advance pay of twenty shillings for each soldier and noncommissioned officer. Later it

[6] French, *First Year,* pp. 62-63; Mass. Prov. Cong., *Journals,* pp. 206-207, 210, 258, 302, 305, 307, 310, 311, note 1, 312, 321-322, 553; *Warren-Adams Letters,* I, 47-48; Warren to Samuel Adams, Cambridge, Mass., May 14, 17, 1775, Samuel Adams MSS; *id.* to New Hampshire Congress, Watertown, Mass., June 15, 1775, and Falmouth Committee of Correspondence to Warren, Falmouth, Mass., June 15, 1775, Force, *American Archives,* 4th ser., II, 1003, 1005.

asked the troops to accept interest-bearing notes of forty shillings instead of twenty shillings cash.[7]

Enforcing discipline and cleanliness in the camps was virtually impossible during these months. When one captain spoke rashly about his company electing a sergeant, the men refused to do duty until the officer apologized in front of them. Fire ships, as the camp followers were called, had to be drummed out of camp, and officers were given orders to stove barrels of liquor in grog shops which were selling in violation of regulations. More serious was the lack of ordinary sanitary precautions, which the discovery of a smallpox case made alarming. Warren, knowing well what an epidemic disease could do in a concentrated population center, was one of the main forces in trying to clean up the camps. John Thomas' camp at Roxbury was in fairly good shape, but James Warren, who had no love for Artemas Ward, found the Cambridge camp "spiritless, sluggish, confused and dirty," except where Joseph Warren and Israel Putnam had been active. On June 1, the general orders instructed regimental officers to inspect daily to see that the barracks or tents and the men were clean.[8]

The British alluded to the American army as a "rustic rout with calico frocks and fowling pieces." The calico frocks were all right—William Prescott wore something like one in his magnificent defense of Breed's Hill—but the fowling pieces were another matter. Arms and ammunition were vital needs in May and June, as indeed they were to be for the next eight years. Congress, in a top-secret resolve, authorized the Committee of Supplies to import military stores, with the hope that some European countries would

[7] Broadside, "Resolved, That each soldier in the Massachusetts Army," Watertown, Mass., June 10, 1775, Chamberlain MSS: Souvenir of Lexington and Memorial of Bunker Hill, p. 119; Elbridge Gerry to Warren, Watertown, Mass., May 1, 1775, Washburn MSS; copy, Warren to Gerry, May 2, 1775, Warren MSS, II; Mass. Prov. Cong., *Journals,* pp. 190, 207-208, 246, 300, 303, note 1, 306-307, 332, 335; Joseph Palmer to Committee of Safety, Cambridge, Mass., June 13, 1775, Force, *American Archives,* 4th ser., II, 978; French, *First Year,* pp. 182-183; broadside, Massachusetts Provincial Congress, Watertown, Mass., April 23, 1775, "RESOLVED, That the Selectmen" (Boston Public Library).

[8] "The Revolutionary Journal of James Stevens of Andover, Mass.," Essex Institute, *Historical Collections,* XLVIII, No. 1 (Jan., 1912), 44; Samuel Haws, "A Journal for 1775," Abraham Tomlinson, ed., *The Military Journals of Two Private Soldiers* (Poughkeepsie, N.Y., 1855), p. 57; "Orderly Book of Colonel William Henshaw," pp. 104, 107; Mass. Prov. Cong., *Journals,* p. 294; *Warren-Adams Letters,* I, 68.

sell to the revolutionary government. Warren, Ward, and Moses Gill wrote to the Continental Congress and to New York for powder, but received only 650 pounds. Warren also asked Samuel Adams to see what he could do about artillery and ammunition in Philadelphia.[9]

The main dependence, however, had to be upon local supplies. Towns, particularly those along the seacoast and on the frontier, were appealing for arms and ammunition, and Warren appointed himself to the committee to recommend measures for alleviating the shortage. Another committee was to consider means of obtaining medicines, as Warren had been able to get only one medicine chest for the Cambridge camp and one for the Roxbury wing of the army. Warren's group recommended that towns furnish guns to soldiers without them, from the town stock or by purchasing them from residents, and suggested that a number of armorers be appointed to repair arms. As the shortage continued, Congress ordered the towns to turn over part of their powder supply and a number of arms to the Committee of Supplies, and Warren and Professor Sewall analyzed a sample of earth which was thought to contain saltpeter. The action of the Congress in December, 1775, of purchasing an old powder mill at Stoughton likely was initiated by a letter to Warren in May, mentioning an elderly powder maker there whose skill might be useful to the colony.[10]

Artillery for the Massachusetts forces was practically nonexistent. On April 29, Warren wrote that there were only six three-pounders and a single six-pounder at Cambridge and sixteen pieces of artillery at Watertown, not all of which were usable. The most important effort to fill this gap was the expedition against Fort Ticonderoga which Warren promoted. In 1774, Gage had written home about putting Ticonderoga and Crown Point in defensible shape, and Dartmouth had sent orders that this be done. In March, 1775, John Brown went to Montreal as an agent of Warren and Samuel Adams, and recommended to them

---

[9] Allan Nevins, *The American States During and After the Revolution, 1775-1789* (New York, 1924), p. 69; Mass. Prov. Cong., *Journals*, p. 198; Force, *American Archives*, 4th ser., II, 906; Warren to Adams, Cambridge, Mass., May 14, 17, 1775, Samuel Adams MSS.

[10] Mass. Prov. Cong., *Journals*, pp. 209-210, 256-257, 298, 299, 321, 323, 336-337; broadside, "Whereas a few of the inhabitants," Watertown, Mass., May 9, 1775 (Boston Public Library); Force, *American Archives*, 4th ser., II, 932, 967, 1284-85.

the seizure of Ticonderoga as soon as hostilities should begin. Men on the New Hampshire grants, he said, were already thinking of such a scheme and he felt that they were in a good position to execute it. When Benedict Arnold arrived in Cambridge after the Battle of Lexington, he talked with Joseph Warren of the cannon about Lake Champlain, and Warren asked him for a detailed report of their numbers. Arnold answered that there were more than 100 pieces, eighty of which were heavy artillery. Through Warren's agency, the Provincial Congress gave Arnold a colonel's commission and £100, with power to recruit 400 men. Arnold long remembered Warren for giving him this opportunity, and contributed a considerable sum of money to support Warren's children after their father's death.[11]

When Benedict Arnold arrived at Lake Champlain, he found a small Connecticut force and Ethan Allen's men already there. By dint of occasional cooperation, and much more of competition for the honor of a victory and the right of command, these forces took Fort Ticonderoga, as well as other weakly fortified points in the area. Warren received news of the capture of Ticonderoga on May 17 and word of Arnold's successful expedition against St. John's about a week later. He sent word of the first victory to John Scollay, and it was this letter that gave Thomas Gage his first knowledge of the loss of the fort.[12]

Warren also had news of the disputes that had broken out between Arnold and others. He was on the committee which cleverly suggested to the Connecticut Assembly that these would be settled if Arnold were appointed to bring some of the cannon to Cambridge where it was badly needed. By late May the Committee of Safety wrote to Arnold instructing him to obey all orders of the Provincial Congress, and in June a commission was sent to investigate "the spirit, capacity, and conduct of the

[11] Carter, ed., *Correspondence of Gage,* II, 177; Force, *American Archives,* 4th ser., II, 243-244, 450, 485; Mass. Prov. Cong., *Journals,* pp. 185, 530-531; Lowell Kerr, "Benedict Arnold and the Warrens," *Americana,* XXX, No. 2 (April, 1936), 324-334.

[12] Mass. Prov. Cong., *Journals,* pp. 696-697, 698-699; Warren to John Scholly [Scollay], Watertown, Mass., May 17, 1775, and Gage to Dartmouth, Boston, May 17, 1775, Gage MSS: English Series, XXIX, also printed in Carter, ed., *Correspondence of Gage,* I, 400; Warren to Committee of Safety, Watertown, Mass., May [25], 1775 (photostat, New York Public Library), also printed in Frothingham, *Warren,* p. 494.

said Arnold." The removal of him from his command was the first of those blows to his vanity which were to be one factor in his treason.[13]

The army before Boston needed the cannon badly, but Warren saw the necessity of treading softly on this problem. After the Committee of Safety ordered Arnold to transport the guns to Cambridge, Warren and Hawley wrote explanations to Connecticut and New York, as well as to the Continental Congress. They assured them that Arnold's orders had been issued "in the hurry and confusion of war," and that Massachusetts had no intention of invading the jurisdiction of a sister colony. They pledged that, if any of the guns did reach Cambridge, the Provincial Congress would be strictly accountable and yield them up to the Continental Congress when requested to do so.[14] The difficulties of moving the captured guns to Cambridge prevented their use on June 17, but little use was made of that artillery which was available.

General Artemas Ward commanded the American forces about Boston, a soldier whose nervousness and indecisiveness contrasted with the reliability and good sense of John Thomas at Roxbury. When a note, intended for officers in the country, was sent to Thomas, ordering him to come to Cambridge with his forces immediately, Thomas maintained his position and sent a message of inquiry to Warren. Benjamin Church had sent this order to Thomas, possibly to open a route for Gage to attack the Cambridge camp. Warren immediately corrected this "very great error," which would have destroyed the American defensive lines, and complimented Thomas on his prudence and good judgment.[15] When a £100,000 fire swept through Boston, Ward wrote Thomas that he feared the British had started it to distract the Americans from some planned attack. To Ward's warning to be on guard, Thomas calmly replied that every day he got information of a plan to take Boston Neck and had his defenses in excellent shape. Warren and Elbridge Gerry felt that "a regular

[13] Mass. Prov. Cong., *Journals*, pp. 233-234, 261, 264, 327-329, 332.

[14] *Ibid.*, pp. 258-260, 265-266; "Letters of John Hancock, Joseph Warren . . . and Governor Trumbull," pp. 303-307.

[15] MS, Warren to John Thomas, Cambridge, Mass., May 10, 1775, inserted in William L. Clement's copy of Joseph Warren, *Oration Delivered March 6, 1775*, also printed in Charles Martyn, *The Life of Artemas Ward: The First Commander-in-Chief of the American Revolution* (New York, 1921), pp. 103-104.

general" was needed to discipline the army, and Warren was anxious that the Continental Congress take over direction of the forces which had been mustered. He thought highly of Charles Lee's military experience, but shared Gerry's view that George Washington was an excellent choice as generalissimo. He suggested to his friends in Philadelphia that the matter be handled with great delicacy to avoid jealousy among the Massachusetts generals. In a letter dated the day after Warren died, John Hancock sent news of Washington's appointment, not mentioning his own jealousy of the Virginian.[16]

Between the fight at Lexington and the action of June 17, there were a few movements and skirmishes. As early as April 27, Warren was writing of the possibility of an attack upon Gage's army. Putnam and other American leaders saw the need for keeping the men busy, and, on May 13, Putnam marched a battalion around Charlestown peninsula within shouting distance of a British man-of-war. Plans were in the making for a large movement, probably an attack upon Boston itself. On May 9 and 10, the Council of War, composed of the Committee of War and the Committee of Safety, called for another 2,000 militiamen from the towns, and ordered all regiments being enlisted to come to Cambridge. The Congress, "meditating a blow against our restless enemies," employed carpenters to build boats and called for oars stored at Concord. Gage and Admiral Graves were also active. The Provincial Congress limited the exportation of fish, because the British were seizing so many provision boats, and dispatched a force to Salem to prevent the sailing of a ship destined to get food for the British army. The Provincial Congress also sent word to New York that British vessels had sailed for that city, in order to prevent the people there from taking the arms and ammunition from the fort.[17] The Provincial Congress simply approved of most of these

---

[16] Artemas Ward to John Thomas, Cambridge, Mass., May 17, [1775], Ward MSS, III (Mass. Hist. Soc. Library); French, *First Year,* p. 188; James T. Austin, *The Life of Elbridge Gerry* (Boston, 1828), I, 79; Warren to Adams, Cambridge, Mass., May 14, 17, 1775, Samuel Adams MSS; *Warren-Adams Letters,* I, 58.

[17] Warren to Arthur Lee, Cambridge, Mass., April 27, 1775, Force, *American Archives,* 4th ser., II, 425; Samuel A. Green, ed., "Amos Farnsworth's Diary," Mass. Hist. Soc., *Proceedings,* XXXII (1897, 1899), 79; "Thomas Boynton's Journal," *ibid.,* XV (1876-77), 254; Mass. Prov. Cong., *Journals,* p. 216 and note 1, 323, 324, 540, 541, 542.

actions, of course, the initiation of them coming from Warren and others of the Committee of Safety.

Gage's first foraging expedition to Grape Island in Boston Harbor on May 14 led the Committee of Safety to recommend that the selectmen of neighboring towns have the islands cleared of livestock. On May 21, word reached John Thomas of a British expedition heading toward Weymouth. He sent three companies to aid the inhabitants, and Warren hurried to the scene. The British landed on Grape Island and the Americans fired at them from the mainland for several hours. As the tide came in, the Americans were able to float boats, which had been aground, and made for the island. The British quickly retreated to their boats, having made off with only a small part of the hay on the island. The Americans burned more than eighty tons of hay, collected all livestock, and returned to the mainland. Warren was in the action, and wrote the news report which appeared in the *Essex Gazette.* Three days after the skirmish, Warren's Committee of Safety urged the Provincial Congress to assume responsibility for removing sheep, stock, and hay from Noddle's Island and others in the harbor.[18]

On May 26, General Ward dispatched several companies under Colonel Nixon to clear Noddle's and Hog's Islands. On Saturday morning, May 27, they ran cattle, horses, and some 400 sheep off Hog's Island, and a small party of men waded across to Noddle's in the afternoon. Sailors aboard British ships sighted them, but they managed to set fire to a house and barn and kill a few head of stock. Admiral Graves sent marines, boats, an armed schooner, and a sloop, but the Americans were able to get back to Hog's Island. They directed a warm fire against the British until sunset, and about nine in the evening Putnam and Warren arrived with re-enforcements, including two artillery pieces. Putnam demanded the surrender of the British schooner *Diana* which had run aground, but was answered by two cannon shot. The Americans turned their two three-pounders against her, and forced the British to abandon ship. In the face of fire from the barges, the Americans set the *Diana* afire, and its magazine exploded about three in the morning. Still, they were able to salvage a few guns

[18] *Ibid.,* pp. 252, 545, 557; Warren to Adams, Cambridge, Mass., May 26, 1775, Samuel Adams MSS; Caleb Haskell, "Caleb Haskell's Diary," *Magazine of History with Notes,* XXII, Extra No. 86, 62.

and several wagonloads of stores from her.[19] Only two or three British were killed and three Americans wounded, two by their own men, in the long fight, a neat commentary on the marksmanship of the men of 1775. Early in June, Warren and Putnam entertained British officers from the warship *Lively* in Charlestown and exchanged prisoners "with the utmost decency and good humour," as Warren put it in the *Essex Gazette.*

During June further raids were conducted on Pettick's and Deer's Islands, from which the Americans removed more than 1,000 sheep and cows.[20] Warren does not appear in these actions, but the troops in Cambridge and Roxbury had had opportunity enough to mark his courage. Here was one politician who was not starting a war that others might fight it. On April 19, he left Boston at dawn, rode to Lexington, and was at the center of the day's hottest fighting. Now he had been in the midst of the fighting at Grape and Hog's Islands. Not satisfied with his position as chairman of the Committee of Safety, in which he played a leading role in planning strategy and ordering the army, he sought a commission as a field officer, and the Provincial Congress appointed him a major general on June 14.

There was no turning back now. Warren had gone too far into politics and the revolutionary crusade to pause at disquieting thoughts about where this war might end for his country or for himself. His medical practice had been destroyed after April 19, and he was deep in debt. On June 16, he signed his final proclamation as president of the Provincial Congress, a paper which alone might have been enough to make the British hang him. It was a reply to Gage's offer of a pardon for all who would lay down their arms, with the exception of Samuel Adams and John Hancock, whose crimes were such as to merit only "condign punishment." In one of his finest state papers, unmarred by the excesses that characterized much of his prose, Warren recited the grievances of the Province. Britain had blockaded the town of Boston, seized the colony's powder supply, dissolved the legisla-

[19] Green, ed., "Farnsworth's Diary," pp. 80-81; "Revolutionary Journal of James Stevens," p. 46; MS, Artemas Ward to John Thomas, Cambridge, Mass., May 27, 1775 (Boston Public Library); French, *First Year,* pp. 191-192; Albert Bosson, "The Battle of Chelsea," Old Suffolk Chapter, Sons of the American Revolution, *Register* (1900), p. 46.

[20] Dixon and Hunter's *Virginia Gazette,* July 1, 1775; "Caleb Haskell's Diary," pp. 63-64.

tive body, and denied the people justice. Finally, on the "ever memorable nineteenth of April," British troops "in a most barbarous and infamous manner" had attacked the inhabitants and destroyed all hope of reconciliation. Warren promised, however, a pardon to all who surrendered to the Massachusetts army, except Thomas Gage, Samuel Graves, and the mandamus councilors who had not resigned. He concluded: "We trust, that the God of armies, on whom we rely for a blessing upon our arms, which we have taken up in support of the great and fundamental principles of natural justice and the common and indefeasible rights of mankind, will guide and direct us in our designs; and at last, in infinite goodness to this his injured people, restore peace and freedom to the American world."[21]

While Warren was preparing to enter active military service, his children were separated from him, seemingly left in the care of Mercy Scollay in Boston when Warren had been forced to flee town. In 1774 this young woman, as charming and tender as his wife Elizabeth had been, visited him as a patient. They were soon deeply in love, and Joseph persuaded her to make use of her lively intelligence in writing for the revolutionary cause. She wrote a satire on the female love of dress, and, had Warren lived and married her, Mercy Scollay might have joined the circle of Abigail Adams and Mercy Warren as one of the leading women of her day. Shortly before his death, Warren asked her to care for his children if anything should happen to him.[22]

Throughout May and early June, the leaders of the opposing armies planned their strategy in the stalemated war and tried to predict enemy moves. Both camps eyed two key heights, one in Charlestown and the other in Roxbury, which commanded the low peninsula of Boston. On April 23, the British, anticipating American occupation of Bunker Hill in Charlestown, began erecting a battery at Copp's Hill on the Boston side of the Charles River. Though Warren and his generals considered some offensive plans, they were primarily concerned about a British attempt to sally into the country, and it was for checking such a march that they planned their defenses. The Committees of Safety and

[21] Broadside, "Whereas the infatuated multitudes," Boston, June 12, 1775 (Mass. Hist. Soc. Library); Mass. Prov. Cong., *Journals*, pp. 330, 344-347.

[22] Mercy Scollay to John Hancock, Boston, May 21, 1776, Warren MSS, II; *Warren-Adams Letters*, I, 33.

of War studied the terrain, and decided, on May 12, that breastworks should be established along the road from Cambridge to Charlestown. Atop Bunker Hill a redoubt would be built, with cannon to annoy the enemy coming out of Boston. Gage had news of this recommendation the day after it was made.[23]

Gage's strategy was to take Dorchester Heights in Roxbury, and then attack the American army at Cambridge. Artemas Ward feared the British would move to these heights as early as May 29. Gage, however, was awaiting re-enforcements, and shortly after their arrival he completed his plan to attack on June 18. Warren's spy system, quite as efficient as the British, obtained word of the British intentions, and by June 15 Ward, Warren, and Putnam began preparations for occupying Bunker Hill.[24]

Colonel William Prescott commanded the 1,000-man force that was charged with fortifying the hill. On June 16, he assembled his men on the parade at six in the evening, and, after a prayer, they moved out toward Charlestown about nine o'clock. The Committee of Safety had ordered the fortification of Bunker Hill, the general name for the heights on Charlestown peninsula. Only the immediate neighbors distinguished the lower hill closest to Boston by the name Breed's. Prescott conferred with his engineer and other officers and decided to erect the redoubt upon Breed's, sending part of his men off to Charlestown, where they took post in the townhouse. Prescott began the entrenchment just before midnight, and the men worked steadily until dawn, between four and five o'clock. By then they had a redoubt of about eight rods on each side, with an angle projecting toward Boston. They were soon sighted by men aboard the British ship *Lively,* which began an artillery bombardment.[25]

On the evening of June 16, Joseph Warren crossed secretly by boat to a wharf in Boston. There he met John Jeffries, a former student of James Lloyd and now one of the best doctors in Boston.

[23] Barker, *British in Boston,* pp. 37-38; Mass. Prov. Cong., *Journals,* p. 543; French, *General Gage's Informers,* p. 119.

[24] Artemas Ward to John Thomas, Cambridge, Mass., May 29, 1775, Ward MSS, III; Howe to ———, Charlestown, Mass., June 22, 24, 1775; Fortescue, ed., *Correspondence of King George the Third,* III, 220; MS, Massachusetts Committee of Safety, Resolution to Take Possession of Bunker Hill, June 15, 1775 (Boston Public Library), also in Martyn, *Life of Ward,* p. 118.

[25] Frothingham, *Seige of Boston,* p. 395; "Thomas Boynton's Journal," p. 255; Green, ed., "Farnsworth's Diary," p. 83; Richard Frothingham, "Remarks," Mass. Hist. Soc., *Proceedings,* XIV (1875-76), 55.

Warren and Jeffries were good friends, the former having proposed his colleague's name for membership in St. Andrew's lodge and deposited a three-dollar membership fee for him. Now Warren tried to persuade Jeffries to return to Cambridge with him to head the American medical service. Jeffries, however, refused and Warren crossed the Charles River again to get a few hours' sleep. The next day Warren attended a Council of War meeting, and expressed his anxiety to be at the scene of the action. Several men present tried to persuade him not to go and volunteered to execute any orders he cared to send, but Warren could not be dissuaded. Bothered by one of his oppressive headaches, he tried to rest for a while, after which he walked through Cambridge toward Charlestown Neck and the entrenchments on Breed's Hill.[26]

When the British command observed the American works shortly after daybreak, there was little to the defensive position but the redoubt. They saw that every hour would give the rebels added strength, yet William Howe, who commanded the British expedition, seems not to have acted with a bit of the swiftness necessary. He laid plans for sending a column along the shore of the Mystic River, which would take the American line in its left flank. When he devised these tactics, such a movement was feasible; by the time he had landed on Charlestown peninsula, the Americans had extended their line to the Mystic and Howe was forced to attack frontally.[27]

Prescott's forces should have been relieved after erecting the defensive positions, but Artemas Ward was fearful of an attack upon Cambridge by way of Roxbury, where Lord Percy was conducting a diversionary artillery attack upon John Thomas. Thus, Ward was sparing even of re-enforcements, and many who were sent to Prescott's aid refused to cross Charlestown Neck. Prescott had

[26] St. Andrew's Lodge, Records, I, May 8, 1766; John Jeffries, "A Tory Surgeon's Experiences, June 17, 1775," *The Boston Medical and Surgical Journal,* XCII, No. 24 (June 17, 1875), 729; "Extracts from Dr. Belknap's Note-Books," Mass. Hist. Soc., *Proceedings,* XIV (1875-76), 92-93; J. S. L[oring], "Reminiscence of General Warren," New Eng. Hist. and Geneal. Soc., *Register,* XII, No. 3 (July, 1858), 230; Richard Frothingham, *The Battle-field of Bunker Hill* (Boston, 1876), p. 42.

[27] Harold Murdock, *Bunker Hill: Notes and Queries on a Famous Battle* (Boston, 1927), pp. 148-149; Charles F. Adams, "Battle of Bunker Hill from a Strategic Point of View," Amer. Antiq. Soc., *Proceedings,* n.s., X, Part 2 (Oct., 1895), 387-398, argues that Howe originally planned a frontal assault.

little artillery to start with, and most of what he did have deserted him. He had good men in Charlestown to hit the British left, and sent the remainder of the Connecticut men to man a breastwork on the left of the redoubt. Stark and Reed, with their New Hampshire boys, quickly built rail fences and bundles of hay into a rough breastwork running down to the Mystic River. Israel Putnam came over from Cambridge, and exerted his energies in preventing desertions and pushing frightened troops forward toward Breed's Hill. Contact with Ward's headquarters was virtually cut off, for the Committee of Safety had no horses available for messenger service. Warren managed to get through on foot in the afternoon, crossing Charlestown Neck, which the British ships were bombarding, and entering the redoubt in his best clothes. The firing was heaviest there and Prescott asked him to leave. Warren refused and also rejected Colonel Prescott's offer to yield the command to him, declaring that Prescott was more experienced and that he came only as a volunteer. His example fired the men about him, and he stayed in the heavily attacked redoubt throughout the battle, treating the wounded, fighting as a common soldier, and probably giving advice to Prescott and others when he was asked for it.[28]

Howe decided to pursue his original plan, but sent back to Gage for re-enforcements, which brought his total force to about 2,200 men. Brigadier General Pigot commanded the British left, which would attack the redoubt defended by Prescott and Warren; Howe directed the flanking movement against the New Hampshire and Connecticut men on the American left. The attack began with a heavy cannonade, and both flanks of the British army moved forward slowly. Looking down from their position on the hill, Warren and Prescott could see the men in Charlestown hitting Pigot's left, until the British set the town afire. The entire line of the British army was impeded in its attack by fences, and Pigot's men fired prematurely and in great confusion, his

[28] Murdock, *Bunker Hill,* pp. 54, note, 148-149; Dexter, ed., *Literary Diary of Ezra Stiles,* I, 576; French, *First Year,* p. 244; [Henry B. Dawson], *The Historical Magazine and Notes and Queries,* n.s., III, No. 6 (June, 1868), 367. The story of Warren being offered the command appears in many statements of soldiers who claimed to have been in the redoubt, but most of them are 1818 or later, the earliest appearance of it being the August 24, 1787, entry in "Extracts from Dr. Belknap's Note-Books," pp. 92-93; in many accounts written in June and July, 1775, he is named as the commander of the American troops, but none of these are by men who were at the scene.

second line pressing up into the first. The Americans in the redoubt also wasted much ammunition, but were finally ordered to hold their fire until the British advanced within thirty yards. They fired then, taking a large toll, and forcing Pigot's troops to retreat. On the left, the Americans held their fire well, and then let go a withering barrage. The light infantry, the best troops in the British army, retreated. Howe, at the head of his troops, experienced "a moment that I never felt before," as he phrased it later.[29]

In the redoubt Prescott and Warren had only about 150 men left. They watched Pigot's men reform and start up again, this time coming in column rather than line. Prescott's men again held their fire, with good reason, for their ammunition supply was failing fast. The British troops broke through on the sides of the redoubt and threatened to encircle it. Still the defenders stayed, hurling stones and using guns as clubs to hold their crude fort. The British bayoneted about thirty of them before Prescott ordered their retreat. Warren was among the last to leave the redoubt, and a short distance down the back of the hill he was hit. The bullet entered the skull, and he probably died instantly, though there was a story four days later that one man had tried to aid him, but Warren, knowing he had but moments to live, urged the man to be off.[30]

The British had the hill, but failed to follow the confused, retreating Americans. Their casualties were high, particularly among the officers, and the rebels were no longer to be mistaken for cowards or rustics in calico frocks. Warren's call to prepare for war had not been in vain. The war had begun in earnest, though Warren did not live to see its end or even the direction it was to take. It was to be nearly a year after his death before his beloved town of Boston was cleared of British troops by the man whom Warren had supported for the post of commander-in-chief of the American army. And it was to be more than a year before independence was proclaimed as the goal of the war.

---

[29] Frothingham, *Seige of Boston,* pp. 395-396; Fortescue, ed., *Correspondence of King George the Third,* III, 222.

[30] "Thomas Boynton's Journal," p. 255; Mass. Hist. Soc., *Proceedings,* XI (1869-70), 227. In 1843, Needham Maynard, at the age of eighty-eight, made an interesting, unsubstantiated statement naming Warren commander of the American forces and claiming to have served as his aide during the battle. Dated June 20, 1843, Warren MSS, II.

Legend has it that Warren's body was identified by John Jeffries, who came onto the field after the action, and that some of the officers suggested cutting off the head, but one who was a mason put a stop to that indignity. Lieutenant Walter Laurie, who had fought at Concord Bridge on April 19, was in charge of the detail to bury the dead. He wrote, "Doctor Warren, president of the Provincial Congress . . . and next to Adams, in abilities, I found among the slain, and stuffed the scoundrel with another rebel, into one hole, and there he, and his seditious principles may remain."[31] In April, 1776, two of Warren's brothers and some friends exhumed the body, which was probably identified by Paul Revere, who had made two false teeth for Warren. A public ceremony was held at King's Chapel, attended by Warren's masonic brethren, and the remains interred in the Granary Burying Ground. In 1825 they were removed to the Warren vault in St. Paul's Church where they rested until they were buried, in 1855, in Forest Hills Cemetery at Roxbury, Warren's birthplace.

A Warren legend was not long in building. Eulogies, acrostic and elegiac poetry, false horoscopes, orations, and sincere expressions of sorrow were delivered. Hugh Henry Brackenridge wrote a play, with a last act of ten scenes, in which Warren gave an elaborate two-page speech after being shot. John Burk wrote another, which John Adams angrily criticized for portraying Warren as a bully and blackguard, instead of a scholar and gentleman. Another critic said its only merit was its brevity. John Trumbull circulated a story that Howe had asked a British colonel if he knew the gentleman in fine clothes retreating down Breed's Hill. The colonel, who later denied the story, was said to have recognized Warren and tried to prevent the troops from firing, but was too late. The number of Americans who stopped to hear dying speeches from Warren would have made a fair-sized crowd. One Amos Foster, in 1825, was certain that Warren had called, "I am a dead man, fight on my brave fellows, for the salvation of your country." George Hewes watched the battle from Boston, but from there he saw an artillery shell hit Warren. A sword allegedly taken from the body and a bullet dug from the skull found ready pur-

[31] Jeffries, "A Tory Surgeon's Experiences," p. 730, which is inaccurate enough to place Howe in Boston during the battle; Charles F. Adams, ed., *Familiar Letters*, p. 91; Walter S. Laurie to John Roebuck, Charlestown, Mass., June 23, 1775, *New England Quarterly*, XXV, No. 3 (Sept., 1952), 367.

chasers. Within days after the battle, Warren's claim was as firmly established as Prescott's or Putnam's for the honor of having commanded the American defense.[32]

The friends who knew him best wrote better epitaphs than the poets, dramatists, and mythmakers of a later day. In his history of the Revolution, William Gordon wrote of Warren, "Neither resentment, nor interested views, but a regard to the liberties of his country, induced him to oppose the measures of government. He stepped forward into public view not that he might be noted and admired for a patriotic spirit, but because he *was* a patriot." Abigail Adams wrote to her husband that none of the havoc and destruction of the British army wounded her as did Warren's death. "We mourn," she said, "for the citizen, the senator, the physician, and the warrior." James Warren also wrote John Adams of their "worthy and much lamented friend," who died with as much glory as James Wolfe at Quebec. Adams' simple reply was the finest epitaph of all: "Our dear Warren has fallen, with laurells on his brows as fresh and blooming as ever graced an hero."[33]

This last chapter of Joseph Warren's life was, to be sure, his finest, but there were others quite as important. Born the son of a Roxbury farmer, he had peddled milk to the Boston market as a barelegged boy. By the age of thirty-four, he was widely known as a competent physician, a skillful politician, and a sincere patriot. As a physician he stood at the top of his profession in Boston, and did much to train the next generation of doctors in Massachusetts, the men who served as army surgeons during the war. In politics Warren ranked with Samuel Adams as one of the two most important men in forming a political party that influenced colony politics for twenty years. Without assuming public office until 1775, he led the Bay Colony in forcing the recall of Francis Bernard, in fighting for local control of offices and poli-

[32] John W. Farwell, "A Horoscope of Dr. Joseph Warren," Col. Soc. of Mass., *Publications*, XX (*Trans.*, 1917-19), 18-21; Brander Matthews, "Introduction," *Bunker-Hill or the Death of General Warren* by John Burk (New York, 1891), p. 6; Daniel Putnam, *A Letter to Major-General Dearborn* (Boston, [1818]), p. 9; William H. Sumner, "Reminiscences Relating to General Warren and Bunker Hill," New Eng. Hist. and Geneal. Soc., *Register*, XII, No. 2 (April, 1858), 118, 122.

[33] Gordon, *History of the Independence of the United States*, II, 49-50; Charles F. Adams, ed., *Letters of Mrs. Adams, the Wife of John Adams* (Boston, 1840), I, 49; *Warren-Adams Letters*, I, 63, 66.

cies, in gaining repeal of parliamentary taxes, and in driving British troops from Boston. Through press, oration, instruction, caucus, committee, and town meeting, he expressed the growing sentiment against the domination of Massachusetts politics by a pro–British party. But Warren was more than a publicist for the revolutionary cause; he was also an able organizer and director of his political party and of the political activities of such groups as the masonic lodges and the North End artisans. He was a key figure in the *Liberty* incident, the Massacre trial, the formation of the committees of correspondence, and the Boston Tea Party. Warren was perhaps the most important man in creating the Provincial Congress; he fought to give Massachusetts a complete, democratic government; and, in his Suffolk Resolves, he sounded the keynote for some of the most important policies adopted by the Continental Congress—nonintercourse with Britain and, if necessary, a defensive war.

Warren's political party would have had but scant success, if a widespread discontent had not existed in Massachusetts. Warren and Samuel Adams articulated the grievances and fears of a people, rather than creating them. The people supported them from 1765 to 1768 and after 1772, because those were the years when the issues of parliamentary taxation and imperial control were most clearly on the tapis. During the intervening years—as in the convention of 1768 and the Massacre trials of 1770—Massachusetts repudiated many of the Warren-Adams policies. Otis, Hancock, John Adams, and other Moderates became noticeably cool toward their extremist friends, and some of them even supported Hutchinson's right to remove the General Court to Cambridge. Their attitude was representative of much of the population of the colony in these years, when imperial issues lay dormant and the economy prospered. Warren, fearing the development of a closed aristocracy that would rule independent of the people, continued to fight the Conservatives from 1768 to 1773. But the general political lethargy of these years made it clear that many people in Massachusetts took this issue less seriously than they did imperial questions, and there was no doubt of Massachusetts' rejection of the Warren-Adams plea for armed resistance.

Joseph Warren and Samuel Adams knew this well, and saw that they would have to appeal to the people on broader grounds than local politics or the dangers of an American aristocracy.

They soon found that only the anti-British issue was popular enough to gain wide support for their party, and, in the committee of correspondence, they created an organization to unify the opposition throughout Massachusetts. The ground upon which they made their appeal is written large across the page of history. It is found in Joseph Warren's list of grievances of 1772, and in the January, 1773, answer of the General Court to Thomas Hutchinson's argument that Parliament must be supreme or the colonists would be independent. Warren's party shaped its program to fit the growing spirit of nationalism and the long tradition of virtual home rule, which Britain had tolerated for many years and was now endangering by trying to impose stricter imperial controls. The response of the people of Massachusetts in 1773 to the Radical program was enough to warm the cockles of the coldest heart among them.

In making this appeal to infant American nationalism, Joseph Warren was one of the most effective men in Massachusetts. His honesty, sincere idealism, and personal belief in the justice of his cause forestalled the charges of avarice and ambition that were hurled at others. He earned the respect of all parties until war brought inevitable criminations and slander. His attractive personality won him a devoted corps of Boston Masons, artisans, and laborers, which served him well in opposing the landing of the tea and in observing British movements and carrying messages before April 19. His patent sincerity, his passionate writing and speaking, and his apparent lack of interest in office brought a respect from the general public that no other Radical leader commanded.

Here was no smuggling merchant, taxed newspaper editor, or southern planter rebelling to cancel debts. Joseph Warren's leadership was effective because he believed in the same things as did the people of Massachusetts. He expressed in his life the nationalism, the desire for home rule, and the demand for a government responsive to the electorate that were becoming articles of a new American faith. These sentiments he crowned at Breed's Hill with the sacrifice of life. His earlier services, no less than this last, added luster to the name which Peter Warren had brought to windswept Monhegan Island 125 years before.

# Bibliography

## I. Primary Sources

### A. Manuscripts

Joseph Warren destroyed some of his own papers when there was danger of his arrest, and others were burned in a fire in Greenfield, Massachusetts. The largest collections of Warren manuscripts are in the Massachusetts Historical Society Library, the Boston Public Library, and the New York Public Library. Several of the other collections listed contain one or more Warren items.


Adams, Samuel-Joseph Warren Letters, a part of the Samuel Adams Papers, New York Public Library.

Bernard, Francis, Official Papers, 13 vols., a part of the Jared Sparks MSS, Houghton Library, Harvard.

Boston, Committee of Correspondence, Minutes, 1772-74, photostats in the Mass. Hist. Soc. Library of 13 vols. of originals, New York Public Library.

British-American Customs Records, 1750-77, 2 boxes of transcripts, Mass. Hist. Soc. Library.

Chamberlain, Mellen, Collection of Autographs, Boston Public Library:
- Adams, John, Sketch of His Life, 1 vol.
- Adams, Samuel and Joseph Warren, Sketches of Their Lives, 1 vol.
- Hancock, John, Sketch of His Life, 1 vol.
- Miscellaneous Papers, 1640-1797, 5 vols.
- Souvenir of Lexington and Memorial of Bunker Hill, 1775-1875, 1 vol.

Gage, Thomas, Manuscripts, William L. Clements Library.

Gay, Frederick Lewis, Gay Transcripts of Material in the Public Record Office, London, 1630-1776, 124 vols., Mass. Hist. Soc. Library.

Green, Samuel A., Green Papers, 1700-1918, 11 boxes, Mass. Hist. Soc. Library.

Harvard College, Collection of Autographs, Houghton Library.

Harvard College, College Records, Harvard Archives:
Admissions Book, 1725-1828, 1 vol.
Book of *Theses* and *Quaestiones,* 1737-1810, 1 vol.
Harvard Faculty Records, II (1752-66).
Room Assignment Records, 1 vol.

Hutchinson-Oliver Papers, 1637-1859, 1 vol., Mass. Hist. Soc. Library.

Instructions to Provincial Governors of Massachusetts, 1631-1775, 8 vols. of transcripts, Mass. Hist. Soc. Library.

Knox, William, Manuscripts, William L. Clements Library.

Lee, Arthur, Papers, 8 vols., Houghton Library.

Lloyd, James, Ledger, 1758-78, 1 vol., Boston Medical Society Library.

Massachusetts Archives, State House, Boston:
Council Records, XVI (1765-74).
Hutchinson Correspondence, XXV-XXVII.

Massachusetts Bay, Suffolk Session of Superior Court of Judicature, Records, 1686-1780, Suffolk County Courthouse.

Massachusetts Historical Society, Bound Miscellaneous MSS, 1621-1908, 21 vols., Mass. Hist. Soc. Library.

Oliver, Peter, The Origins and Progress of the American Rebellion, Gay Transcripts, Mass. Hist. Soc. Library.

Quincy, Josiah, Jr., Papers, 1635-1852, 1 vol., Mass. Hist. Soc. Library.

Rowe, John, Diary, 1764-79, Mass. Hist. Soc. Library.

Roxbury, Town Records, II (1730-90), Archives, Boston City Hall.

Saint Andrew's Lodge, Records, 1756-1809, 3 vols., Mass. Grand Lodge Library, Boston.

Seventy-Six Society, Massachusetts Papers, 1769-77, 1 vol., Mass. Hist. Soc. Library.

Sparks, Jared, Manuscripts: New England Papers, Houghton Library.

Suffolk County, Probate Records, Suffolk County Courthouse.

———, Suffolk Deeds, Suffolk County Courthouse.

———, Inferior Court of Common Pleas, Records, Suffolk County Courthouse: Court Files.
Court Files: Executions.

Ward, Artemas, Papers, 1684-1775, 8 vols. and 1 box, Mass. Hist. Soc. Library.

Warren, John, Papers, 1776-1815, 1 vol., Mass. Hist. Soc. Library.

Warren, Joseph, Ledgers, 1763-68 and 1774-75, 2 vols., Dr. Richard Warren, on deposit at the Mass. Hist. Soc. Library.

———, Oration on the Boston Massacre Delivered March 6, 1775, Mass. Hist. Soc. Library.

———, Warren Family Papers, 1738-1921, 131 vols. and 3 boxes, Mass. Hist. Soc. Library.

Washburn, Alexander, Collection of Autographs, 1639-1884, 26 vols., Mass. Hist. Soc. Library.

Williams, Israel, Papers, 1730-80, 2 vols., Mass. Hist. Soc. Library.

B. PRINTED SOURCES

Adams, Charles F., ed., *Familiar Letters of John Adams and His Wife Abigail Adams During the Revolution* (Boston, 1875).

———, ed., *The Works of John Adams, Second President of the United States, with a Life of the Author* (Boston, 1856), 10 vols.

Adams, Randolph G., ed., "New Light on the Boston Massacre," Amer. Antiq. Soc., *Proceedings,* n.s., XLVII, Part 2 (Oct., 1937), 259-354.

[Almon, John], *A Collection of Interesting, Authentic Papers Relative to the Dispute Between Great Britain and America* (London, 1777), often cited as *Prior Documents.*

Baker, Sarah Breck, ed., "Extracts from the Ames Diary," *Dedham Historical Register,* I, No. 1 (Jan., 1890), to III, No. 3 (July, 1892).

Barker, John, *The British in Boston,* notes by Elizabeth E. Dana (Cambridge, Mass., 1924).

"Bennett's *History of New England,*" Mass. Hist. Soc., *Proceedings,* V (1860-62), 108-126.

[Bernard, Francis, Thomas Gage, and Samuel Hood], *Letters to the Ministry* (Boston, 1769).

Bolton, Charles K., ed., *Letters of Hugh Earl Percy from Boston and New York, 1774-1776* (Boston, 1902).

Bosson, Albert, ed., "The Battle of Chelsea," Old Suffolk Chapter, Sons of the American Revolution, *Register* (1900), appendix.

Boston. *A Report of the Boston Record Commissioners, Containing the Roxbury Land and Church Records* (Boston, 1881).

———. *A Report of the Record Commissioners of the City of Boston, Containing the Boston Town Records, 1758 to 1769* (Boston, 1886).

———. *A Report of the Record Commissioners of the City of Boston, Containing the Boston Town Records, 1770 Through 1777* (Boston, 1887).

———. *A Report of the Record Commissioners of the City of Boston, Containing the Selectmen's Minutes from 1769 Through April, 1775* (Boston, 1893).

"Boston Marriages," New Eng. Hist. and Geneal. Soc., *Register,* XIX, No. 1 (Jan., 1865), 29-32.

"Boston Records," *ibid.,* XVI, No. 1 (Jan., 1862), 45-49.

"Boyle's Journal of Occurences in Boston, 1759-1778," *ibid.,* LXXXIV (1930), 142-171, 248-272, 357-382, and LXXXV (1931), 5-28, 117-133.

[Bradford, Alden E., ed.], *Speeches of the Governors of Massachusetts from 1764 to 1775* (Boston, 1818).

Burnett, Edmund C., ed., *Letters of Members of the Continental Congress* (Washington, 1921-36), 8 vols.

Carter, Clarence E., ed., *The Correspondence of General Thomas Gage* (New Haven, Conn., 1931-33), 2 vols.

Channing, Edward and Archibald Coolidge, eds., *The Barrington-Ber-*

*nard Correspondence and Illustrative Material, 1760-1770,* vol. 17, *Harvard Historical Studies* (Cambridge, Mass., 1912).

Clements Library, *Documents of the American Revolution: Lexington and Concord* (Ann Arbor, Mich., [1946]).

"College Customs Anno 1734-5," Col. Soc. of Mass., *Publications,* XXXI *(Collections: Harvard College Records,* III), 383-384.

Cunningham, Anne Rowe, ed., *Letters and Diary of John Rowe, Boston Merchant, 1759-1762, 1764-1779* (Boston, 1903).

Cushing, Harry A., ed., *The Writings of Samuel Adams* (New York and London, 1904-08), 4 vols.

[Dawson, Henry B.], *The Historical Magazine and Notes and Queries,* n.s., III, No. 6 (June, 1868).

*Detail and Conduct of the American War, The,* 3rd ed. (London, 1780).

Dexter, Franklin B., ed., *The Literary Diary of Ezra Stiles* (New York, 1901), 3 vols.

"Diary of Ezekiel Price," Mass. Hist. Soc., *Proceedings,* VII (1863-64), 185-262.

Dickerson, Oliver M., ed., *Boston Under Military Rule, 1768-1769, as Revealed in "A Journal of the Times"* (Boston, 1936).

Donne, W. Bodham, ed., *The Correspondence of King George the Third with Lord North from 1768 to 1783* (London, 1867), 2 vols.

Drake, Francis S., *Tea Leaves* (Boston, 1884).

"Extracts from Dr. Belknap's Note-books," Mass. Hist. Soc., *Proceedings,* XIV (1875-76), 92-98.

[Force, Peter, ed.], *American Archives,* 4th ser. (Washington, 1837-46), 6 vols.

Ford, Worthington C., ed., "John Wilkes and Boston," Mass. Hist. Soc., *Proceedings,* XLVII (1913-14), 190-215.

———, "Letters of Catherine Macauley, William Bollan, and Thomas Pownall, Relating to the Boston Massacre," Col. Soc. of Mass., *Publications,* VIII (*Trans.,* 1900-1902), 211-215.

Fortescue, John, ed., *The Correspondence of King George the Third from 1760 to December 1783* (London, 1927-28), 6 vols.

French, Allen, ed., *A British Fusilier in Revolutionary Boston* (Cambridge, Mass., 1926).

[Frothingham, Richard, ed.], "Correspondence, in 1774 and 1775, Between a Committee of the Town of Boston and Contributors of Donations for the Relief of the Sufferers by the Boston Port Bill," Mass. Hist. Soc., *Collections,* 4th ser., IV, 1-278.

———, comp. [Documents on the Battle of Bunker's Hill], Mass. Hist. Soc., *Proceedings,* XIV (1875-76), 68-91.

[Galloway, Joseph], *Historical and Political Reflections on the Rise and Progress of the American Rebellion* (London, 1780).

*General Gage's Instructions of 22nd February 1775 to Captain Brown* (Boston, 1779).

Gordon, William, *The History of the Rise, Progress, and Establishment, of the Independence of the United States* (London, 1788), 4 vols.

Great Britain, Privy Council. *Acts of the Privy Council of England: Colonial Series, 1613-1783* (London, 1908-12), 6 vols.

Green, Samuel A., ed., "Amos Farnsworth's Diary," Mass. Hist. Soc., *Proceedings,* XXXII (1897, 1899), 74-107.

———, "Minutes of the Tea Meetings, 1773," Mass. Hist. Soc., *Proceedings,* XX (1882-83), 10-17.

Hagelin, Wladimir and Ralph A. Brown, eds., "Connecticut Farmers at Bunker Hill: The Diary of Colonel Experience Storrs," *New England Quarterly,* XXVIII, No. 1 (March, 1955), 72-73.

Haskell, Caleb, "Caleb Haskell's Diary," *The Magazine of History with Notes and Queries,* XXII, Extra No. 86, pp. 61-110.

Heath, William, *Memoirs of Major-General Heath* (Boston, 1798).

[Hollis, Thomas], *The True Sentiments of America* (London, 1768).

Hutchinson, Peter O., ed., *The Diary and Letters of His Excellency Thomas Hutchinson, Esq.* (Boston, 1884).

[Hutchinson, Thomas], *Copy of Letters Sent to Great Britain* (Boston, 1773).

———, *The History of the Colony and Province of Massachusetts-Bay,* ed. Lawrence S. Mayo (Cambridge, Mass., 1936), 3 vols.

Jensen, Merrill, ed., *English Historical Documents: American Colonial Documents to 1776* (London, 1955).

Kidder, Frederic, *History of the Boston Massacre* (Albany, N.Y., 1870).

"The Laws of Harvard College [1767]," Col. Soc. of Mass., *Publications,* XXXI (*Collections: Harvard College Records,* III), 347-383.

"Letters Illustrating the Battle [of Breed's Hill]," Mass. Hist. Soc., *Proceedings,* XIV (1875-76), 79-91.

"Letters of John Hancock, Joseph Warren, Thomas Gage, James Warren, and Governor Trumball," Mass. Hist. Soc., *Collections,* 5th ser., X (Boston, 1888), 283-312.

Lister, Jeremy, *Concord Fight* [ed. Harold Murdock] (Cambridge, Mass., 1931).

Massachusetts Grand Lodge of Ancient Free and Accepted Masons. *Proceedings, 1733-1953* (Boston and Cambridge, 1871——), 89 vols. to 1953.

Mass. Hist. Soc., *Letters and Papers of John Singleton Copley and Henry Pelham, 1739-1776* ([Boston], 1914).

———, *Warren-Adams Letters* (Boston, 1917, 1925), 2 vols.

Mass. Prov. Cong., *The Journals of Each Provincial Congress of Massachusetts in 1774 and 1775* (Boston, 1838).

Matthews, Albert, ed., "Documents Relating to Captain Thomas Preston and the Boston Massacre," Col. Soc. of Mass., *Publications,* VII (*Trans.,* 1900-1902), 2-21.

Matthews, Albert, ed., "Documents Relating to the Last Meetings of the Massachusetts Royal Council, 1774-1776," *ibid.,* XXXII (*Trans.,* 1933-37), 460-504.

———, "Letters of Dennys De Berdt, 1757-1770," *ibid.,* XIII (*Trans.,* 1910-11), 293-461.

Mayo, Catherine B., ed., "Additions to Thomas Hutchinson's 'History of Massachusetts Bay,' " Amer. Antiq. Soc., *Proceedings,* LIX, Part 1 (April, 1949), 11-74.

Motte, Ellis L., *et al.,* eds., *Records of the Church in Brattle Square, Boston, with Lists of Communicants, Baptisms, Marriages, and Funerals, 1699-1872* (Boston, 1902).

Mumby, Frank A., *George III and the American Revolution: The Beginnings* (Boston and New York, 1923).

[Murdock, Harold, ed.], *Late News of the Excursions and Ravages of the King's Troops on the Nineteenth of April, 1775* (Cambridge, Mass., 1927).

*Orations Delivered at the Request of the Inhabitants of the Town of Boston to Commemorate the Evening of the Fifth of March, 1770* (Boston, [1785]).

"Original Letters of Hugh, Earl Percy and Afterwards Duke of Northumberland, Between April 17, 1774 and July 11, 1778," Boston Public Library, *Bulletin,* X, No. 4 (Jan., 1892), 317-327.

*Proceedings of the Most Worshipful Grand Lodge of . . . Massachusetts* (Boston, n.d.).

"The Revolutionary Journal of James Stevens of Andover, Mass.," Essex Institute, *Historical Collections,* XLVIII, No. 1 (Jan., 1912), 41-71.

Roxbury. *Vital Records of Roxbury to the End of the Year 1849* (Salem, Mass., 1925), 2 vols.

Sargent, Winthrop, ed., "Letters of John Andrews, Esq. of Boston," Mass. Hist. Soc., *Proceedings,* VIII (1864-65), 316-412.

Seventy-Six Society, *Papers Relating to Public Events in Massachusetts Preceding the American Revolution* (Philadelphia, Pa., 1856).

Sparks, Jared, ed., "Destruction of the Tea, in the Harbor of Boston, December 16, 1773," Mass. Hist. Soc., *Collections,* 4th ser., IV, 373-389.

———, "Extracts from an Original Diary by Thomas Newell, Boston, 1773, 1774," Mass. Hist. Soc., *Proceedings,* IV (1858-60), 216-224.

Stevens, B[enjamin] F., *Facsimiles of Manuscripts in European Archives Relating to America, 1773-1783* (London, 1889-98), 25 vols.

Suffolk County. *Suffolk Deeds* (Boston, 1880-1906), 14 vols.

Tudor, William, ed., *Deacon Tudor's Diary* (Boston, 1896).

U.S. Continental Congress, *Journals of the Continental Congress, 1774-1789,* eds. Worthington C. Ford *et al.* (Washington, 1904-37), 34 vols.

Warren, Joseph, *An Oration Delivered March 5th, 1772,* 2nd ed. (Boston, 1772).

———, *An Oration Delivered March Sixth, 1775* (Boston, 1775).

[———. James Bowdoin, and Samuel Pemberton], *A Short Narrative of the Horrid Massacre in Boston* (Boston, 1770).

Warren, Mercy, *History of the Rise, Progress and Termination of the American Revolution* (Boston, 1805), 3 vols.

Willard, Margaret W., ed., *Letters on the American Revolution, 1774-1776* (Boston, 1925).

C. Newspapers

The American Antiquarian Society has the fullest files of colonial newspapers, an increasing number of which are now available on microfilm. The collections of Boston newspapers at the Boston Public Library and the Massachusetts Historical Society provide a virtually complete file, and the Dorr file of the *Boston Gazette* at the latter library contains marginal notes by its eighteenth-century collector which help in identifying pseudonymous articles and letters.

*Boston Chronicle, The*

*Boston Evening-Post, The*

*Boston Gazette, The*

*Boston Post-Boy, The*

*Massachusetts Gazette, The*

*Massachusetts Spy, The*

## II. Secondary Works

A. General Works

This section lists only a few books which were particularly helpful or germane to the present study. The bibliographies in the books listed below by John R. Alden and Lawrence H. Gipson, and the bibliographies and guides mentioned therein, cover the large literature of British and colonial history before 1775.

Adams, James T., *Revolutionary New England, 1691-1776* (Boston, 1927).

Alden, John R., *The American Revolution, 1775-1783* (New York, 1954).

Bridenbaugh, Carl, *Cities in Revolt: Urban Life in America, 1743-1776* (New York, 1955).

Brown, Robert E., *Middle-Class Democracy and the Revolution in Massachusetts, 1691-1780* (Ithaca, N.Y., 1955).

Dickerson, Oliver M., *The Navigation Acts and the American Revolution* (Philadelphia, Pa., 1951).

Gipson, Lawrence H., *The Coming of the Revolution, 1763-1775* (New York, 1954).

Hart, Albert B., ed., *Commonwealth History of Massachusetts* (New York, 1927-30), 5 vols.

Knollenberg, Bernhard, *Origin of the American Revolution, 1759-1766* (New York, 1960).

Labaree, Leonard W., *Royal Government in America: A Study of the British Colonial System Before 1783* (New Haven, Conn., 1930).

Miller, John C., *Origins of the American Revolution* (Boston, 1943).

———, *Triumph of Freedom* (Boston, 1948).

Namier, L[ewis] B., *England in the Age of the American Revolution* (London, 1930).

———, *The Structure of Politics at the Accession of George III* (London, 1929), 2 vols.

Ritcheson, Charles R., *British Politics and the American Revolution* (Norman, Okla., 1954).

Trevelyan, George O., *The American Revolution* (New York, 1899-1908), 3 vols.

Van Tyne, Claude H., *The Causes of the War of Independence* (Boston and New York, 1922).

Ward, Christopher, *The War of the Revolution,* ed. John R. Alden (New York, 1952), 2 vols.

B. Special Studies

This section lists monographs and popular works, the latter being occasionally useful for local color, obscure details, and reminiscences and contemporary accounts printed in them. Most of the commemorative addresses and memorial volumes on Lexington, Bunker Hill, and the like have been omitted, as has the large, controversial, and generally valueless literature of the nineteenth century on the subjects of who fired first at Lexington, where the first resistance to British troops was made, and who commanded at Breed's Hill.

Adams, Randolph G., *Political Ideas of the American Revolution: Britannic-American Contributions to the Problem of Imperial Organization, 1765 to 1775,* 2nd ed. (New York, 1939).

Anderson, Troyer S., *The Command of the Howe Brothers During the American Revolution* (New York and London, 1936).

Ayer, Mary F., *Early Days on Boston Common* (Boston, 1910).

Bakeless, John, *Turncoats, Traitors, and Heroes* (Philadelphia, Pa., and New York, 1959).

Baldwin, Alice M., *The New England Clergy and the American Revolution* (Durham, N.C., 1928).

Batchelder, Samuel F., *Bits of Harvard History* (Cambridge, Mass., 1924).

Boston. *Monument to Joseph Warren, Its Origin, History and Dedication, 1894-1904* (Boston, 1905).

Boston City Council. *Celebration of the Centennial Anniversary of the Battle of Bunker Hill* (Boston, 1875).

Brennan, Ellen E., *Plural Office-Holding in Massachusetts, 1760-1780:*

*Its Relation to the "Separation" of Departments of Government* (Chapel Hill, N.C., 1945).

Burnett, Edmund C., *The Continental Congress* (New York, 1941).

Coburn, Frank W., *The Battle of April 19, 1775, in Lexington, Concord, Lincoln, Arlington, Cambridge, Somerville and Charlestown, Massachusetts,* 2nd ed. (Lexington, Mass., 1922).

Cushing, Harry A., *History of the Transition from Provincial to Commonwealth Government in Massachusetts,* vol. 7, No. 1 [No. 17] in Columbia University, *Studies in History, Economics and Public Law* (New York, 1896).

Davidson, Philip, *Propaganda and the American Revolution, 1763-1783* (Chapel Hill, N.C., 1941).

Drake, Francis S., *The Town of Roxbury* (Roxbury, Mass., 1878).

Drake, Samuel A., *Old Boston Taverns and Tavern Clubs* (Boston, 1917).

———, *Old Landmarks and Historic Personages of Boston,* 8th ed. (Boston, 1895).

Drake, Samuel G., *The History and Antiquities of Boston* (Boston, 1856).

Duffy, John, *Epidemics in Colonial America* (Baton Rouge, La., 1953).

Duncan, Louis C., *Medical Men in the American Revolution, 1775-1783* (Carlisle Barracks, Pa., 1931).

Farrington, Charles C., *Paul Revere and His Famous Ride* (Bedford, Mass., 1923).

Fay, Bernard, *Revolution and Freemasonry, 1680-1800* (Boston, 1935).

Fleming, Thomas J., *Now We Are Enemies: The Story of Bunker Hill* (New York, 1960).

French, Allen, *The Day of Concord and Lexington: The Nineteenth of April 1775* (Boston, 1925).

———, *The First Year of the American Revolution* (Boston and New York, 1934).

———, *General Gage's Informers: New Material upon Lexington & Concord, Benjamin Thompson as Loyalist & the Treachery of Benjamin Church, Jr.* (Ann Arbor, Mich., 1932).

———, *Historic Concord: A Handbook of Its Story and Its Memorials with the Story of the Lexington Fight* (Concord, Mass., 1942).

———, *The Seige of Boston* (New York, 1911).

———, *The Taking of Ticonderoga in 1775: The British Story* (Cambridge, Mass., 1928).

Frothingham, Richard, *The Alarm on the Night of April 18, 1775* ([Boston, 1876]).

———, *Battle of Bunker Hill* (Boston, 1889).

———, *The Battle-Field of Bunker Hill, with a Relation of the Action by William Prescott and Illustrative Documents* (Boston, 1876).

———, *History of the Seige of Boston, and of the Battles of Lexington, Concord, and Bunker Hill* (Boston, 1851).

Guttridge, George H., *English Whiggism and the American Revolution,* vol. 28, University of California, *Publications in History* (Berkeley and Los Angeles, Calif., 1942).

Hale, Richard W., Jr., *History of the Roxbury Latin School* (Cambridge, Mass., 1946).

Halko, Henry J., "The British Understanding of the American Constitutional Position, 1763-1776" (thesis, Brown University, Providence, R.I., 1957, University Microfilms).

Harrington, Thomas F., *The Harvard Medical School: A History, Narrative and Documentary, 1782-1905* (New York, 1905), 3 vols.

Haywood, Harry L. and James E. Craig, *A History of Freemasonry* (New York, 1927).

Hill, Hamilton A., *History of the Old South Church (Third Church) Boston, 1669-1884* (Boston and New York, 1890), 2 vols.

Hinkhouse, Fred J., *The Preliminaries of the American Revolution as Seen in the English Press, 1763-1775,* No. 276, Columbia University, *Studies in History, Economics and Public Law* (New York, 1926).

Hudson, Charles, *History of the Town of Lexington, Middlesex County, Massachusetts from Its First Settlement to 1868* (Boston, 1868).

Hunt, Agnes, *The Provincial Committees of Safety of the American Revolution* ([Cleveland, Ohio], 1904).

*Inauguration of the Statue of Warren, by the Bunker Hill Monument Association, June 17, 1857* (Boston, 1858).

Montross, Lynn, *The Reluctant Rebels: The Story of the Continental Congress, 1774-1789* (New York, 1950).

Morgan, Edmund S. and Helen M., *The Stamp Act Crisis: Prologue to Revolution* (Chapel Hill, N.C., 1953).

Morison, Samuel E., *Three Centuries of Harvard, 1636-1936* (Cambridge, Mass., 1936).

Morse, Sidney, *Freemasonry in the American Revolution* (Washington, D.C., 1924).

Mullett, Charles F., *Colonial Claims to Home Rule (1764-1775): An Essay in Imperial Politics,* vol. 2, No. 4, University of Missouri, *Studies* (Columbia, Mo., 1927).

———, *Fundamental Law and the American Revolution, 1760-1776,* No. 385, Columbia University, *Studies in History, Economics and Public Law* (New York, 1933).

Mumford, James G., *A Narrative of Medicine in America* (Philadelphia, Pa., 1903).

Murdock, Harold, *Bunker Hill: Notes and Queries on a Famous Battle* (Boston, 1927).

———, *The Nineteenth of April, 1775* (Boston, 1923).

Nelson, William H., "The Loyalist View of the American Revolution" (thesis, Columbia University, New York, 1958, University Microfilms).

Nevins, Allan, *The American States During and After the Revolution, 1775-1789* (New York, 1924).

Newcomer, Lee N., *The Embattled Farmers: A Massachusetts Countryside in the American Revolution* (New York, 1953).

Packard, Francis R., *The History of Medicine in the United States* (Philadelphia, Pa., 1901).

Ray, Sister Mary Augustina, *American Opinion of Roman Catholicism in the Eighteenth Century,* No. 416, Columbia University, *Studies in History, Economics and Public Law* (New York, 1936).

Saint Andrew's Lodge. *The Lodge of Saint Andrew and the Massachusetts Grand Lodge* (Boston, 1870).

Scaife, Lauriston L., *Milton and the Suffolk Resolves* ([Milton, Mass.], 1921).

Schlesinger, Arthur M., *The Colonial Merchants and the American Revolution, 1763-1776* (New York, 1957).

———, *Prelude to Independence: The Newspaper War on Britain, 1764-1776* (New York, 1958).

Shipton, Clifford K., ed., *Biographical Sketches of Those Who Attended Harvard College* (Cambridge and Boston, Mass., 1873-1958), 10 vols. to date, cited by its short title *Sibley's Harvard Graduates.*

Spencer, Henry R., *Constitutional Conflict in Provincial Massachusetts: A Study of Some Phases of the Opposition Between the Massachusetts Governor and General Court in the Early Eighteenth Century* (Columbus, Ohio, 1905).

Stark, James H., *The Loyalists of Massachusetts and the Other Side of the American Revolution* (Boston, 1910).

Tatsch, J. Hugo, *Freemasonry in the Thirteen Colonies* (New York, 1933).

Taylor, Robert J., *Western Massachusetts in the Revolution* (Providence, R.I., 1954).

Thomas, Isaiah, *The History of Printing in America, with a Biography of Printers and an Account of Newspapers,* 2nd ed. (Albany, N.Y., 1874), 2 vols.

Thwing, Annie H., *The Crooked and Narrow Streets of the Town of Boston, 1630-1822* (Boston, 1930).

Thwing, Walter E., *History of the First Church in Roxbury, Massachusetts, 1630-1904* (Boston, 1908).

Toner, Joseph M., *The Medical Men of the Revolution with a Brief History of the Medical Department of the Continental Army* (Philadelphia, Pa., 1876).

Tourtellot, Arthur B., *William Diamond's Drum: The Beginning of the War of the American Revolution* (Garden City, N.Y., 1959).

Van Doren, Carl, *Secret History of the American Revolution* (New York, 1941).

Van Tyne, Claude H., *The Loyalists in the American Revolution* (New York, 1929).

Viets, Henry R., *A Brief History of Medicine in Massachusetts* (Boston and New York, 1930).

W.P.A. Writers' Program (Massachusetts), *Boston Looks Seaward: The Story of the Port, 1630-1940* (Boston, 1941).

Wallace, Willard M., *Appeal to Arms: A Military History of the American Revolution* (New York, 1951).

Warren, George W., *The History of the Bunker Hill Monument Association During the First Century of the United States of America* (Boston, 1877).

Wheildon, William W., *History of Paul Revere's Signal Lanterns* (Concord, Mass., 1878).

Winsor, Justin, ed., *The Memorial History of Boston, Including Suffolk County, Massachusetts, 1630-1880* (Boston, 1882-83), 4 vols.

C. Biographies

The present study of Joseph Warren is the first since 1865. Because of this, and because some things which are of no value to the biographer may be of interest to the intellectual historian concerned with such subjects as hero worship, a virtually complete bibliography of the writings on Warren is included in this and the following section. However, it should be emphasized that the book by Richard Frothingham is the only biography of any value, and the articles by Lowell Kerr and M. P. Webster are the only ones about Warren which are worth reading. Everything written before Frothingham's biography was outdated by it, and everything written since its publication depends upon it as the principal, if not sole, authority.

Alden, John R., *General Gage in America, Being Principally a History of His Role in the American Revolution* (Baton Rouge, La., 1948).

Allan, Herbert S., *John Hancock, Patriot in Purple* (New York, 1948).

Austin, James T., *The Life of Elbridge Gerry* (Boston, 1828-29), 2 vols.

Boardman, Samuel Lane, *Peter Edes: Pioneer Printer in Maine* (Bangor, Me., 1901).

Bostonian, A [Samuel Adams Wells], *Biographical Sketch of Gen. Joseph Warren* (Boston, 1857).

Bowen, Catherine D., *John Adams and the American Revolution* (Boston, 1950).

Brown, E. Francis, *Joseph Hawley, Colonial Radical* (New York, 1931).

Brown, Rebecca (Warren), *Stories About General Warren in Relation to the Fifth of March Massacre and the Battle of Bunker Hill* (Boston, 1835).

Carroll, Warren H., "John Adams, Puritan Revolutionist: A Study of His Part in Making the American Revolution, 1764-1776" (thesis, Columbia University, New York, 1959, University Microfilms).

Eliot, John, *A Biographical Dictionary Containing a Brief Account of the First Settlers* (Salem, Mass., 1809).

Everett, Alexander H., *Joseph Warren*, Jared Sparks, ed., *Library of American Biography* (Boston, 1838), 1st series, X, 91-183.

Forbes, Esther, *Paul Revere and the World He Lived In* (Boston, 1942).

Frothingham, Richard, *Life and Times of Joseph Warren* (Boston, 1865).

Goss, Elbridge H., *The Life of Colonel Paul Revere* (Boston, 1891), 2 vols.

Holland, Henry W., *William Dawes and His Ride with Paul Revere* (Boston, 1878).

Kelly, Howard A. and Walter L. Burrage, *American Medical Biographies* (Baltimore, Md., 1920).

Knapp, Samuel L., *Biographical Sketches of Eminent Lawyers, Statesmen, and Men of Letters* (Boston, 1821).

Lee, Richard H., *Life of Arthur Lee, L.L.D* (Boston, 1829), 2 vols.

Loring, James S., *The Hundred Boston Orators* (Boston, 1853).

Magoon, Elias L., *Orators of the American Revolution* (New York, 1848).

Martyn, Charles, *The Life of Artemas Ward: The First Commander-in-Chief of the American Revolution* (New York, 1921).

Miller, John C., *Sam Adams, Pioneer in Propaganda* (Boston, 1936).

Partridge, Bellamy, *Sir Billy Howe* (London, 1932).

Quincy, Josiah, *Memoir of the Life of Josiah Quincy Junior of Massachusetts Bay, 1744-1775* (Boston, 1875).

Rogers, Thomas J., comp., *A New American Biographical Dictionary*, 2nd ed. (Easton, Pa., 1823).

Sabine, Lorenzo, *Biographical Sketches of Loyalists of the American Revolution, with an Historical Essay* (Boston, 1864), 2 vols.

Thacher, James, *American Medical Biography* (Boston, 1828), 2 vols.

Vering, Alice, "James Otis" (thesis, University of Nebraska, Lincoln, Neb., 1954, University Microfilms).

Warren, Edward, *The Life of John Warren, M. D.* (Boston, 1874).

Warren, John C., *Genealogy of Warren with Some Historical Sketches* (Boston, 1854).

Wells, William V., *The Life and Public Services of Samuel Adams* (Boston, 1865), 3 vols.

D. ARTICLES

Adams, Charles F., "The Battle of Bunker Hill from a Strategic Point of View," Amer. Antiq. Soc., *Proceedings*, n.s., X, Part 2 (Oct., 1895), 387-398.

Adams, James T., "Joseph Warren," *Dictionary of American Biography*, ed. Dumas Malone (New York, 1936), XIX, 482-483.

Amery, J. S., "The Warrens of Headborough and Their Descendants," Devonshire Assoc. for the Advancement of Science, Literature and Art, *Transactions*, XXVIII (1896), 494-502.

Anderson, George P., "Ebenezer Mackintosh: Stamp Act Rioter and Patriot," Col. Soc. of Mass., *Publications*, XXVI (*Trans.*, 1924-26), 15-64.

Anderson, George P., "A Note on Ebenezer Mackintosh," *ibid.*, pp. 348-361.

Andrews, Charles M., "Boston Merchants and the Non-Importation Movement," *ibid.*, XIX (*Trans.*, 1916-17), 159-259.

Appleton, Marguerite, "The Agents of the New England Colonies in the Revolutionary Period," *New England Quarterly*, VI, No. 2 (June, 1933), 371-387.

Bacon, Gaspar G., "Joseph Warren," *Government and the Voter* (Boston, 1931), pp. 150-158.

Batchelder, Samuel F., "Harvard Hospital-Surgeons of 1775: A Study in the Medical History of the American Revolution," *Harvard Alumni Bulletin*, XXII, No. 22 (Feb. 26, 1920), 501-513.

Blake, John B., "Smallpox Inoculation in Colonial Boston," *Journal of the History of Medicine and Allied Sciences*, VIII, No. 3 (July, 1953), 284-300.

Bradford, Charles, "Doctors Afield: Joseph Warren," *New England Journal of Medicine*, CCL, No. 9 (March 4, 1954), 383-386.

Brennan, Ellen E., "James Otis: Recreant and Patriot," *New England Quarterly*, XII, No. 4 (Dec., 1939), 691-725.

Bridenbaugh, Carl, "Baths and Watering Places of Colonial America," *William and Mary Quarterly*, 3rd ser., III, No. 2 (April, 1946), 151-181.

Cadbury, Henry J., "Quaker Relief During the Seige of Boston," Col. Soc. of Mass., *Publications*, XXXIV (*Trans.*, 1937-42), 39-179.

Cheever, David, "The Warren Stock and Some of Its Scions," *The New England Journal of Medicine*, CC, No. 17 (April 25, 1929), 857-863.

"Contributors to the Science of Medicine: John Warren, Joseph Warren and John Collins Warren," *Medical Journal and Record*, CXXVI, No. 8 (Oct. 19, 1927), 509-511.

Crawford, Mary C., "The Warren Family," *Famous Families of Massachusetts* (Boston, 1930), II, 52-71.

Dickerson, Oliver M., "The Commissioners of Customs and the 'Boston Massacre,'" *New England Quarterly*, XXVII, No. 3 (Sept., 1954), 307-325.

———, "John Hancock: Notorious Smuggler or Near Victim of British Revenue Racketeers?," *Mississippi Valley Historical Review*, XXXII, No. 4 (March, 1946), 517-540.

———, "Use Made of the Revenue from the Tax on Tea," *New England Quarterly*, XXXI, No. 2 (June, 1958), 232-243.

———, "Writs of Assistance as a Cause of the Revolution," Richard B. Morris, ed., *The Era of the American Revolution: Studies Inscribed to Evarts Boutell Greene* (New York, 1939), pp. 40-75.

"Dr. Joseph Warren's Day-Book," *The Boston Medical and Surgical Journal*, XCII, No. 24 (June 17, 1875), 725-726.

Edes, Henry H., "Memoir of Dr. Thomas Young, 1731-1777," Col. Soc. of Mass., *Publications,* XI (*Trans.,* 1906-07), 2-54.

Farwell, John W., "A Horoscope of Dr. Joseph Warren," *ibid.,* XX (*Trans.,* 1917-19), 18-21.

Frese, Joseph R., "James Otis and the Writs of Assistance," *New England Quarterly,* XXX, No. 4 (Dec., 1957), 496-508.

Frothingham, Richard, "Remarks," Mass. Hist. Soc., *Proceedings,* XIV (1875-76), 53-68.

Gipson, Lawrence H., "Aspects of the Beginning of the American Revolution in Massachusetts Bay, 1760-1762," Amer. Antiq. Soc., *Proceedings,* LXVII, Part 1 (April 17, 1957), 11-32.

Green, Samuel A., "The Boston Massacre, March 5, 1770," *ibid.,* n.s., XIV, Part 1 (Oct., 1900), 40-51.

Greene, J. Evarts, "The Roxbury Latin School: An Outline of Its History," *ibid.,* n.s., IV, Part 4 (April, 1887), 348-366.

Harper, Lawrence A., "The Effect of the Navigation Acts on the Thirteen Colonies," Richard B. Morris, ed., *The Era of the American Revolution: Studies Inscribed to Evarts Boutell Greene* (New York, 1939), pp. 3-39.

Hersey, Frank W. C., "Tar and Feathers: The Adventures of Captain John Malcom," Col. Soc. of Mass., *Publications,* XXXIV (*Trans.,* 1937-42), 429-473.

Hickman, Emily, "Colonial Writs of Assistance," *New England Quarterly,* V, No. 1 (Jan., 1932), 83-104.

Hosmer, James K., "The Debt of Massachusetts to Thomas Hutchinson," Col. Soc. of Mass., *Publications,* XII (*Trans.,* 1908-09), 238-245.

Jeffries, John, "A Tory Surgeon's Experiences, June 17, 1775," *The Boston Medical and Surgical Journal,* XCII, No. 24 (June 17, 1875), 729-730.

Jensen, Merrill, "Democracy and the American Revolution," *Huntington Library Quarterly,* XX, No. 4 (Aug., 1957), 321-341.

Kerr, Lowell, "Benedict Arnold and the Warrens," *Americana,* XXX, No. 2 (April, 1936), 324-334.

Kimball, James, "The One Hundredth Anniversary of the Destruction of Tea in Boston Harbor," Essex Institute, *Historical Collections,* XII, No. 3 (July, 1874), 197-239.

Longley, Ronald S., "Mobs in Revolutionary Massachusetts," *New England Quarterly,* VI, No. 1 (March, 1933), 98-130.

Matthews, Albert, "Notes on Early Autopsies and Anatomical Lectures," Col. Soc. of Mass., *Publications,* XIX (*Trans.,* 1916-17), 273-290.

———, "The Solemn League and Covenant, 1774," *ibid.,* XVIII (*Trans.,* 1915-16), 103-122.

"Memoirs of Major-Gen. Joseph Warren," *The Polyanthos,* III, No. 6 (Nov., 1806), 217-224.

Miller, John C., "The Massachusetts Convention, 1768," *New England Quarterly,* VII, No. 3 (Sept., 1934), 445-474.

Miller, John C., "Religion, Finance, and Democracy in Massachusetts," *ibid.,* VI, No. 1 (March, 1933), 29-58.

Moore, Cornelius, "Joseph Warren," in *Leaflets of Masonic Biography; or Sketches of Eminent Freemasons,* 3rd ed. (Cincinnati, Ohio, 1864), pp. 9-48.

Morgan, Edmund S., "Colonial Ideas of Parliamentary Power, 1764-1766," *William and Mary Quarterly,* 3rd ser., V, No. 3 (July, 1948), 311-341.

———, "Thomas Hutchinson and the Stamp Act," *New England Quarterly,* XXI, No. 4 (Dec., 1948), 459-492.

Murdock, Harold, "The British at Concord, April 19, 1775," Mass. Hist. Soc., *Proceedings,* LVI (1922-23), 70-94.

Page, Elwin L., "The King's Powder, 1774," *New England Quarterly,* XVIII, No. 1 (March, 1945), 83-92.

Parke, Frederic W., "Bullet Taken from the Body of Gen. Warren Who Was Killed at the Battle of Bunker Hill," New Eng. Hist. and Geneal. Soc., *Register,* LII (Jan., 1898), 147-148.

Rantoul, Robert S., "The Cruise of the 'Quero': How We Carried the News to the King," Essex Institute, *Historical Collections,* XXXVI, No. 1 (Jan., 1900), 1-30.

Sandham, William R., "General Joseph Warren, for Whom Warren County, Ill. Was Named," *Journal of the Illinois State Historical Society,* XVIII, No. 4 (Jan., 1926), 1053-55.

Scheide, John H., "The Lexington Alarm," Amer. Antiq. Soc., *Proceedings,* n.s., L, Part 1 (April, 1940), 49-79.

Schlesinger, Arthur M., "Liberty Tree: A Genealogy," *New England Quarterly,* XXV, No. 4 (Dec., 1952), 435-458.

———, "A Note on Songs as Patriot Propaganda, 1765-1776," *William and Mary Quarterly,* 3rd series, XI, No. 1 (Jan., 1954), 78-88.

———, "Propaganda and the Boston Newspaper Press, 1767-1770," Col. Soc. of Mass., *Publications,* XXXII (*Trans.,* 1933-37), 396-416.

Sheirr, Rodman J., "The Death of Major-General Joseph Warren," *Potter's American Monthly,* IV, No. 44 (Aug., 1875), 571-574.

Shryock, Richard H., "Eighteenth Century Medicine in America," Amer. Antiq. Soc., *Proceedings,* n.s., LIX, Part 2 (Oct. 19, 1949), 275-292.

Stalker, Hugh, "The Warrens of New England and Their Friends," *New England Journal of Medicine,* CCXXII, No. 13 (March 28, 1940), 517-529.

Sumner, William H., "Reminiscences of Gen. Wm. H. Sumner," New Eng. Hist. and Geneal. Soc., *Register,* VIII, No. 2 (April, 1854), 187-191.

Sumner, William H., "Reminiscences Relating to General Warren and Bunker Hill," *ibid.,* XII, No. 2 (April, 1858), 113-122.

Viets, Henry R., "Some Features of the History of Medicine in Massachusetts During the Colonial Period (1620-1770)," *Isis,* XXIII, No. 2 (Sept., 1935), 390-405.

Walett, Francis G., "The Massachusetts Council, 1766-1774: The Transformation of a Conservative Institution," *William and Mary Quarterly,* 3rd ser., VI, No. 4 (Oct., 1949), 605-627.

[Warren, John C.], "Joseph Warren," Abraham Rees, ed., *The Cyclopedia; Or Universal Dictionary of Arts, Sciences, and Literature* (Philadelphia, Pa., n.d.).

Webster, M. P., "The Suffolk Resolves," *New England Magazine,* n.s., XXVII, No. 3 (Nov., 1902), 353-372.

Wolkins, George G., "The Seizure of John Hancock's Sloop *Liberty,*" Mass. Hist. Soc., *Proceedings,* LV (1921-22), 239-284.

# Index